# The Theatrical Rambles of Mr. and Mrs. John Greene

By Charles Durang

## The Theatrical Rambles of Mr. and Mrs. John Greene

The Greenes represent a class of journeymen actors, rewarded with but little attention by chroniclers of the early Nineteenth Century. Along with hundreds of their day, they were living, breathing craftsmen, undergoing frequent moments of tribulation and rare occasions of triumph, respectable artists who bore the almost daily vicissitudes as an expected part of their theatrical practice. They traveled from place to place applying their craft, working with many of the major theatrical performers of the period. These Rambles were transcribed from Mrs. Greene's memoirs by Charles Durang, who supplied additional material obtained from his experiences as actor, prompter and dancing master.

**A Borgo Press Book
Edited by William L. Slout**

# THE THEATRICAL RAMBLES OF MR. AND MRS. JOHN GREENE

Second Edition, Revised and Expanded

CLIPPER STUDIES IN THE THEATRE
ISSN 0748-237X * Number One

by

**Charles Durang**

**Edited by William L. Slout**

The Borgo Press
An Imprint of Wildside Press

MMVII

Copyright © 1987, 2007 by William L. Slout

All rights reserved.
No part of this book may be reproduced in any form
without the expressed written consent
of the author and publisher.
Printed in the United States of America

Library of Congress Cataloging in Publication Data for the First Edition:

Durang, Charles.
    The theatrical rambles of Mr. and Mrs. John Greene / by Charles Durang ; edited by William L. Slout. – 2$^{nd}$ ed., rev. and expanded.
    p. cm. — (Clipper studies in the theatre, ISSN 0748-237X ; no. 1)
    Includes bibliographical references and index.
    1. Greene, John, d. 1860. 2. Greene, John, Mrs., 1800-1862. 3. Actors—United States—Biography. I. Slout, William L. (William Lawrence). II. Title. III. Series.
PN2287.G676D8 1987                                    84-11165
792'.028'0922 [B]—dc19                                      CIP

SECOND EDITION

## CONTENTS

*Preface*   9

*Chronology*   14

**I.**   16
Mrs. Greene—The War of 1812—Spencer H. Cone as an Actor—Advised to Go on the Stage by a Bishop—Trouble About a Part—A Theatrical Riot—Cone Leaving the Profession—Appearance of John Duff, Etc.

**II.**   26
Death of George Frederick Cooke—Opening of the Baltimore Holliday Theatre—Mrs. Mason and Mr. Entwistle—Bombardment of Fort McHenry—Anne Joins the Beaumont Corps of Thespians—Married to a Brute—Anne's Union with John Greene, Etc.

**III.**   36
The Actors in Pennsylvania—Charles S. Porter's Apprenticeship—The Greenes Join the Willis Troupe—A She Devil—Big Scott—Failure of an Expedition by Scott and Porter, Etc.

**IV.**   45
The Poisoned *Corps*—The Country Hostelry—A Double Chalking Landlord—Arrested—John Greene "Took in"—Among the Mad Chaps—Games of the Sports—Playing Again—A Final Scene with Mrs. Willis—The Drama in New Orleans—Mr. J. H. Caldwell—Theatrical Riot—English Opera—Jane Placide, Etc.

**V.**   59
Going Down the Ohio—Getting an Audience—More Trouble with a Landlord—A Redeeming Trait—First Floating Theatre—The Four Roads—No Baggage Smashers Needed—Getting a Quiet Meal—The Dark Side of Humanity—Hardships of an Actor's Life.

**VI.**     **66**
Sad Prospects—No Toll—Kean and His Aquatic Performance—A Good Samaritan—In Clover—Change of Fortune—On the Boards Again—Big Thing—Many Presents—Webb Found Drowned.

**VII.**     **75**
Blanchard's Company—Roughing it in the Backwoods—Mixed Audiences—Curious Currency—Enthusiasm of THE Indians—A Love Affair—Chicago Then and Now—With Turnbull in Canada.

**VIII.**     **82**
Montréal Theatre—An Insult Remembered—Just Reproof—A Return to the States—Mrs. Drake and the President—Dramatic Readings in New England, Etc.

**IX.**     **89**
A Minor Theatre—In the Ballet—Old Times in Philadelphia—Mrs. Greene at Baltimore—James Wallack—Theatricals in Maryland—Coffee and Cakes for the Players—The Great Race Between the North and South—Wood and Warren.

**X.**     **99**
A Lady as Hamlet—Death of Mrs. Lafolle—The Placides—Master Edwin Forrest—James H. Caldwell—Southern Theatres—The Rise of Young Forrest, Etc.

**XI.**     **108**
Season in New Orleans—A Friend in Need—Theatrical Performances—Little Marian Russell—Tom Placide, Failure—Stuck in the Mud—Furious Traveling—Mrs. Bloxton, Etc.

**XII.**     **116**
Up the River—Rebellion—Alabama—Painful Scene from the Past—A "Great" Explosion, and Funny Effect—The Edmund Kean Controversy.

**XIII.**     **125**
An Insult Remembered—Just Reproof—Mr. Wm. C. Mac-ready—Mr. and Mrs. George Barrett—The Boy in *William Tell*—Native Talent—Fresh Arrivals—Miss Latimer—Gen. Sandford and His Great Amphitheatre—Phillips, the Vocalist, Etc.

**XIV.** **139**
Importations—Competition from Wemyss—Cooper's Farewell—Reconciliation—Wilmington Too Good—Stars at Baltimore.

**XV.** **146**
Novel "Cure for the Heart Ache"—Extraordinary Circumstance—Trials of Professionals—Greene's Management at the Walnut Street—The West Indian Dramatic Corps—Josephine Clifton—Damaged Wardrobes, Etc.

**XVI.** **156**
A Merry Governor—Family Disputes—How to Settle Them—Money Plenty—*Black-Eyed Susan*—Miss Clifton Withdraws, Etc.

**XVII.** **163**
A Voyage to Old England—American Actors on the British Stage—Josephine Clifton in London—A Country Fair—Stage Coach Travel—An Englishman's Opinion of America.

**XVIII.** **170**
A Strange Visitor—The Great Bare Back Rider—Reunited with Herr Cline—Bearded Indians—Visiting the Theatres—T. P. Cooke—A Real Tragedy, Etc.

**XIX.** **176**
Arrival Home—Nosey Phillips—Drilling the Supes—Miss Waring—Stingy Gates—About *The Hunchback*—A Nice Little Fight—Greene Arrested, Etc.

**XX.** **183**
Arch Street Theatre—Something Wrong About the Monkey—A Bad Break—Fire—Unfortunate Remark—At Niagara Falls—Stage Coach Adventure, Etc.

**XXI.** **192**
A Tragedy Indeed—Murder of Mr. Duffy—A Suit at Law and Its Results—Fanny Jarman Compared with Ellen Tree.

**XXII.** **200**
With Rufus Welch—Acquitted of Duffy—Spectacles at the Walnut

Street Theatre—Vache, His Eccentricities—Miss Ellen Tree—Pittsburgh Theatre, Etc.

### XXIII. 210
The Batemans—Characteristics of a New Orleans Audience—Mrs. Greene's Benefit—Melancholy Finale to a Successful *Début*—The Stage and Pulpit—Courage of an Actress.

### XXIV. 218
Weighty Actors—Metamora and the Indians—A Ludicrous Scene—General Jackson and the Actors—A Traveling Scheme, Etc..

### XXV. 225
Down the River—The Jefferson Family—Silver Cup Versus Tin Cup—Free and Easy Hotel Accommodations, Etc.

### XXVI. 233
The City of the Dead—A Return to New Orleans—A Most Awful Scene—The Two Fannies—The Comedienne and the *Danseuse*—George Holland as Mine Host.

### XXVII. 241
*London Assurance*—Stage Dresses and Dressing—English Opera Company—Joe Cowell as a Boniface—A Serenade and Its Results—A Conflagration—A Man Overboard—The Little Magician—The Bonnet of 76—Duverna at the Chatham—Anderson, the Stage Manager—Back to New Orleans.

### XXVIII. 254
Josephine Clifton—From Gay to the Grave—A Corpse—Forrest's Farewell to New Orleans—The McVickers—The Drama, Its Earlier History in Chicago—Mrs. Hunt in *Macbeth*—Chicago Scavenger Law—Back to New Orleans—The Case of the Angry Canine and Dead Richard III—Brief Biography of Booth the Elder.

### XXIX. 264
Illness and Death of the Elder Booth—Greene's Personal Appearance—The Mayor of Trenton Receives a Blessing—A Management Speculation—The Cholera—Julia Dean and Eliza Logan—A Breakfast Scene—Miss Charlotte Cushman.

**XXX.** 275
Charlotte Cushman Criticized—An Accident Taken Advantage of—The Drama at Nashville—Chanfrau's Success—A Terpsichorean Sheriff—A Generous Offer—Last Days and Death of John Greene—Death of Mrs. Greene—The End.

*Bibliography* 287

*Index* 292

*Theatrical Rambles of Mr. & Mrs. Greene*, Charles Durang

## PREFACE

These *Theatrical Rambles* originally appeared in the New York *Clipper,* with weekly chapter installments covering a period from February 18, 1865, through October 13, 1865. They were prepared "expressly" for the paper, and, according to the editor's announcement, "will not appear in any other form, the copyright being held by us." The *Clipper* was a sporting and theatrical weekly, which at the time was placing particular emphasis on reminiscences of performers and other aspects of amusement history.

The *Clipper* was first published on April 30, 1853, by Harrison Fulton Trent to serve a readership for whom the daily papers did little detailed reporting. Sporting subjects included boating, prize fighting, baseball, pedestrianism, and even such non-physical events as chess and checkers. The paper's theatrical news increased in emphasis during the 1860s, when war necessitated shutting down the popular *Spirit of the Times* because of its large circulation in the South. Practically speaking, the *Clipper* was the only theatrical paper in America during the decade of 1865 to 1875. At the turn of our century it was the most complete chronicler of amusement activities, and continued to be until competition from the *Billboard* forced its demise in 1924.

The *Clipper* was sold to Frank Queen in 1855, who, as sole proprietor and editor, soon established it as a major organ for sporting and theatrical reportage, with a reputation for reliability. Under Queen's guiding force the paper befriended the popular amusements neglected by other publications. In addition to its dramatic interests, it became the major source for circus, minstrel, and variety news, a position it held throughout the century. When vaudeville evolved from the old variety performances, the *Clipper* responded by be-

*Theatrical Rambles of Mr. & Mrs. Greene*, Charles Durang

coming the journalistic organ for it. Through active exploitation of circus, minstrelsy, and vaudeville, the New York *Clipper* became known to those in the entertainment world as "The Old Reliable" and "The Showman's Bible."

In writing these *Theatrical Rambles,* Durang made use of the memoirs of Mrs. Greene; however, he also supplied much additional material obtained from his experiences as actor, prompter, and dancing master. Born into a show family, he spent the greater part of his life on the Philadelphia stage, which was second only to New York City in theatrical significance. Consequently, he had the advantage of mingling with the leading entertainers and of being privy to the theatrical table talk of his day. He utilized these experiences when his retirement from the stage allowed him time for writing about the theatre and theatre folk, his most useful effort being *The Philadelphia Stage from the Year 1794 to the Year 1855,* published serially in the Philadelphia *Sunday Dispatch.*

Durang represents the theatrical spirit of his time. His life and career spanned the vigorous years of the nineteenth century, when dramatic activity expanded from within a few principal cities along the eastern seaboard to the new settlements of the western frontier. Born in 1794, the year the famed Chestnut Street Theatre in Philadelphia opened its doors, he lived through seventy-six years of theatrical change, dying on May 15, 1870.

His professional career began at the age of nine when he danced in *The Tale of Mystery* at the Chestnut Street Theatre. In 1815 he joined Holman's company at the theatre in Charleston, and he was there the following year when James Caldwell and Miss Latimer were brought over from England. In 1817 he was part of the Caldwell-Entwistle troupe performing in Alexandria, Washington, and Baltimore. He jointly managed the Raleigh theatre with his brother Ferdinand in 1820 with a company largely made up of a thespian society. The same year he was back in Philadelphia at the Walnut Street Theatre when Edwin Forrest made his theatrical debut as Young Norval in *Douglas.*

Although he spent most of his mature years in and

*Theatrical Rambles of Mr. & Mrs. Greene*, Charles Durang

around Philadelphia, Durang was occasionally connected with the New York playhouses. Ireland assumes it was Charles Durang who appeared at the Park Theatre in February of 1812 as "Harlequin" in the pantomime, giving great satisfaction "by his grace and dexterity." In the summer of 1827 he appeared at the Broadway Theatre in a "grand ballet of action," and as Jean Louis in *The Deserter* and Bilker in *The Hundred-Pound Note.*

Durang and the Greenes were fellow artists. They were professionally together during the Greenes' various engagements in Philadelphia, beginning in 1820. In his *Philadelphia Stage,* Durang recalled an earlier association with them as performers in a company in Frederickstown, Maryland. Of John Greene he commented:

> John Greene is a very good reader, has good judgment, and clever literary tastes. But his personal requisites may not have hit the general idea that the tragic muse requires in stilted dignity. He, however, succeeded in making a name in another department of dramatic walks. His features are very strongly marked, but rather of an iron cast, the opposite characteristics of his heart, which are benevolent and companionable.

And of Mrs. Greene:

> This lady was also in her novitiate. She subsequently became a most useful and talented actress. She had a commanding figure and very pretty features, and altogether won approbation from an amiable interest with which she invested her personations in comedy and tragedy. The latter walk she often supported with force and vigorous expression. Both on and off stage she was ever admired as a good actress and an amiable and an unassuming woman. Mrs. Greene had the misfortune in after life to be afflicted with deafness, a great evil to a performer.

> Mr. and Mrs. Greene are representatives of a class of journeymen actors without whom the theatre could not

*Theatrical Rambles of Mr. & Mrs. Greene*, Charles Durang

function, but who have been rewarded with only slight attention by the chroniclers of early nineteenth century performing. The predominance of the star system, beginning with visitations from England of such luminaries as Cooke, Kean, Macready, Miss Kemble, Miss Tree, and innumerable others who came to these shores to revitalize depleted treasuries, has obscured the role of the common player in the cooperative art of the theatre. The stock actor of a hundred and fifty years ago has been somewhat dehumanized to an item in the theatre property room, or at best raised no higher than an unfamiliar name on an old playbill. The Greenes, along with hundreds of supporting performers in their lifetime, were living, breathing craftsmen, undergoing frequent times of tribulation and rare moments of triumph, respectable artists who bore the almost daily vicissitudes as an expected part of their theatrical existence.

The Greenes were able and useful stock actors. Anne Greene excelled in tragic heroines. Ireland has observed of her stage work:

> She possessed no great diversity of talent, but in the highest range of walking ladies, the serious mothers, the distressed wives, and stately baronesses of the stage, we have never seen her surpassed .... In personal appearance, she was tall and commanding, and her costume was generally elegant and appropriate. Mrs. Greene has been well known at our minor theatres, where she often moved like a goddess among the mortals that surrounded her.

Henry Dickinson Stone, in recalling her performances in Albany, deemed her "a great favorite, a lady of the highest dramatic attainments, and a model woman in public as well as private life." He noted that she "seldom failed to work upon the sympathies of her audience," this being accomplished "by throwing such intensity of feeling and earnestness in the characters as to have the entire audience in tears, and not infrequently in audible sobs."

John Greene attained professional acclaim for his portrayal of Irishmen. Wemyss recalled that he was "for many years a favorite in the city of Philadelphia." Durang described him as "one of nature's actors, and, as a representative of low Irishmen, was without a compeer .... He had the peculiar talent of bringing forth all the prominency of interest and coloring of a principal ten length part." Ireland felt that before the emergence of the great English comedian, Power, and is famous Irish characterizations, Greene had acquired a high reputation, and as Dennis Brulgruddery he had "never seen him surpassed."

Charles Durang was not a man of literature. In all probability he had little formal education. Consequently, his writing style is cumbersome and ambling. Frequently he stops his narrative to deal with peripheral material or to defend the acting profession against a critical and suspicious public. He is writing as an actor of the early American theatre, not as a skilled compositor of ideas. In addition, he was an old man when he compiled these *Rambles,* having just turned seventy. Despite this, his efforts remain a significant contribution. The theatrical life of the Greenes, a typical yet model acting couple, is certainly revealing in terms of the active theatre of their time, its *modus operandi* in the first half of the nineteenth century.

This manuscript has undergone substantial editing. Liberty has been taken with syntax as well in an effort to improve on clarity and to allow the narrative to flow more easily. It is believed that these changes have in no way altered Durang's intentions, and it is hoped that it has not obscured his personal style. Furthermore, it is our best wish that *The Theatrical Rambles of Mr. and Mrs. John Greene* will furnish the reader with a full and satisfying experience of early American theatrical life.

—William L. Slout

*Theatrical Rambles of Mr. & Mrs. Greene*, Charles Durang

## CHRONOLOGY

1800    Anne Nuskey born March 23 at Boston, Massachusetts.

1815    The Nuskeys move to Norfolk, VA, where Anne makes her first appearance on stage. Marries Henry Lewis, a minor British actor, who brutalizes her.

1817    Lewis abandons his wife in Charleston, SC. She returns to her family in Baltimore.

1818    Meets and marries American actor, John Greene, beginning a relationship of 42 years. They join Willis's group.

1820    They tour the American Northwest, including Detroit, Green Bay, Chicago (then a collection of mud huts), and Canada, particularly Montréal.

1821-4    The Greenes join the Walnut Street Theatre in Philadelphia, and the Chestnut Street Theatre in Baltimore.

1825    They arrive at New Orleans (Jan.), where John is seriously ill. They then sail up the Mississippi, thence to Alabama, and back to the Northeast.

1830-5    They make a tour through the West Indies, and thence to England (Aug. 1, 1830), returning to New

*Theatrical Rambles of Mr. & Mrs. Greene*, Charles Durang

          York in Jan. 1831. Greene becomes stage manager at Albany, NY.

1836-9  A brief interlude in Canada is followed by a trip down the Ohio and Mississippi Rivers to New Orleans (1839), and thence to Louisville and Nashville.

1840    A tour through Illinois, Iowa, and Wisconsin.

1841-2  Back to New Orleans. J. Greene now regarded as a star.

1845-7  In the Northeast. They return to New Orleans (1847).

1848-51 A season in Chicago playing with obscure actors, and thence back to the Northeast and Nashville by 1851.

1851-60 The Greenes reside primarily in Nashville and 'Memphis, TN, where John manages several theatres. He dies in Memphis on May 28, 1860, and Anne in Nashville on Jan. 19, 1862.

*Theatrical Rambles of Mr. & Mrs. Greene*, Charles Durang

## I.

MRS. GREENE — THE WAR OF 1812—SPENCER H. CONE AS AN ACTOR — ADVISED TO GO ON THE STAGE BY A BISHOP —TROUBLE ABOUT A PART — A THEATRICAL RIOT — CONE LEAVING THE PROFESSION — APPEARANCE OF JOHN DUFF, ETC.

Mrs. Greene, whose memoirs furnish many incidents to these rambling sketches, was an offspring of New England's Pilgrims. Her name was Anne Nuskey. She was born in the capital of old Massachusetts, on March 23, 1800. On Mrs. Greene's final retirement from the stage at Nashville, about the year 1859, she was the oldest American actress on it and had traveled further and acted in more theatres than any other lady of the profession at that day. It may thus be seen at a glance what a rich and varied store of anecdotes and dramatic reminiscences such a career must furnish, especially from a female point of view, the sex being acute observers. We may venture to say that Mrs. Greene, whose notes we frequently refer to, was a woman of shrewd observation and possessed a keen faculty of description and raconteur. Therefore, there are sufficient relations of a curious nature to while away an idle hour in these itinerant sketches; if not, the fault must be in the narrator.

During the War of 1812, Anne Nuskey, with her mother, brother and sister, resided in the vicinity of Baltimore in a rustic cottage on the margin of Jones' Creek (or Falls), being within the shadows of Howard's lovely park, on a site of one of the many hills which so romantically encircle that then truly rural city. A well-stocked orchard of peach and cherry trees was attached to their dwelling, where Anne

## Theatrical Rambles of Mr. & Mrs. Greene, Charles Durang

studied her school lessons and where she oft indulged in viewing the distant gleaming of the Patapeco, or the flashing waters of the Chesapeake bay.[1] Thus did her girlish fancy first receive the impressions of romance, those poetical idealisms that amaze the tender mind and so imprint and shape youthful aspirations that mold and confirm the destinies of life. Here in this secluded retreat of health, of purity, of innocence and ease she passed the happiest days of her life.

But these scenes of happiness and contentment were doomed to be destroyed by the rude blasts of war's alarms, the clash of arms, the roar of cannon and the flash of bomb shells. The deadly struggle between America and England was then in progress and war's wild blast blew throughout the land and around their flower-clad and tree-embosomed cottage. On September 11th, while the girls were arranging their dinner table under the trees in the garden, the serenity of their blissful domestic scenes, like a stroke of magic, was suddenly over-clouded with the sorrows and presence of the bloody battle field. The signals from the city announced the approach of the British fleet, and the brother had to hasten to join his volunteer regiment at the rendezvous in Gay Street. Everything was in confusion; every cart, dray, or wagon that could be procured was engaged to carry furniture and valuables to the country parts adjacent. York road, Governstown road, in fact every avenue leading to the city was crowded with families departing with their household goods; while volunteers from the country were pouring down the same roads armed with rifles, muskets and every weapon that they had been able to procure.

Although there were but few Americans on the stage at this time, those that were on it volunteered in defense of their country; amongst whom were Spencer H. Cone, Thomas A. Cooper, my brother, Ferdinand Durang, Joseph Harris, and myself.[2]

Mr. Cone graduated at Princeton College at an early age, and in his 17th year developed remarkable physical qualities of strength and activity with fine mental elements. His love of literature and the sciences thus early shaped his first vocations, and he became an instructor of

## *Theatrical Rambles of Mr. & Mrs. Greene*, Charles Durang

youth and prepared many scholars for college. From an acquaintance with that good and truly venerable minister of the Gospel, Dr. Abercrombie, Principal of the celebrated old Academy in North 4$^{th}$ street, Philadelphia, he became through that divine's solicitation an active assistant in that "High School," where some of our professional men of the past generation received their education.[3]

In 1805, either from inclination or the fascination of the drama to the youthful, cultivated mind, or, for the prospect of a larger income than that which is given to a teacher, Mr. Cone turned his attention to the stage and made his first appearance in July of that year as Achmet in the tragedy of *Mahomet*,[4] making a most successful impression as a novice. The debut was made at the old Chestnut Street Theatre, Philadelphia, then in its zenith. He soon became a popular favorite; a native feeling for the young aspirant flowed deeply in the current of public sentiment. The performers were all English, prejudices were strong, but he bent the barrier and Cone was one of the first Thespians that gave birth to that predilection for so called "native talent" that has since echoed and re-echoed through the land.

With the ladies he was quite an Adonis. He was not tall of figure, about 5 feet 7 inches in height, symmetrically stout, of great muscle in the limbs, with thin, pale features, regular, but not strongly marked or of impassioned expression; hence his tragedy was not forcible or deeply imbued with the genius of passionate illustration. His voice was silvery and musical. His aspect was pleasing but his action had been spoiled, or rendered stiff and awkward, through early instruction in the angular gesticulation of the academical schools, where the arms are taught a windmill-like motion, in constant whirling circular action. His filial affections for his mother and sisters were of the most exemplary character; and probably those virtues were not more sacredly exalted or embalmed in his heart when he assumed the heavenly functions of the preacher than when he wore the tragic *cothurnus* or buskin.

His sons have given to the public a very minute and elaborate biography of their father, wherein they touch deli-

## *Theatrical Rambles of Mr. & Mrs. Greene*, Charles Durang

cately that very interesting portion which embraced his youthful theatrical career, and became apologetic of his youthful aberration of the proprieties of his vocation by qualifying the peculiar claims of the profession as to respectability that Mrs. Warren—the Siddons of the American stage—was the only performer's house he visited.[5] "It's lawyers, poets, artists, etc., did congregate there." They might have truthfully said that in such a galaxy of talent and private worth he found professional brethren and sisters in every relations of cultivation and moral attributes worthy of his association even after he assumed the sacerdotal robe.

It would seem from the history of his life that a Bishop of the Episcopal Church was instrumental in his embracing the theatrical profession. Waiting upon the reverend gentleman who had often given him fatherly advice, and wishing further council as to his future pursuits, the bishop advised him to study for the church, as nature had bestowed on him great advantages for it, and offering, if he accepted the advice, to see that he was provided for during the period of his theological studies. He described warmly the advantages that presented themselves to him—position, ease, reputation, etc. This was a tempting offer to one in need. But the Baptist form of religion overruled that of the Episcopalian and he declined. The good bishop then said, "There is but one thing more that I can advise you to do; it is to go on the stage. Your voice and physical abilities eminently fit you for it." The advice was taken and he went on the stage and thereby gained reputation, applause, fame, and money to support respectably a mother and sisters which he could not do as an obscure teacher.

At the period that Mr. Cone undertook juvenile tragedy and comedy, the stage was occupied in every department, male and female, by English performers. The great trouble in all theatrical companies is what is technically called casting the pieces, assigning to each actor employed in the *dramatis personae* their appropriate character, which is called "a line of business"; that is, the kind of characters which the performers especially engage to act, which is distinctly mentioned in their articles of engagement. This stipulates to have

*Theatrical Rambles of Mr. & Mrs. Greene*, Charles Durang

certain parts in all plays wherein they exist, to the exclusion of any other performer.

From this casting power, which lies with the manager or his stage representative, a difficulty arose with Mr. Cone and the Warren dynasty about the disposition of a part claimed by Mr. Cone as his right by precedent and the terms of his engagement. The result was a belligerent demonstration of Mr. Cone's friends on the night of the piece's performance, wherein Mr. Cone's part was assigned to another. On the night in question, the friends of Mr. Cone assembled in formidable forces, having posted on the corner of the streets, on the pillars of the colonnade in front of the old theatre, and other places, hand bills inscribed "Cone or No Play." The excitement was very great and as the house filled up its intensity increased to violence and rage; thundering noises with sticks, hisses, yells, and deafening screams of savage calls made a most terrific scene. The players could not be heard at all. All personal appeals from the stage proved fruitless. Mr. McKenzie, a very good actor, was playing Richmond in *Richard III*.[6] This was demanded as Mr. Cone's part. Mr. McKenzie went forward and stated that he did not cast the plays, that the stage manager did agreeable to the rules of theatrical government; and he was obliged, from the tenor of his engagement, to obey orders or to forfeit a week's salary and be discharged. This explanation had no effect. The tumult only gathered strength, denouncing the management for breaking faith with their cherished *protégé*. The assaults of noise and riotous uproar continued through three acts, the people calling upon the managers to address Mr. Cone's grievances and that then their hostilities would cease.

Warren and Wood yielded to this enraged audience and sent for Mr. Cone, who was at a distance from the theatre. He ran in breathless haste to answer the summons. A brief interview with the managers restored a good understanding and Mr. Cone consented to address the audience to calm if possible their popular indignation. The curtain having fallen on what might be called the "pantomime of Richard the Third," Mr. Cone addressed the audience in eloquent

## *Theatrical Rambles of Mr. & Mrs. Greene*, Charles Durang

terms, requesting them to suspend their hostilities for the present, that negotiations were pending to settle the difficulty which, no doubt, would be amicably arranged in a few days. The managers agreed to refer the affair to two gentlemen, who decided in Mr. Cone's favor; and thus was the theatrical rebellion crushed and the old *entente cordiale* restored. The outbreak clearly declared the great popularity of Mr. Cone, the higher classes of society largely supporting him.

In 1810 he became dissatisfied with the theatrical profession. Taking a very superficial view of it, he perceived that members of it were subjected to be criticized by fools and fellows who could hardly write their own names, yet considered themselves privileged to judge! approve! condemn! or hiss! having paid their dollar, fifty, or twenty-five cents. Those thoughts, though not very philosophical, were in some measure true, but every business of life has its dark side.

In 1811 his desire to abandon all dramatic temples increased; but he doubted the policy of resigning the situation that afforded him a generous remuneration, although not congenial to his disposition. But the pursuit that should take the place of the player's vocation seemed a mooted point; certainly none of the many that suggested themselves offered the pecuniary equivalent to the despised sock and buskin. He was puzzled to choose in this business call to another sphere of life. A circulating library in Baltimore was much wanted and many friends suggested it as in consonance with his habits and tastes. But that depended upon uncertain success, as the establishment could only progress slowly and bring in small returns at first. His expenses were absolute and could not wait on contingencies.

He then thought of his maiden profession of teacher and commenced a subscription for a school. Having obtained pupils enough in advance to warrant the opening in June, he proceeded to obtain the manager's leave to absent himself from the morning rehearsals and only to appear at night, as he was still under contract to Warren and Wood. But the permission of the managers he did not obtain. The rules of the theatre were as rigid for attendance at rehearsals as for the performances at night. At that day the entrances and exits

*Theatrical Rambles of Mr. & Mrs. Greene*, Charles Durang

had to be made at the proper places and the language as closely spoken at rehearsal as before the audience at night. Thus was his academy repudiated.

He subsequently proposed a plan of English and classical education; but it was coldly received. He was much mortified at the failure. Mr. Cone was then offered a share in a commercial dictionary, then on the eve of publication. This issue depended upon the event of hostilities being commenced. But war! war! was the cry. So the dictionary remained in *status quo*.

During the latter end of the year of 1812 he seceded from the drama's temple. His benefit receipts were $460. In his farewell address on this occasion he glanced at a want of public favor, a lack of advancement in the theatre, among the other alleged reasons for leaving it.[7] At the close of his engagement, he received the office of bookkeeper and treasurer to the *Baltimore American*. This paper was then in a most flourishing condition and Mr. Cone's duties were heavy and responsible.

During the summer of 1812 Mr. Chandler Price, the uncle of Miss Morrel, died. As he had violently opposed her union with Mr. Cone, this death removed one of the difficulties to their marriage, which took place about two years after. After he was one year in the employ of the *Baltimore American* establishment, John Nowel, Esq., brother-in-law to Mr. Cone (having married his sister), proposed to him to purchase the *Baltimore Whig*. They did so and zealously supported the Madison administration and defended the war principles of 1812 with much ability. Mr. Cone pursued his patriotic military pursuits and commanded the Baltimore Union Artillery Company, having been elected its captain.

The season of 1811 and 1812 was a disastrous one. The benefits at the close of it were generally failures. It was during the benefits that John Duff—the very paragon of a great general actor,[8] the unique Elliston of our stage, and one of the most imposing, showy comedians that ever trod the stage, with great personal qualities, and a voice that was music itself—appeared and charmed our audiences for many years. He made his bow in Macbeth and Jeremy Didler[9] to a

*Theatrical Rambles of Mr. & Mrs. Greene*, Charles Durang

poor house of about $120. The hit he made was tremendous; and such was the excitement to see him that, in this season when the theatres had been deserted, when the actors could not draw half the expenses, Mr. Duff with *Three and the Deuce* brought $624. In *The School of Reform* and *The Critic*, $750; *Three and the Deuce* repeated, $560; and on his own benefit night playing *Alexander the Great* to the enormous receipts of $1,102. His success was extraordinary.[10]

The Walnut Street Theatre was now in the full tide of successes, a powerful rival to old "Drury."[11] They refused Mr. Duff an appearance there when he first applied and which they afterwards regretted. The Capitolian stars of 1811 and 1812 destroyed all the stock company's combined efforts and their benefit boons. Cooper played nine nights, alternating with Dwyer, the former averaging about $500 a night, the latter $450. The youthful star, John Howard Payne, averaged for nine nights $400; the great Cooke for 12 nights, $1,177, $1,121, $1,000, $917, $780, etc. His Shylock drew the largest houses. *Richard III*, his last and 12th, $1,180. Cooke's benefit (last night) was $571. On the 1st of January, 1812, *The Lady of the Lake*[12] was first produced to about $1,200. It proved a great success, and a save-all to the management. Amongst benefit failures, Cone's was a sad one. Another was given him to retrieve his losses when was produced for the first time in America Diamond's beautiful drama of *The Peasant Boy*,[13] which, with a powerful appeal to his friends and the public by S. H. Cone, produced $740.

This was his last season in the theatre. He was always a kind friend, an affectionate son and brother, a religious and honorable man while in the theatrical profession. He could be no more in the theological one, and his after life was a refutation of all slanders against the former, as it did not pollute or unfit him for the latter.

**NOTES**

[1]The Patapsco River empties into Chesapeake Bay and, in 1812, was just south of the city.
[2]The shelling began with an attack on Ft. McHenry, September 12, 1814. The newly erected and yet not completed

*Theatrical Rambles of Mr. & Mrs. Greene*, Charles Durang

Baltimore theatre operated throughout the siege. A benefit performance was offered by the proprietors, Warren and Wood, in early October, the funds to support the defense of the city. Cone made his acting debut in Philadelphia when a detachment of the Chestnut Street Theatre was performing at the Southwark in June of 1806. "Flattered with his success," as Durang put it, he accompanied the company to Washington and Alexandria. He remained with them through the season of 1812, performing juvenile tragedy and second men in comedy. Cone died in New York City on September 4, 1855. Thomas Apthorpe Cooper (1776-1849), unappreciated in London, was brought to the Chestnut Street Company by Wignell in 1796. Handsome, talented, and with a fine voice, he was successful in both comedy and tragedy, and was one of the leading actors during the first quarter of the century. By 1838 he had left the stage and taken an appointment as Custom House officer in New York. He died in Bristol, PA, age 73. Ferdinand Durang (1796-1831) first appeared at the Chestnut Street Theatre. A performer without possessing extraordinary merit, he was useful in almost every line—a good swordsman and dancer, excelling in melodramatic and French characters. Joseph Harris was the adopted son of Mr. and Mrs. Francis, performers in the Warren and Wood Company. He was probably a minor actor in the same company.

[3]It was Dr. Abercrombie who performed the marriage of William B. Wood and Miss Juliana Westray, January 30, 1804.

[4]Sometimes called *The Impostor*, the piece was first performed in America during the Revolution by military actors. Various versions of it were produced in both England and America, including those by Garrick and Miller.

[5]Mrs. Warren (1769-1808), nee Miss Brunton, daughter of the manager of the Norwich Theatre, married Robert Merry, 1792; married Thomas Wignell, 1803; married William Warren 1806.

[6]McKenzie, a native of Scotland, was connected with Philadelphia theatricals for several years, where he performed in second tragedy and "parts requiring dignity and

*Theatrical Rambles of Mr. & Mrs. Greene*, Charles Durang

firmness of deportment." His habits were intemperate; after a period of despondency, he drowned himself in the Delaware River.

[7] Cone's line of parts was taken over by Barrett.

[8] John Duff was a respected actor in Dublin before coming to America and making his debut in Boston in 1810. After introducing his wife to the public in 1823, her success eclipsed his. Duff died in Philadelphia in 1831.

[9] Jeremy Didler was a character in *Raising the Wind*, a farce by Kenney.

[10] *Three and a Deuce* was a farce by Prince Hoare which offered an actor three roles in one, Pertinax Single, Penegrine Single, and Percival Single. *School of Reform*, a comedy by Thomas Morton; *The Critic*, a farce by R. B. Sheridan; *Alexander the Great; or, The Rival Queens*, a tragedy by Nathaniel Lee.

[11] Both the Park Theatre, New York, and the Chestnut Street Theatre, Philadelphia, were affectionately designated "old Drury" after the Drury Lane Theatre, London.

[12] *The Lady of the Lake*, a melodrama by W. J. Dibdin, was adapted from the Walter Scott poem.

[13] *The Peasant Boy* was a melodrama by William Dimond (or Diamond).

*Theatrical Rambles of Mr. & Mrs. Greene*, Charles Durang

## II.

DEATH OF GEORGE FREDERICK COOKE — OPENING OF THE BALTIMORE HOLLIDAY THEATRE — MRS. MASON AND MR, ENTWISTLE — BOMBARDMENT OF FORT MC HENRY — ANNE JOINS THE BEAUMONT CORPS OF THESPIANS — MARRIED TO A BRUTE — ANNE'S UNION WITH JOHN GREENE, ETC.

Why wears the stage this unaccustomed gloom?
Why rises on the view the distant tomb?
What grief has taught Thalia's tears to flow,
And clothed the Tragic Muse in deeper woe?
The mighty master of the scenic art,
The great portrayer of the human heart,
Cooke is no more! The inmate of his breast,
His active spirit, seeks eternal rest;
Seeks in a happier, and a holier sphere
Relief from trials, toils, and triumphs here.
His genius claimed crooked Richard for his own;
Resplendent through the dark Glenalvon shone;
Joined Cawdor's treachery to Cawdor's fear,
And sparkled in the diadem of Lear;
With Pierre gave interest to a traitor's cause,
And gained for Cato more sublime applause.
Then every tragic trophy nobly won,
He shone the comic Muse's favorite son;
Falstaff's conflicting qualities combined,
The grossest body, and the liveliest mind;
Faultless appeared his Caledonian Knight
Where sternest critics said that all was right.
Various his talents. If in that rich mind
Some human frailties scrutiny can find,
Such is the lot to every mortal given;

*Theatrical Rambles of Mr. & Mrs. Greene*, Charles Durang

> Error with man, forgiveness lies with heaven.
> Peace to his ashes! Distant realms combine
> Thou great Tragedian thus to honor thine.
> Friends of the drama! be it yours to mourn,
> And place fresh chaplets on the funeral urn;
> For your applause he ploughed the Atlantic wave
> And found a welcome, where he found a grave.[2]

The Baltimore Holliday Street Theatre opened under the management of Warren and Wood. The house was unfinished, it being a new one erected on the site where the old wooden one had stood.[3] The seats of the second and third tier were only rough boarded, yet the theatre was nightly filled with the army encamped in and about the city, which amounted to twenty-five or thirty thousand men. Mr. Entwistle and Mrs. Mason were members of the company at this time. Mrs. Mason had a very fine figure, very ugly face, and very fascinating manners. Notwithstanding her want of beauty, she monopolized the attention of all the *beaux*, some of whom were young enough to be her sons.

Mrs. Mason, Mr. Entwistle, and Mr. Stewart[4] boarded in the same house. Mr. Entwistle had a singular face, well calculated for low comedy. The Widow Mason used to be much amused at what she called "his comical phiz," and wasted more sarcasm on it than ever Beatrice did on Benedict.

"Suppose we get married?" said Entwistle as they were sitting after dinner one day.

"Suppose we do!" was her reply, laughingly taking it as a joke.

The next day after dinner Entwistle exclaimed, "I've got it!" and produced a marriage license.

She reprimanded him for wasting money on such a joke. However, Stewart resolved to carry the joke on, got all the performers to join in it, and they walked into the green room the next morning with wedding favors on their breasts to congratulate the happy couple. The lady got angry but the gentleman ordered cake and wine and passed all off as a joke. The excitement was over and circumstances forgotten when, some weeks after, Mr. Entwistle and Mrs. Mason con-

*Theatrical Rambles of Mr. & Mrs. Greene*, Charles Durang

sidered the matter over and thought they might as well use the license. They went to church, stood before the altar, where they were joined in holy wedlock.[5]

It was on the 11th of September, 1814, while the citizens were in church, that the signal guns were fired. The following day the bombardment of Fort McHenry commenced, which lasted during the entire night. While the author of the "Star Spangled Banner" was a prisoner on board of one of the British vessels, the situation he was placed in suggested the words of that ever popular hymn![6] In the confusion occasioned by the times, the cottages around Baltimore and all the out houses were converted into bedrooms. Families even slept in the carriages that had conveyed them from the foe. Any place for a shelter was acceptable.

Whilst madam rumor was continually giving the alarm of defeat to the tortured minds of those who had friends in the fray, in this state of mind did Mrs. Greene's family remain in anguished contemplation with many other families whose husbands, brothers, and friends were absent on the battle field and not yet heard from, not knowing whether they were dead or alive. All were anxiously awaiting tidings from them and thus could only hope and pray in silence.

One moonlight night, while the family was assembled beneath the same trees where a lost loved one had bidden them a hasty farewell with tearful fondness, they were recalling his last words and looks, when they were startled by a faint exclamation of "Mother! Dear mother!" All started up with the expectation of seeing a disembodied spirit, so unearthly seemed the voice, when the pale moon's light fell on a death-like face and a figure covered with blood streaming from his fearful wounds fell at their feet. On raising him up, they recognized the lamented brother. With lightning speed his wounds were dressed. That night mingled joy and sorrow pervaded the household, joy that his life was spared and sorrowing and lamenting over his wounds.

The family remained safe in their retreat until peace was proclaimed in 1815. Then they removed to Norfolk, and there the tender years of Anne Nuskey met the turning point

*Theatrical Rambles of Mr. & Mrs. Greene*, Charles Durang

of her destiny. The widowed mother's means were small and meager, as they were depending for their resources upon the eldest daughter. Anne, with independence and feeling, expressed a desire to aid in the support of the family by adopting the profession of the stage, for which art she had a very strong predilection and felt an instinctive capability of being able to successfully sustain herself.

An opportunity offered itself in the presence of a small *corps* of regular Thespians under the management of Mr. de Jersey Beaumont,[7] from the Edinburgh Theatres, who made his first appearance in Philadelphia about 1810 for a few nights as Rolla, Octavian, the Stranger, etc. He was a fine figured man and a showy performer but possessed no talent for acting. He subsequently became, for a brief season, manager of the Walnut Street Theatre. His wife, Mrs. Beaumont, was an actress of much excellence in tragedy, and starred it at the old Chestnut Street Theatre with great *éclat*. She played in London with great success.

Beaumont's *corps* at once offered an opportunity for the ordeal of a trial. And being introduced to the majestic manager, an arrangement was soon made. Miss Nuskey's personal requisites of symmetrical figure and beauty of expression of face at once struck him as a valuable acquisition to his *rôle d'équipage*. Her mother opposed the attempt but the bland and polished Beaumont soon won the slow and unwilling consent of the wary parent to her daughter's first appearance. The debut was successfully made and Anne Nuskey finally became an enrolled member of this dramatic *corps*.

On the same night of our fair debutante's *entrée*, a new foreign actor made his appearance in America, Mr. Henry Lewis,[8] a son of the celebrated Mr. Lewis of Covent Garden Theatre, London, who for a period of thirty-six years held the rank of first comedian of the British stage and whose boast it was that during his long career "it had never once been his misfortune to fall under the displeasure of the public." A rare truth for an actor's lot.

As the ablest representative of high life and fashion in all its various phases, he never had his peer. His Copper Captain in *Rule a Wife*[9] was said to be one of the finest speci-

*Theatrical Rambles of Mr. & Mrs. Greene*, Charles Durang

mens of pure acting that was seen from the days of Garrick to the Kembles. He was a native of Dublin and had all the brilliancy of the true Irish gentleman.

But this son of his had none of the father's excellent qualities on or off the stage. He was short of stature, slim of figure, with a round, unmeaning face, red hair and beard, and a faint imitation of his father's manner, with a perfect lack of genius, and sorrowful to say, wholly bereft of any principle of honor or propriety of conduct that should mark the man or the gentleman.

Henry Lewis, though many years older than Miss Nuskey, succeeded in winning her affections. She was inexperienced and unfortunately became his wife. But after a course of brutal treatment of many months, savage cruelties that would fill a volume, she was compelled to leave him and return to her home. It was afterwards ascertained that he had a wife and family in his native country.

In 1817 this Lewis arrived in Charleston, South Carolina (after he had married her at Norfolk) in a small schooner, in pursuit of professional employment. It was Mr. Holman's first season after the war of 1812. Mr. Lewis played Jeremy Didler, Dr. Dablancour,[10] and two other comedy parts with poor success. He had no money and left his wife (Miss Nuskey that he had married in Norfolk) on board the vessel, deserted and forlorn, while he fed and lodged at the Planter's Hotel. He had beaten her until she was black and blue, tore her earrings from her ears, and destroyed her clothing. Let humanity and disgust cease to dwell further upon so revolting a topic.

At length the captain of the craft, being about to sail, was touched with her situation, seeing she was without any home but his rude cabin and its rough accommodations. He appealed to her husband, but in vain; his feelings were perverted from that of man to a brute! The captain then sought some of the actors to communicate to them the situation of the unfortunate young lady. The first of this class that he fell in with was the well known Charles Young,[11] in his day a histrion of infinite popularity, with the figure of a Hercules, the heart of a lion in courage, yet with pulses which beat with

*Theatrical Rambles of Mr. & Mrs. Greene*, Charles Durang

a woman's softness and tenderness. The case was made known to him by this son of the ocean; and with true Christian feelings for the unfortunate, Charles Young and his theatrical brethren sought and relieved her from her tribulations. Thus rescued, she returned to her mother.

Lewis' father, the great comedian, realized a fortune of £55,000. During his life he kept up an elegant establishment in London. It was no light expense but his high associations and noble social position required this mode of life. He was the author of *The Monk* and several other works. Many of the old play editions of *The Midnight Hour* contain his full length portrait as "The Marquis" in that pleasing little comedy. The likeness was taken by Martin Arthur Shea, and now adorns the National Gallery in London. It was a valuable and interesting bequest from a son of Mr. Lewis (an elder brother of the sad case that came to this country) to the trustees of that admirable institution of art. So should private worth and public merit be ever perpetuated.[12]

After Mrs. Lewis wended her way to the North and reached her mother's humble but protecting home, her elder sister married an actor of the name of Bignall, one of the descendants of the Bignalls who early introduced theatricals into Virginia and North Carolina.[13]

Their father, an Englishman, built the first regular theatre at Norfolk, which was a substantial edifice but meagerly furnished with scenery, etc. It stood in an isolated situation in the suburbs of the town in the midst of a cornfield and vegetable garden. It looked desolate and deserted of every human care when we performed in it in 1830. On this building the Bignall family put in claims of ownership. Thus it went into ruin while in a state of litigation, but the family lost the suit through the quibbles of the law.

John Bignall was a prompter and actor and a member several times of Warren and Wood's company. At the time of Mrs. Greene's sister's marriage with John Bignall, the Bignall family resided in Baltimore and kept a boarding house. Mr. John Greene and a company with which he had been making a theatrical tour through Virginia, of which company John Bignall and wife had been members, returned

## *Theatrical Rambles of Mr. & Mrs. Greene*, Charles Durang

to Baltimore for a recess and to recruit, and most of the company took up their quarters at the Bignall boarding house.[14]

It was at this time that Anne Nuskey, or rather Mrs. H. Lewis, paid a visit to her sisters, Mr. John Greene being temporarily absent in Philadelphia, where sometimes he plied his profession of printer during his acting apprenticeship. Here she was hourly regaled with extravagant eulogies upon Greene's merits, personal, and professional, his promising talents as an actor, his manly and benevolent qualities, till she grew tired of hearing his name and disgusted with the theme. Greene's mind, also, through the waggery of the family, received unfavorable impressions of her personal qualities and crooked ill tempered disposition. All this, as pertaining to her, were false representations, so much so that when her friends insisted on obtaining a divorce from that prodigal son (to give him no harsher name), her timid nature shrunk from the step, but her friends were resolute.

John Greene's personal aspect bore a very strange contrast to his genial disposition, for he had a heart filled with the milk of human kindness. His figure was rather dwarfish, stout about the shoulders, and the breast of Hercules. The muscle in the torso was remarkable, which tapered down to the lower limbs with a feminine delicacy. His head was very large, disproportioned to his stature. A phrenologist would probably declare too much brain. The face was peculiarly marked with iron sternness, expressive of strong will, a desperate, courageous nature, and an anti-humane temperament unmistakably delineated in every line. He was the reverse of all these demoniac indications that a Lavater would have recognized. His views were liberal to a fault.

When his wife was first introduced to him she was so struck with his strong inhuman expression of countenance that she shunned all intercourse with him. But soon love triumphed over appearances, for Greene's suavity of manners and conversational powers, with his good nature and merry humors, won her affections, and the sparks from cupid's flame warmed the twain, which daily interviews fanned into a blaze and at length culminated into a genuine old fashioned attachment. Here was a capricious caper for love to play! for soon Hymen's torch waved his conjugal fire over the pair and they wedded for better or worse, which union united them during forty-two years but was severed by the shafts of death at last.[15]

John Greene was a native of Philadelphia, born in Southwark, from whence so many bright geniuses have sprung to adorn the professions, the arts and the science, where naval architecture flourishes in all its beauty and ingenuity. It was there that our warships of the United States Navy of 1798 were modeled and built, and there, we may add, our enlightened Ironsides, John Greene, took in the first respiration of this breathing world.

John Greene served an apprenticeship and practiced the type art there and became early initiated in Faust's mysteries that have so enlightened the world. And, like all the disciples of Laurentius Coster (who first gave birth to printing 426 years ago), took to the sock and buskin instinctively, as it is a profession that derives its impulses from letters and intellectual elements, the printer's food and drink.[16]

After their marriage, Mr. and Mrs. Greene joined a company of Thespians under the management of Mr. Willis.[17]

## NOTES

[1]The Philadelphia season opened on September 28, 1812, with *The Constitution; or American Tars Triumphant*, a play celebrating the first naval victory of the war. The companion piece was *The Soldier's Daughter*. The Baltimore season began on March 23, 1812, and was concluded on June 7. The company then removed to Washington, performing there from June 15 to August 10.

[2]The tribute to Cooke occurred on October 2, 1812. The bill for the evening was *The Stranger*, after which was offered this *Tribute to Departed Genius; or, The Tears of Thalia Helponene*. The stage was set with "an extensive view of the Cathedral, richly illuminated," and "a statue of the immortal Shakespeare." On one side of the stage was a bust of Ben Jonson. In front was an elevated mourning platform on which was exhibited Sully's full-length picture of Cooke as

*Theatrical Rambles of Mr. & Mrs. Greene*, Charles Durang

Richard III. The painter Thomas Sully was the son of actor Matthew Sully, Sr. As a child he appeared with his parents at the Charleston Theatre. But in 1808, after studying art, he moved to Philadelphia where his artistic career was carried on.

[3] The new Baltimore theatre was opened on April 20, 1814. The season lasted until June 10.

[4] It is questionable as to the identity of Stewart. He may have been the John Stewart, an Englishman, who made his debut in America with the strolling Kenna family in 1792, and who was known on both sides of the Atlantic as "Walking Stewart."

[5] Entwistle had performed at the Boston theatre and then, in the spring of 1814, at the Anthony Street Theatre, New York. He eventually died in New Orleans by suicide. Mrs. Mason made her American debut at the Park Theatre, October 23, 1809, in the Edward Moore tragedy, *The Gamesters*. She also died in New Orleans in 1835. Entwistle and Mrs. Mason were married in 1816, a union that was unsuccessful and lasted barely a year. At this time Mrs. Mason was believed to have a comfortable sum of money. This misconception led Entwistle into theatre management, which proved unfortunate. Mrs. Mason later married an actor by the name of Crooke.

[6] Soon after the "Star Spangle Banner" was composed, the piece was sung by Charles and Ferdinand Durang from the stage of the Holliday Theatre. The performance was received so enthusiastically by the Baltimoreans that it was repeated every night for several weeks.

[7] de Jersey Beaumont, a manager of a company in the Virginia circuit, first appeared in New York in June of 1814. Ireland called him "handsome and showy" but much inferior to his wife. The Beaumonts were with the Warren and Wood Company in 1810-11. Mrs. Beaumont was, as described by Durang, "a fine, dashing actress," but weak in tragedy.

[8] Henry Lewis attempted his father's line of roles at the Chestnut Street Theatre in 1816, but was unsuccessful. Wood calls him a "faint imitation of his-father's manner" who

*Theatrical Rambles of Mr. & Mrs. Greene*, Charles Durang

"failed to conceal the want of genius, or the disadvantages of a person not gracefully made."

[9] *Rule a Wife and Have a Wife*, was a long popular piece by John Fletcher.

[10] Dablancour, in *The Budget of Blunders*, was a farce by Greffulhe.

[11] Not to be confused with the Charles Young of the English stage. The American Charles Young first appeared in New York at the Park Theatre on December 23, 1805. In 1826 he was stage manager for the Bowery Theatre, NYC, and last appeared in that city at the Richmond Hill Theatre in 1833.

[12] Durang has confused the actor William Thomas "Gentleman" Lewis with Matthew Gregory "Monk" Lewis. The latter rose to fame with the publication of his Gothic novel, *The Monk*. M. G. Lewis, presumed to be homosexual, had no children. *The Midnight Hour; or, Ruse Contra Ruse* was a comedy by Mrs. Inchbald.

[13] The Bignall family occupied theatres along the eastern coast. In 1793 they were in Charleston, managing as West and Bignall. Mrs. West led in tragedy, Mrs. Bignall in comedy. The family was later connected with the Chestnut Street Theatre. John Bignall, married to Mrs. Greene's sister, was prompter at the Chestnut Street Theatre in 1830-31.

[14] Greene had only recently made his theatrical debut (1818) at Frederickston, Maryland.

[15] The Greenes were married in 1818.

[16] Printing seems to have been a second trade for many actors—John H. McVicker, William Forrest, Charles Porter, William Burton, and George Frederick Cooke being just a few examples.

[17] Mr. and Mrs. Willis are a puzzle. There was a Mr. Willis that was an equestrian performer at this time. There were people by the name of Willis connected with the Chestnut Street Theatre and Wemyss's Pittsburgh theatre in the 1830s. Ludlow mentions a George Willis, circa 1818, with a company formed in Nashville. I have found nothing to confirm our Willis's identity with any of the above.

*Theatrical Rambles of Mr. & Mrs. Greene,* Charles Durang

## III.

THE ACTORS IN PENNSYLVANIA — CHARLES S. PORTER'S APPRENTICESHIP — THE GREENES JOIN THE WILLIS TROUPE — A SHE DEVIL — BIG SCOTT — FAILURE OF AN EXPEDITION BY SCOTT AND PORTER, ETC.

In 1819 while manager Willis and the Greenes were occupying the grounds of the Cumberland valley, Entwistle formed another scheme with the intention of making a circuit in the state of Pennsylvania.[1] He opened in Lancaster and there failed most gloriously when his debts lodged him in durance vile, whence he was delivered through the benefit of the then insolvent act.

Mr. Charles S. Porter entered his first stage apprenticeship with Entwistle. He had been a member of much promise in the old Moretonian Dramatic Society that occupied the old South Street Theatre in days of yore.[2] The society took its name from the favorite actor, John Pollard Moreton, a member of the first Chestnut Street Theatre of 1794, whose elegant and engaging traits of personal deportment and finished histrionic powers made him the model of perfection of the art critics and all play goers. From the easy dignity of his figure and manners, Gilbert Stuart, the distinguished painter of George Washington's full length portrait, selected Moreton to stand as model for the outlines of "the father of his country."

This actor, who did much to elevate his profession, both by his public talent and private worth, died in the season of 1797. His health was ever delicate, and while performing Lothario in *The Fair Penitent*[3] on one of the coldest nights of that severe winter, he had to lie on the stage in his thin dress

## *Theatrical Rambles of Mr. & Mrs. Greene*, Charles Durang

for a great length of time ere the curtain fell. When he was raised he was found totally insensible. He was borne to his dressing room and thence home in a torpid state. It was observed that his acting had for ever passed. He lingered a few weeks and expired.

After Entwistle's failure, Mr. Porter and his brethren formed a traveling *corps*, playing at Little York, Gettysburg, Chambersburg, Hagerstown, etc., where they soon formed a junction with manager Willis and the Greenes, who were on the Virginia side of the Potomac holding forth in the towns in the Shenandoah Valley.

The manager's wife, Mrs. Willis, was a very handsome woman, but of a very shrewish temperament, wishing to be independent and govern in all things, fond of power and its uncontrolled exercise, a very despot in her theatrical rule, snatching her husband's managerial thunder and using it to hurl at the poor players, as she considered her right as the Juno of the mimic throne. "Her vaulting ambition" too often, however, "o'er leaping itself, fell on the others." Her jealousy, like Othello's, without any objective cause, was often aroused and perplexed to madness. But her strongest passion was that of money power, suffering no rival near the till of the box office. This *autocratrix* insisted on being the sole treasurer, not only in holding the sinews of the war, the cash, but assuming the stage manager's function of casting the plays, arranging the bill of performances, and to propose or veto any measure that did not meet her views. Thus holding all managerial control, she sold the tickets night after night, and pocketing the proceeds postponed the salary day to pay the performers and mechanics as suited her royal pleasure. Her arbitrary conduct of paying or non-paying brought the business to a halt, leaving her husband to pay the people in promises, the only currency left him (she took all the coin and paper money).

One by one the members seceded from their allegiance. Mr. C. S. Porter had met J. M. Scott (called by way of distinction Big Scott).[4] This notable histrion of the day was then plying his skill as a master tailor, with six or seven journeymen working in his establishment. But his unfortunate dramatic proclivities caused him to neglect his cutting

## Theatrical Rambles of Mr. & Mrs. Greene, Charles Durang

shears and artful measures—and as Mrs. John Wood exclaims, in *Pocahontas*,[5] "Oh! scissors, how it cuts." His indulgences in dramatic callings cut off all his customers and finally involved him in pecuniary embarrassments, so at last he flew by night from the hills and valleys of Shenandoah with Charles Porter, who was one of the seceders from Mrs. Willis.

J. M. Scott was much attached to Charles Porter and they prepared to perform a pilgrimage to Baltimore, where Scott said he had scenery and wardrobe laid snugly up *incog*. Porter, being young and verdant, agreed to everything suggested by his mentor, who fixed the time for their departure at midnight. No baggage, but a wallet-shaped knapsack was given to Porter to pack his wardrobe in and a couple of small bundles were made up by Scott at this arrangement. Porter was astonished.

"Why not go in the stage by the way of Frederick Town to Baltimore?" asked the greenhorn.

"Oh, no, Charles," said Scott, "I have a motive for this secret and midnight move which I will explain to you as we perambulate toward Alexandria, where I have negotiated for the old Theatre."

At the appointed time, away they went. They crossed over the Potomac and took up the line of march for Alexandria. Money seemed scarce with the new manager. Animated, however, with theatrical ambition and braced by youthful limbs and spirits to endurances, they reached Alexandria, where, it would seem, disappointment awaited the incipient movements of manager Scott. Porter began to despond. A wet blanket had fallen over Scott's brilliant prospectus of theatres, but he cheered up Porter's lagging prospects with what Baltimore would do. Away they hied to the City of Monuments, still moving on the stroller's carriage, the legs.

They arrived at their destination, when Scott took Porter to Federal Hill to a lonely row of dilapidated houses built on speculation when it was thought the city was going that way. Here he showed Porter his treasures. On opening the room, some faded scenery, soaked in the rain of months, was seen and some trunks filled with seedy, moth eaten

*Theatrical Rambles of Mr. & Mrs. Greene*, Charles Durang

dresses. Porter became clairvoyant and the old rhyming enigma crossed his mind:

> Without a bridle or a saddle
> Across a thing I ride a straddle;
> And those I ride, by help of me,
> Though almost blind, are made to see
> The solution—A pair of spectacles.

So common sense saddled his nose with her spectacles that opened his eyes to humbugging. Meeting a friend who was going to Philadelphia, and who took him under his care, they arrived home in health and spirits, with his mind much improved by his maiden excursion in Thespian freaks.

Mrs. Willis saw the extermination of their company with dismay, and they had to rest awhile till they could receive fresh forces. Mrs. Greene was the only lady performer left in the company. Thus left alone in all her glory, with only Mrs. Greene to contend with in all the various lines of female business, the queen of all she surveyed in casts, she grew jealous of Mrs. Greene, the sole representative of the female *repertoire*. This devil incarnate saw that the youthful actress was nightly developing that talent that would elevate her to a high position, and she sought to check it. This Xantippe—like the wife of Socrates—one day at dinner, where at least twenty persons were seated, emptied a tureen of calves-head soup upon the head of her Thespian lord, who only exclaimed, with the Grecian stoic and philosopher "after thunder there generally falls rain"; and this only for the reason that he had cast Mrs. Greene to the part of Juliet, in *Romeo and Juliet*, without asking her managerial leave.

On the night of its performance she was in front as usual, watching the door-keepers. During the garden scene of *Romeo and Juliet*, Juliet exclaims:
"Oh, Romeo, Romeo!"
Mrs. Willis cried out from the front boxes, "Stop calling him, for there he stands before you—that faithless husband of mine."

## *Theatrical Rambles of Mr. & Mrs. Greene*, Charles Durang

Confusion worse confounded seized upon all the audience and performers at this outrage. However, the scene went on. At the ending of the speech by Juliet:

"Romeo, doff thy name, and for that name, which is no part of thee, take all myself!"

To which Romeo replies, "I take thee at thy word. Call me but love, and I'll be new baptized; henceforth I never will be Romeo."

While this dialogue was going on, this termagant of fiery sprites ran behind the scenes and before Romeo spoke the last line rang down the curtain. The audience, disgusted, hastily retired, and the performances ceased.

One night, when Mrs. Greene was performing the part of Floranthe in *The Mountaineers*,[6] Floranthe says, "I love thee for thy heart, dear Sadi!"

"I know you do, you seducer of other women's husbands," shouted the talking termagant.

In her rage she attempted to strike Mrs. Greene in the face in a most artistic pugilistic style, as Powhatan would say to his gentle savage in Brougham's extravaganza of *Pocahontas*. But Mr. Greene stepped before his lady and received the Amazonian blow.

The houses were well attended. The audiences were of the most respectable citizens of the town, where the orderly conduct of its inhabitants was like the harmony of a well regulated family—where the idea of a police officer's power was a thing never dreamt of, or this domestic tyrant would probably have been escorted to lodgings for the night by a gentleman in uniform. But such a thing never occurred to those unsophisticated people, even when she would frighten them by crying "fire" on nights when the house was full if anything occurred to displease her. Her little whims, as they called them, were not interfered with personally, although she degraded herself in their opinion. Her husband was her victim on all occasions, as she constantly insulted him, and in one of her pretty pets she broke his wrist across the bedstead.

It may be asked, why did Mr. and Mrs. Greene remain under this annoying and vulgar brutal tyranny when

## *Theatrical Rambles of Mr. & Mrs. Greene*, Charles Durang

other theatres of note might have availed themselves of their services? They were then in their novitiate. A field in this strolling *corps* was open to study, practice, and improvement thereby. The regular theatres then in existence were very few. There were only four or five of our principal cities that could support theatres, and in those the business of the respective lines was fully monopolized by the thoroughly practiced, *viz.*, English actors. For native performers of any grade above mere expletives, or supernumeraries, there was but little encouragement or courtesy. The theatres were few and far between and salaries bearing no proportion to the sums now paid to even mediocrity or the lower grades of a theatre. The salaries of the three leading theatres of the country about 1817 and 1818—*viz.*, the Park, New York, the Chestnut Street, Philadelphia, and the Federal Street, Boston—were nearly on a par, ranging from $30 to $28 and $25 for leading performers, and benefits at charges, and only one in the season.

    The Charleston Theatre, South Carolina, was the fourth principal theatre in the Union, where the salaries were on rather a larger scale, for the reason of living expenses being higher, traveling more costly, and a shorter season in consequence of the lengthened hot weather and its unhealthiness of climate. This was under the management of Mr. A. Placide, the father of the present talented family of histrions.

    In returning to the Greene fix, in the case of their manageress, we have shown from the paucity of theatres and other circumstances, it was difficult to procure an engagement elsewhere, while their "poverty and not their will" compelled them to remain with their royal mistress.

    The Willis' management moved the company to a distance of 22 miles from their last stopping place in Virginia to a lone village near Baltimore. It being in the month of August and the weather extremely hot and sultry, the journey promised much discomfort, especially as there was no stage or any other conveyances to be found. The only resource was a sort of chair-wheels used to carry the dead to the common cemetery, the farmers having only rough wagons and ox carts for all purposes of work or pleasure trips. This chair-wheel

## *Theatrical Rambles of Mr. & Mrs. Greene*, Charles Durang

vehicle the *autocratix* monopolized for herself and luggage.[7] The Greenes thus being unable to hire any conveyance at all, they agreed with the gentlemen of the company and a lady who played the old dames, to walk the whole distance in a hot sun to the next town, where they were to perform that very night.

Thus did they make a virtue of necessity. At one point of their journey they had to wade through the Potomac, the river being very low made it fordable. An old Negro man, who was bobbing for eels, seated on a boulder, generously offered to ferry the two ladies across the river in his leaky bateau. This the females accepted. The gentlemen with their boots off, trousers rolled up, and bundles on their heads, waded. But a mishap occurred to the boat. She struck a hidden rock and bilged. The shock threw the ladies into the water. They were rescued from their bath by the wading players and carried in their arms, saturated with bright Potomac's waters, and safely landed. Thus wet and disordered in personal aspect, they pursued the journey in a hay wagon.

Arriving at the town they were to play at that night, they were received by the lady manageress with coolness and ironical questions, "Well, how did you like your pedestrian journey, eh? Your vehicular conveyance must have been very agreeable?"

The best and only answer to these demoniac inquiries from a human fiend was their awful plight, their bruised sore feet, their jaded limbs and wearied looks. They looked an animated group of misery and despair.

The business was excellent here. The hall was filled every evening. And as they had agreed to play on shares, they anticipated a handsome sum to each person at the end of the week, some consolation in their afflictions. But the wily female treasurer retained her financial post and usual system of taking the lion's share, and the poor actors received scarcely enough to pay their board. Their clothing was worn out and no prospect of procuring a renewal.

The next move was to Cumberland on the mountains in Maryland, from which wild and romantic crest the eye beholds one of the most picturesque vales in Christendom—so

*Theatrical Rambles of Mr. & Mrs. Greene*, Charles Durang

beautifully checkered with richly cultivated farms, whose golden sheaves of various grains dot the fields.

A large old building that had been used as a drug store the company converted into an extemporary theatre. Here the spouting young men were in the habit of congregating in their hours of leisure to play cards and drafts, etc. One of the party of an inquisitive nature, in rummaging the shelves and boxes, found a bottle of fine old wine. Exultation seized upon the party at this apropos discovery of what was supposed to be an aged bottle of vinous fluid, placed there by the physician as a reserved comfort. So joyously impressed was this party with their new found wine that they ardently imitated their supposed predecessors, bathing their drooping spirits in delight beyond the bliss of dreams.

## NOTES

[1] Shortly after his marriage to Mrs. Mason, Entwistle became disenchanted with their positions at the Chestnut Street Theatre. In 1817 they left the company to take on the management of the Pittsburgh theatre. When Caldwell leased the Alexandria theatre later that same year, he entered into partnership with Entwistle, the managers pooling their companies for engagements in Alexandria and Washington. In the spring of 1818, the Caldwell-Entwistle group joined forces with Pepin's circus *corps*. Charles Durang was an actor with the Alexandria and Washington Company.

[2] The Moretonian Society, an amateur and juvenile acting group, named in honor of Moreton, could boast of such actors as Charles Webb and Edwin Forrest. John Pollard Moreton was an American actor, musician, and painter who was engaged in England by Thomas Wignell for the Philadelphia stage. After making his debut in this country at Annapolis in 1793, he developed into becoming what W. B. Wood called "the best actor of easy comedy" he had ever seen. He died of consumption in Philadelphia on April 4, 1898, still a young man.

[3] *The Fair Penitent*, a tragedy by Nicholas Rowe, was performed at the Chestnut Street Theatre in the spring of 1798.

*Theatrical Rambles of Mr. & Mrs. Greene*, Charles Durang

[4] John M. Scott, professionally known as "Long Tom Coffin," because of his role at the Chatham Theatre, NYC, of Long Tom Coffin in *Paul Jones, the Pilot of the German Ocean* by W. H. Wallack, was a native of Philadelphia. He performed in tragedy, but was particularly famous for nautical characters. At one time he was manager of the Cincinnati and Vicksburg (MS) theatres. Scott died in New York on March 1, 1849. Charles S. Porter (1797-1867) was born in Newark, NJ. He first stood before an audience in the winter of 1816 when he performed dramatic dialogues. His Philadelphia debut was at the South Street Theatre the following year as Sir Bertrand in Hodgkinson's *The Man of Fortune*, but didn't appear in New York until 1828, when at the Park Theatre he enacted Malcolm in *Macbeth*. In 1837 he performed at the National Theatre, NYC, as Gulliver in David Garrick's farce, *Gulliver in Lilliput*, where he was advertised as "a Kentuckian, 7 feet 6 inches high, his first appearance on the stage." He retired from the stage in 1862.

[5] *Pocahontas*, an historical drama in 5 acts, is attributed to Robert Dale Owen.

[6] *The Mountaineers*, was a melodrama by Colman the younger.

[7] Probably a *chaise*, or one-horse shay—a light, open, two-wheeled carriage.

*Theatrical Rambles of Mr. & Mrs. Greene*, Charles Durang

## IV.

THE POISONED *CORPS* — THE COUNTRY HOSTELRY — A DOUBLE-CHALKING LANDLORD — ARRESTED — JOHN GREENE "TOOK IN" — AMONG THE MAD CHAPS — GAMES OF THE SPORTS — PLAYING AGAIN — A FINAL SCENE WITH MRS. WILLIS — THE DRAMA IN NEW ORLEANS — Mr. J. H. CALDWELL — THEATRICAL RIOT — ENGLISH OPERA — JANE PLACIDE, ETC.

One of the party of this social circle began to feel symptoms of approaching nausea at the stomach, another similar feeling, and so a third one. Qualmishness became like an epidemic. All were seized. Each one looked his fellow inquiringly in the face with the same silent question and answer, "What had they been drinking?"

The idea of poison flashes upon their minds. The peculiar expression of each face, as frightened to death, was apparently alarming! It was a scene ludicrously serious. Death had cast his unerring darts among them. One of the youths, with indignant writhing exclaimed he hated to die like a dog by strychnine. A few became penitent and were anxious to be shrived, another made a hearty confession of sins, another, who had been the very personification of morality, steady and grave through life, thought it was a judgment for his cheating at cards. The alarm was given and physicians were forthwith called in, who examined the bottle's sediment. The investigation resulted in relieving their patients' fears and anxieties. Instead of fine aged wine of rare quality, it proved to be only antimonial wine, which only affected them as an endemic and a cathartic, relieving their inner corporeal parts of so much whiskey.

*Theatrical Rambles of Mr. & Mrs. Greene*, Charles Durang

The theatre where this ludicrous scene happened was like the cabin of a passenger ship in a gale of wind—seasick patients tossing and rolling about its floors, grasping for wash basins, buckets, etc., to relieve their stomachic afflictions. *Mal de mer* is a bad sickness.

The company's next stopping place was to be Union Town. It was arranged that the gentlemen, like Oliver Goldsmith's strolling player, should use their feet machinery, the readiest and cheapest locomotive that dame Nature has furnished to poor humanity, and now most *apropos* to these itinerant thespians. Mrs. John Greene, now the aspiring tragedienne, was to precede them in the stage wagon to engage board and to settle other preliminaries. These matters were all satisfactorily negotiated ere the perambulating troupe arrived.

The host of the inn where they were to sojourn was an Irishman, as whimsical as Dennis Brulgruddery,[1] as solicitous for custom to the "Red Cow," but lacking his generous nature, as the sequel will show. The board was engaged at $4.00 for each person. The beds were arranged in hospital fashion, all in a row. The married couples hung up shawls by way of partition screens. The next day the footsore histrions arrived, while the virago of a manageress and her Dolly spouse brought up the rear in an old-fashioned Virginia chariot of George II's reign, drawn by a span of worn out bay and white coach horses, the Jehu a facsimile of an Uncle Tom. Four post-bills, posted on the old court house and the principal corners of the town, announced the opening of the theatre. The houses for six nights were crowded; but, at the end of that time, the purses of the public became drained of their circulating medium which brought this curt but profitable season to an end.

The scenery was taken down and rolled up on long poles, and the wardrobe packed in baskets and placed in the wagon for a start to the next performing place. The tavern bills were ordered, which the wily and double-chalk host readily produced. His charges were frightfully exorbitant to all, but John Greene emphatically took

## Theatrical Rambles of Mr. & Mrs. Greene, Charles Durang

strong exceptions to his charges as being far beyond the agreement made by Mrs. Greene. To that agreement John inflexibly adhered and would not pay one cent more. His bill of sundries was greatly overcharged, such as: cigars of the common weed, charged at three cents, or at Havana prices; Cognac brandy, manufactured from bad whiskey, six cents per glass; and all other items of bar refreshments in the same enhanced ratio. The washing done by Nance, the colored chambermaid, was charged $1 per dozen, for which they paid her 50¢ as a private perquisite, but which he claimed as his hired slave. This Mr. O'Dougherty, the host, met all Greene's reasoning and arithmetic with low jest and laughter, persisting vigorously with his unjust demands. Neither party would yield.

*The corps,* being ready for a start in their usual mode of exodus, began to move, the landlord threatening Greene if they departed with the vengeance of the law. Greene, whose person and strong facial expression were remarkable, bade defiance, and the male performers with Greene made their *exeunt omnes* down the road on "Shank's" mare. Mrs. Greene was to follow the next day by the stagecoach. But Paddy O'Dougherty was on the *qui vive;* and not thus to be circumvented, he dispatched six of his cudgel-armed myrmidons in pursuit of the party to coerce the actors into a settlement of his unjust demands, thus taking law into his own hands. The volunteer police overtook the and *corps,* and *vi et armis,* arrested the whole body. Greene, however, resisted the arrestors with manly courage and refused to submit. But the sham officers, being stalwart men, seized Greene bodily and threw him on a horse and secured him. Thus enthroned, he was ignobly conveyed back to the village, where he was arraigned before a magistrate, who was in villainous alliance with this dishonest Irishman.

John Greene, with his native force and just indignation, pleaded his own cause in a strain of eloquence and logic that made this ignorant Dogberry wince and the impudent host to cower at Greene's keen and searching cross-examination of Doublechalk's charges and false swearing. It would have impressed any impartial jury with

## *Theatrical Rambles of Mr. & Mrs. Greene,* Charles Durang

the defendant's innocence and the falsity the publican's suit. As was said before, John Greene's *personnel* was very remarkable—of a demoniac, scowling aspect to the stranger, a massive forehead wherein we set two large, black piercing eyes, overshadowed with huge, wiry eyebrows of similar hue, a contour of face iron-cast, and dark inflexibility of purpose, without the light of one benevolent expression to assure the gazer of one tender feeling in his heart to beat responsive to human misery and woe. Yet, with all these negative signs of humanity, never did a more feeling heart, throbbing with every beneficent attribute for his fellow man, beat beneath so rough an exterior. He was the quintessence of manhood. In reference to his strongly marked aspect, a captain of a ship wherein he was a passenger said of him, "His black look and savage look would quell a ship crew's mutiny."

But to return from this episode to the trial scene of the Irish Shylock and the poor, wronged player, with all Greene's apt quotations from Shakespeare, his sarcastic denunciations of Shylock's false oaths and proceedings, the actor was defeated.

During this droll trial the following whimsical colloquy occurred between the plaintiff and defendant, which is very characteristic:

"You said to me on the night, sir, after I played Dennis Brulgruddery, that I must certainly be an Irishman, as I played the character up to the handle—for you loved the *honest* Irishman and that Dennis was *one*, faith—you would "trate" all hands in the barroom for the pleasure I gave you and that you would give me, free gratis, one of your best drinks every day while I stayed, for the honor of old Ireland."

"Be aisy and don't play actor-like, be hatching up lies to please the people, as ye do in the play house. Please, your honor, it is all a lie, as your honor may see."

"Oh, yes, these showmen make all their shows big lies. Faith, calling wooly dogs, with their hair half trimmed off their bodies, lions."

## *Theatrical Rambles of Mr. & Mrs. Greene*, Charles Durang

Green here replied in another burst of rage to his rogueries, when the landlord exclaimed to the Justice, "I call upon your honor to protect me from the abuse of this vagabond, for that he had a *character* to lose."

"When that's gone you'll get another, and that's a damned impertinent roguish landlord!"

"Will you again swear to your account?"

"Aye," replied Doublechalk, and took up the Bible with the cross marked on the corner and made his solemn kiss thereon.

"Enough!" responded the judicial Solon. "I give judgment in your favor, Mr. O'Dougherty *versus* this insane showman. So pay the judgment with costs or you go to jail."

Greene answered in the negative, so the learned Justice consigned poor Greene to prison for the crime of poverty and honesty. This jail was also used for an insane asylum, where Greene (who now figured in tragedy) had a fine opportunity of studying Lear from nature in the person of an aged individual who was the very personification of intense madness; and who, in one of his violent fits selected Greene's head as the target to every missile that lay within his reach, keeping up a shower of old shoes, chips, bricks, hats, etc., till his supply of ammunition and physical power became exhausted.

As John Greene was leaving the magistrate's office for the prison, the landlord offered to furnish him with meals at a fair price while in durance vile.

Greene replied thus, "I'll tell you what, Mr. O'Dougherty, it's my notion, in summing up your last accounts, that when you begin to dot, ould Nick will carry one ___, and that's yourself, my darling!" [*exit to prison*]

Mrs. Greene remained near her husband in his tribulations, begging him to pay the extra money unjustly demanded rather than submit to the painful alternative of imprisonment. But he continued to reject her sensible counsel. Like Pickwick, he preferred suffering for conscience's sake, although enduring a martyrdom the very antipodes of boarding at a first-class metropolitan hotel.

*Theatrical Rambles of Mr. & Mrs. Greene*, Charles Durang

The town and its inhabitants were of the most primitive description, the buildings quaint in form and simple of materials in architecture; room and comfort rather than its ornaments seemed the prevailing taste of that day. The prison and mad house, being the same edifice, had an extensive yard appropriated to manifold purposes; *per example*, a portion was partitioned off by a slight railing for the physical amusements of trap ball, with a bowling alley which was the daily resort of the "fast men" and idlers who vegetate in these small towns and their environs. Here in the afternoon these gay gentlemen amused themselves with ball playing against the prison walls and in the bowling alley for small bets of liquor and money. In these sports John Greene, of social habits, mingled freely. All were pleased with his geniality during the games, the libations being solemnized in deep draughts of whiskey and brandy toddies. John was even invited by the victors in these Olympic sports to libate with them.

When the sporting *Chevaliers* were about to exit for home, Greene would laughingly exclaim, "Gentlemen, I would cheerfully accompany you, but bars and bolts forbid such a liberty on my part."

At length, the ball visitors appealed to the prison custodian to suffer Dennis Brulgruddery, as they named him, to promenade with them as a welcomed outsider. So that watchful *Cerberus* declared John Greene a "prisoner at large," and promised that he might go when and where he pleased. So he did. Cavalierly, under the patronage of the prison *bon vivants,* Greene, on "ticket of leave" absence, triumphantly returned to his wife's lodging.

They hastened to join their company, now performing to good houses some fifty miles distant. The Greenes were fresh recruits to the *corps* and proved attractive. The old grievances of the performers remained in *status quo,* with large audiences but no salaries forthcoming at the end of the week, the usual result where the Willis management governed supreme. And things remained in this deranged state till the *corps* arrived in their peregrinations

*Theatrical Rambles of Mr. & Mrs. Greene*, Charles Durang

at Wellsburgh, a small dilapidated town on the banks of the Ohio. Here they were to open with the *Honey Moon*.[2]

The house was rapidly filling while Madame Willis resumed her old station of ticket selling, thus taking the money but never relinquishing it. This mode of non-payment eventually caused Greene to lose his temper. Patience ceased to be a virtue and "rebellion lay in his way." One night Mrs. Greene was dressed for Juliana[3] and Mr. Greene, having completed his stage toilet, threw his cloak over his costume and passed to the front to eye the financial operations. There he found Mrs. Willis engaged as usual in selling tickets and receiving the money, which she deposited in a large satchel at her side. Several patrons came up the stairs and handed Greene their tickets, taking him for the door keeper. Mrs. Willis, like an enraged virago, rushed at him and snatched the cards out of his hands, at the same time firing a volley of abuse, demanding his business there. To this rude question Greene made no answer; but passing to the rear of the stage where the dressing rooms were, he quickly divested himself of his stage habiliments, donned his street clothes, and went directly to Mrs. Greene's dressing room and desired her to do the same, briefly relating the circumstances. Within a few moments they left the theatre into the darkness and away from Mrs. Willis's evil designs. Madame Willis, astounded, inquired into the abandonment of their duties. She received no answer but the scornful looks of the company. Here was a *dramatique nonplus*! The comedy could not be performed without a Juliana. The curtain could not rise on this distracted *corps* of comedians. The lady manageress, covetous soul, received a death wound in being obliged to refund the money to the ticket holders and so dismissed auditory. This was the closing scene of the Greene's engagement with this shameful dynasty. Their sufferings had been great through her tyranny and dishonesty, and this last act of drama of dollars and cents caused the catastrophe as related.

The English drama was first introduced into the city of New Orleans in 1817 by a commonwealth company. The manager was Mr. Noah M. Ludlow. The *corps*

*Theatrical Rambles of Mr. & Mrs. Greene*, Charles Durang

consisted of Messrs. Morgan, John Vaughan, Lucas, Bainbridge, Henry Vaughan, Mrs. Ludlow, Mrs. Morgan, Mrs. Vaughan, and some others.

A temporary theatre was erected, which was afterwards converted into a ballroom. Aaron Phillips, of Philadelphia, took a company there in 1818 of a respectable caliber in talent, and occupied the French theatre in Orleans Street. But he had to encounter a strong opposition in the outset of this very season, which threw his exertions *hors du combat*.

Mr. James H. Caldwell, the Achilles of theatrical enterprise in the Southwest, built more theatres and put them in operation than all the American managers together.[4] Mr. Caldwell, himself of host in tragedy and comedy, had a tolerably strong company. The first occupied the St. Philips Street Theatre, and afterwards moved to the Théâtre d'Orléans, which he played in three evenings of each week, alternating with the French company. A compromise was effected with Mr. A. Phillips, who dissolved his *corps*, himself and the principal members thereof entering into the Caldwell management, making, thus combined, a strong dramatic working company.[5] Mr. Thomas A. Cooper, the great American star of that day, played in New Orleans this season for the first time to houses averaging above $300 nightly.[6]

Certainly, as a theatrical impresario, not one of that class can compare with Mr. Caldwell. This gentleman's first appearance in America was in Charleston, S.C., in 1816-17, when his celebrated *émeute* against Holman during this season occurred about the character of Hamlet, which Caldwell claimed as his right to act. He had become a great favorite at the Palmetto City and unjustly claimed the full right to all leading lines. As Mr. Holman held the right of tragic leading parts to himself, the result was that the theatre, located on the banks of the Ashley river, was completely gutted in the audience department, and closed for two or three weeks for repairs. And thus closed Mr. Caldwell's first engagement in America.[7]

## *Theatrical Rambles of Mr. & Mrs. Greene*, Charles Durang

The stage department was saved from destruction through the spirited and defensive conduct of the company entrenching themselves behind the canvas streets, woods, palaces, and prisons; wherein, with courageous remonstrances, appealing to the rioters' better feelings and warlike show to defend the manager's property, they ultimately gave respite to the savage onslaught, and there was a final retreat after the destruction of the front.

The company, however, demanded their salaries from Mr. Holman during the time the theatre was closed for repairs, to which Mr. Holman yielded under protest. The company, however, thought proper to place the onus of the common calamity on the manager's stubborn will not to yield to Caldwell's demand of the right to act Hamlet or "no play," as the *vox populi* so declared; although the manager was the wronged party, whatever Mr. Caldwell's popularity may have demanded.

At this time Caldwell was a fine, dashing-looking young man of good manners but of very reserved social habits. His figure was very imposing: about five feet eleven, well made, of the Apollo cast, a face of pallid hue, yet often flushed with a hectic glow, indicative of consumption. His features, although small and regular, were vivid, lighted with a fine blue eye. His temperament was frigid, his life marked by a studied temperance. His mental capacities were ever engaged in some scheme of enterprise, either for the drama or the development of mechanical invention or scientific usefulness. His mind was cultivated, but he inclined rather to the pedantic above his fertile intellect. On the whole, his life had been characterized by great energy and devotion to enterprises of all kinds.

When he first arrived at Charleston he was quite *entre* in his street costume that attracted attention from all. His Belcour in *The West Indian*[8] was a very clever piece of acting, as was also his Singles in *Three and the Deuce*, his fencing being particularly great.

He acted as a star in New York and commenced his managerial career in Washington City in 1818. In 1835 he erected and opened the St. Charles Theatre, the largest theatre in size and magnificence then in America, equal-

*Theatrical Rambles of Mr. & Mrs. Greene*, Charles Durang

ing or comparing with our opera temples in New York, Boston, and Philadelphia, and surpassing in elegance anything of the kind in London, Paris, Naples, St. Petersburg, or any of the continental dramatic temples.[9] In March, 1842, this edifice was burnt down, leaving nothing on its site but its ashes to tell of its former greatness. It is almost impossible to enumerate the various theatres that he built and opened in the West and Southwest—often without the adequate funds on hand, only his indomitable energies and skillful financial habits. In Virginia, Louisiana, Alabama, Mississippi, Tennessee, Ohio, Missouri, Arkansas, in all the principal cities of those states, with their adjacent towns, he successfully unfurled the Thespian banner. His untiring energy in 1833 at New Orleans produced a version of the opera of *Cinderella*, a clever concoction of Rossini's great original work of that name, with choice bits extracted from *William Tell* and other productions from the same author.[10]

This was an era in the theatrical annals, or, rather, in operatic exhibitions, being, it was said, the first grand opera in the English language produced in the South. The cast was: the Prince, J. M. Field; Dandini, Mr. Caldwell; Baron Pompolini, Mr. Thorne; Pedro, Mr. Russell; Cinderella, Miss Jane Placide; Thisbe, Mrs. Rowe; Clorinda, Mrs. Russell; Fairy Queen, Miss Nelson (the present Mrs. Brougham). This opera met with great success.[11]

Miss Jane Placide benefited much by the professional experience of Mr. Caldwell, both in music and eloquence. He instructed her in the manner of the great Siddon's acting of Lady Macbeth and her other tragic roles, and she was an apt pupil.

Mr. Caldwell then conceived the idea of lighting New Orleans with gas, and to that end entered into a contract with the municipal authorities of that city. He went to England, there to gather such information and aid on the subject as to enable him the more successfully to carry out his plans. His scheme succeeded to a charm, and Messrs. Russell and Rowe became his successors on his theatric throne.

*Theatrical Rambles of Mr. & Mrs. Greene*, Charles Durang

He took the very talented Miss Jane Placide to London, where she made her debut at Covent Garden in the part of Elvira in 1834. The English papers were very much in her favor, remarking that in person and manner she reminded them of Parodi. Poor girl! With tragic powers of the highest order and bright prospects for the future, she returned to New Orleans with Madame Celeste and Mr. Caldwell. In the fall of that year she died.[12]

Caldwell successfully illuminated New Orleans and Mobile with gas and made many other improvements. After the destruction of the St. Charles Theatre in 1842, he retired from the stage as actor and manager. On the 14th of January, 1843, he took his final leave of the stage in the character of Vapid in *The Dramatist*,[13] and became the Recorder of the second municipality of the city, where he lived honored and respected.

Mr. Caldwell was twice married, first to the dashing widow Twomley of Rose Hill at Fredericksburg, Virginia. This lady was handsome and accomplished and a great admirer of Mr. Caldwell. During the season she occupied the stage box every evening of his performance. One night the alarm of fire was raised in front of the theatre during the representation of *The Soldier's Daughter*.[14] In the alarm the widow Twomley sprang from the box toward the stage. Mr. Caldwell, who was playing Frank Heartall, caught her in his arms to break the fall. An introduction took place, and she became Mrs. Caldwell very soon after. It was reported that she was rich, but it proved her greatest wealth was her beauty, as her first husband left all the property to their son, allowing her only a life interest in it. The Union with Caldwell produced his son Shakespeare, a name and genius which he adored, and which he seemed desirous to perpetuate in the person of this scion of his own image. Whether he floats in poetry or rides Pegasus up Mount Parnassus or swims in Helicon's stream is not known, but Caldwell himself was a whole team. His second marriage was with Miss Rowe of theatrical parentage.

**NOTES**

*Theatrical Rambles of Mr. & Mrs. Greene*, Charles Durang

## NOTES

[1] Dennis Brulgruddery was an Irish character in *John Bull; or, the Englishman's Fireside* by Colman the younger. It was John Greene's most popular character. *John Bull* was first performed in America in New York, November 21, 1803. Dunlap called it "one of the richest pieces of comic acting we have ever witnessed."

[2] *The Honey Moon*, a comedy by John Tobin. It was produced in America for the first time for Mr. Darley's benefit, May 29, 1805, and was a popular piece for nearly a century thereafter.

[3] Juliana was a character from *The Honey Moon*.

[4] As early as 1806 an actor named Rannie took a large room for performances in the city of New Orleans. In 1811, John Duff brought a troupe into the St. Philips Street Theatre, which was previously occupied by a French speaking company. Ludlow did not arrive until January of 1818. Lucas was a minor actor. He was engaged by Ludlow as early as 1817 to play old men. The brothers Henry and John Vaughan were in partnership with Ludlow in 1817. Both died shortly thereafter.

[5] When Caldwell appeared in New Orleans in 1820 with a superior company, Phillips was unable to meet the competition.

[6] Cooper was engaged at this time for sixteen performances. According to Caldwell, it was necessary to add eight more nights. The engagement began on March 23, 1821, with *Macbeth*. Caldwell claimed that the average nightly gross was $700, and thus made "an impression which it required a generation (about the period of an actor's fame) to obliterate."

[7] Holman brought Caldwell to America in the autumn of 1816. After Caldwell established a local reputation, he insisted on playing the first parts in both tragedy and comedy. Manager Holman resisted this attempt. The public, the majority of whom were in sympathy with Caldwell, encouraged the disturbance. Placards reading, "Caldwell, or no play," were posted everywhere. When the performance was an-

*Theatrical Rambles of Mr. & Mrs. Greene*, Charles Durang

nounced with Caldwell's name missing, the aroused supporters filled the theatre, creating a tumult when the performance was attempted. They called the manager forward, demanding redress for the injured stranger, whose rights had been violated. After asking the ladies to leave, the mob demolished the interior of the theatre. Joseph George Holman (1764-1817) was born in England. He made his professional debut at Covent Garden as Romeo at the age of 20. He came to America in 1812 and opened at the Park Theatre. He married Miss Latimer on August 22, 1817, and died of apoplexy two days later.

[8] *The West Indian*, a comedy by Richard Cumberland.

[9] The first St. Charles Theatre, which opened in 1835, lighted by 250 gas jets, represented an investment of about $325,000.

[10] Sol Smith called the production of *Cinderella* a hodgepodge of Rossini's work, *Cenerentola* and other compositions, a first attempt at Grand Opera in English in the South, forming "an era in theatrical annals."

[11] James Thorne, from Drury Lane Theatre, London, first appeared in America as a tenor singer at the Park Theatre. He gave up singing in 1834 to manage the Cincinnati theatre with John M. Scott. He died at sea in 1843 while returning to England. Richard Russell was a versatile comedian, performing mostly in Boston, Cincinnati and New Orleans. He made his New Orleans debut for Caldwell in 1821. J. M. Field was an actor, theatrical manager, and journalist. He wrote for the New Orleans *Picayune* under the heading of "Straws." At one time he was an assistant editor of the New York *Evening Post* and also edited the St. Louis *Reveille*. He managed theatres in St. Louis and Mobile. He was married to actress Eliza Riddle. Field died in Mobile on January 28, 1856. Mrs. Rowe is probably the former Rosina Seymour. She was married to James Rowe, treasure for Caldwell until he went into management with Richard Russell. Miss Nelson came from the English stage, making her debut in New Orleans in *The Fairy Queen*, astonishing patrons from the delicacy of her hands and feet. She later went into management briefly at the Richmond Hill Theatre, NYC called Miss Nelson's Theatre. She became Mrs. Brougham in 1847.

*Theatrical Rambles of Mr. & Mrs. Greene*, Charles Durang

[12] Elvira is a character in R. B. Sheridan's adaptation of *Pizarro*. Miss Placide (1804-1835) was at Covent Garden in the role in 1834. The reference is to Signorina Teresa Parodi, the *prima donna*, who made her American debut at the Astor Place Opera House in 1850.

[13] *The Dramatist*, a comedy by Frederick Reynolds.

[14] *The Soldier's Daughter*, a comedy by Andrew Cherry.

*Theatrical Rambles of Mr. & Mrs. Greene*, Charles Durang

## V.

GOING DOWN THE OHIO — GETTING AN AUDIENCE — MORE TROUBLE WITH A LANDLORD — A REDEEMING TRAIT — FIRST FLOATING THEATRE — THE FOUR ROADS — NO BAGGAGE SMASHERS NEEDED — GETTING A QUIET MEAL — THE DARK SIDE OF HUMANITY — HARDSHIPS OF AN ACTOR'S LIFE.

Shortly after leaving the Willis management the Greenes became part of a traveling scheme, performing in towns along the Ohio River. Thus did they descend by days and sometimes by night the gentle Ohio, enjoying in the strolling actor's way "the feast of reason and the flow of soul" to the no small amusement of two coarse boatmen who worked the boat. At night they would make their dramatic ark fast to a gigantic oak on the river's bank near to some hamlet or populous settlement. And thus did they "star it" during the day by the presence of Sol's light, and at night by Diana's chaste light and a pound of penny dips. So would they tragedize and comedize to a motley group of white bushwhackers and Negroes at one of such landing locations too insignificant to have a geographical name.

A very unpleasant incident occurred here, of so pointed a character as to impress its locality indelibly upon the memory of this nomadic tribe of Thespians who took up their temporary quarters at a public shanty and gave the landlord a number of tickets to dispose of. The performances were duly announced to the assembled multitude before the shanty and the exhibition was given to the great satisfaction of all.

## *Theatrical Rambles of Mr. & Mrs. Greene*, Charles Durang

At the end, a ticket settlement was requested from the landlord, when, with much *naïveté*, he exclaimed, "I did my best for you. I collected all the folks within 10 miles. I executed your orders and gave every ticket away, not keeping one for myself."

Here was a *dénouement* to the drama of real life that enraged the *corps dramatique*. In the miserable state of their treasury it was a cruel disappointment, when their prospects of remuneration were so flattering, promising to relieve their wants. Harsh words ensued and reparation of some kind demanded. But the country folks who formed the audience took sides with the landlord who had acted so generously in furnishing them with so novel a treat gratis. The players spiritedly remonstrated and met with the response of a shower of missiles of various sorts. They found discretion the better part of valor and retreated to their floating theatre on the Ohio, where they found a safe asylum in casting off the boat's moorings and floating her out to the middle of the stream. The company, thus impounded, resolved to up anchor and float off at once from so inhospitable a place.

As bright Phoebus shed his golden rays over their deck the next morning, to their surprise they beheld a flag of truce waving on the shore as a token of peace and desired communication. The theatrical ark was hauled to shore and, to their astonishment, the inhabitants, headed by the host of ticket benevolence, came to the boat's landing with large baskets filled with hams, eggs, chickens, vegetables, fruits, breads, etc.; in short, with every variety of edibles and luxuries that that fertile country afforded, and all given with a blunt and cordial courtesy as an atonement for their them. Their repentance and the amends was truly characteristic of the Western people at that day, who were then behind their present savage treatment of the poor showmen who had behaved so kindly to civilization, or that refinement since reached by them. The dramatic action of real life now represented was of an exhilarating nature. A banquet fit for a Persian court was spread on the rotten deck of the boat, at which the merry, wayward sons and daughters of Thespis, with hearts as light as their purses, did ample justice to the

*Theatrical Rambles of Mr. & Mrs. Greene*, Charles Durang

viands and their dainty accompaniments. No class of society more literally fulfills the scriptural injunction in taking "no thought for the morrow" than that of the stage profession, or so it was once.

The *corps* continued their professional descent of the Ohio till the receipts would no longer meet their expenses and it became clear that their frail boat was no longer sea worthy, requiring more repairs than she was truly worth. They resolved to sell her out, if possible. This was soon effected for a mere trifle. This dramatic ark was the first of the kind (a very primitive one it was) that history mentions. The idea was followed in about 26 years after by William Chapman Sen., on the Ohio, which for a period was successful, but he died in Cincinnati in 1841 while constructing a new steam one.[1]

The floating *corps* having dissolved water acting, a new process of system and travel had now to be adopted, not, indeed, a new one, but a resort to their original perambulation of travel. And thus organized as ancient strolling players, they plodded their weary way to parts unknown, while their baggage, neither very heavy nor cumbrous, was equally divided among the rank and file—some had knapsacks, others bundles enveloped in pocket handkerchiefs, *à la* Dick Dowlas.[2]

Thus loaded like mules, they trudged on with light hearts in bitter cold winter weathers—mother earth wrapped in a mantle of snow—with not sufficient means to pay for a night's lodgings even in the straw bed of a barn, blighted in all prospects of relief, no tinge of friendly hands in the melancholy distance to be seen extended to give their tottering footsteps a welcome and shelter. Yet, so oppressed, hope still animated their jaded energies. Thus tossed on the stormy sea of circumstances did they plod on, looking furtively at the substantial farm houses they passed by with a sigh, but lacked the boldness or heart to ask the charity of an humble lodging. Despair at length seized upon the forlorn wayfarers, and they all agreed that it would be best to part and individually to seek their fortunes.[3]

They came to this resolution at the meeting of Four Roads, a circumstance that seemingly suggested the wisdom

*Theatrical Rambles of Mr. & Mrs. Greene*, Charles Durang

of that course. Poor O'Neil[4] first essayed to leave the distressed group and took the right-hand path. But a sudden revulsion of feeling seized upon all as they beheld his forlorn and manly form departing, recalling to their memory and hearts the tribulations and fitful pleasures they had shared with that noble-hearted young man. As this nobleman of nature was descending the road, the females burst into tears, nor could the men suppress their emotions, but with sympathies thus wrought upon did all in one simultaneous burst, exclaim, "O'Neil, return to us. Oh! Do not leave us."

He halted, turned towards them and came back, when Greene spoke thus, "Together we have wandered, together we have suffered, together we'll meet the future storms of adversity as we have the past and present."

He consented to remain, with tears in his eyes, for this proof of friendship in his forlorn companions; and they as joyfully responded as if he had brought thousands to alleviate their distresses. As Rolla exclaimed in *Pizarro*, "Oh! holy nature, thou dost never plead in vain," when he wins over the Spanish sentinel to humanity, not through gold, but parental feeling.[5]

The itinerant players now ascended the course of the Ohio River by land, and after innumerable difficulties they reached Steubenville, on the river, then, 1819, a growing manufacturing town. Here Mr. Braydon and P. O'Neil, being expert printers, obtained employment.

Mr. and Mrs. John Greene were reduced to what they carried on their persons, so shabby and seedy that it required some art to keep them from falling from their bodies So decayed was the clothing, which comprised a large woolen wrapper something of the cut of the present mantilla, a covered ragged skirt of Meg Merrilies[6] hue and texture. Worn out slippers were laced to her feet like sandals, with rope yarn to keep them on. John Greene had on a pair of salmon-colored stage tights and a pair of tragedy crimson buskins with Charles II tops, which he contrived to hide from the eye by a large pair of woolen dingy socks; and he was covered with a huge drab, ten-caped greatcoat—a *facsimile* of the elder Kean's overcoat when he first came up to London in

## *Theatrical Rambles of Mr. & Mrs. Greene*, Charles Durang

1814 to make his trial in Shylock at Drury Lane, so well described by Leigh Hunt in his life of that nonpareil tragedian.

The Greenes, thus bowed down with fatigue, want of food, and lack of sleep, appeared the very poorest of foot travelers of a gypsy caste. Faint and penniless, they saw a cottage in their approaches to the town that seemed most inviting to their eyes as offering rest and relief to their destitute state. They at once resolved to go to its benevolent inmates and ask for refreshment and temporary repose. They reached the door and craved entrance of the woman who answered. They humbly solicited the favor of some refreshments and repose to fagged and way worn wanderers who had met with untoward misfortunes. The woman listened to their request with seeming complacency and readily prepared the repast asked and served it to them, which they devoured with avidity. At the end of this frugal but substantial meal, they returned the hostess their thanks and to Providence the proper grace. If they prevaricated to the hostess, it may be excused on the great law of dire necessity. It was obvious to the Greenes that the woman so seemingly charitable looked for the payment of the meal. This touched their honor. Hunger made them unscrupulous in asking and they felt it the more. They did not previously inform the woman of their penniless state lest it would have been refused and with it a night's shelter.

The woman flew into a terrific rage at their deceit, calling it a robbery of the poor and insisted upon remuneration of some kind or she would have them arrested for vagabonds. The sensibilities of the Greenes were dumbfounded. What could they give? They had no clothing, not even a bundle! No money, jewels, nor extra clothing, naught but the shabby apparel upon their persons. What a dilemma for a heroine and hero of tragedy, the Macbeth and lady Macbeth of a strolling company of actors to be subject to the vulgar abuse, scorn and scolding vituperation of an ill mannered country landlady of a two-roomed cottage. All the wardrobe the Queen in *Hamlet* could boast of was on her back and consisted of a tattered flannel petticoat, a faded gown, and a worn-out cashmere shawl.

## *Theatrical Rambles of Mr. & Mrs. Greene*, Charles Durang

After a candid explanation of their state by the Greenes to this gentle virago of affected benevolence at first, her anger softening, she said to Mrs. Greene, "Give me your petticoat (after examining her clothes) and you may go. I'll take that as payment."

To this the poor tragedienne agreed, divesting herself of the only comfortable garment she had on, which made her look as slim and spare of figure as the starved apothecary in *Romeo and Juliet*, there being no crinoline in those days to balloonize a female's slender form. And so denuded, this Christian hostess turned the twain out of doors in a raging storm. Charity with this Good Samaritan truly began at home.

At this time Mrs. Greene was young and a very pretty woman. Ugly women seldom like or love a beautiful one. Greene and wife had not as yet belonged to a regular company of comedians. Their entree had been made in an itinerant *corps* of straggling regulars and amateurs. In such primitive theatrical associations they had arrived at the moral dignity of very useful and talented people as leading performers in their respective lines, undergoing with great philosophy of temper and complacency the vicissitudes of a strolling player's life.

### NOTES

[1] Durang is in error regarding the Chapmans. Graham dates the "first deliberately planned showboat" of William Chapman at 1831. The Greene's river venture could very well have been the first of its kind.

[2] Dick Dowlas was a character in Colman the Younger's comedy, *The Heir at Law*.

[3] Traveling on foot from town to town was not uncommon for the early American stroller. During his formative years, while performing with an itinerant company, the great Edwin Forrest was forced to walk 20 miles from Lebanon to Cincinnati, only to play to a house of $7.

[4] O'Neil was an actor of obvious obscurity.

[5] *Pizarro*, a tragedy by William Brinsley Sheridan.

*Theatrical Rambles of Mr. & Mrs. Greene*, Charles Durang

[6] Meg Merrilies was a popular role for an actress in *Guy Mannering*, a melodrama adapted from Sir Walter Scott by Daniel Terry.

*Theatrical Rambles of Mr. & Mrs. Greene*, Charles Durang

## VI.

SAD PROSPECTS — NO TOLL — KEAN AND HIS AQUATIC PERFORMANCE — A GOOD SAMARITAN — IN CLOVER — CHANGE OF FORTUNE — ON THE BOARDS AGAIN — BIG THING — MANY PRESENTS — WEBB FOUND DROWNED.

Thus did the subjects of these memoirs seek the bubble reputation of histrions through such degrading, painful tribulations that pave the actor's social paths, lonely wanderers begging their way till they arrived at Chilicothe on a Sunday afternoon. The day was gloomy and the snow was heavily falling as they passed the cheery dwellings of the suburbs, wherein could be seen the cheerful blazing firesides encircled by the merry laughing family. The ringing joy of youthful felicity at the parental tales and funny reminiscences of their boyish and girlish sports with their family history were in dead contrast with our miserable fagged pedestrians. John Greene, with manly sensibilities and cheering example, consoled his poor wife's despondency in this sharp crisis of their youthful struggles, cheered her on with some apt quotations from the dramatic writers, with some lines from Goldsmith's muse.

As Mrs. Greene heaved a sigh for a domestic hearth, John exclaimed, "We may yet have such home happiness as those household scenes so glowingly show our eyes, that so painfully contrast with our wretched state. Providence may have in reserve for us the family blessings those houses exhibit to our impoverished senses. If our lives continue honest and virtuous, we may yet be seated—

Around our fire an evening group to draw,
And tell of all we felt and all we saw;

## *Theatrical Rambles of Mr. & Mrs. Greene*, Charles Durang

And as a hare, whom hounds and horns pursue,
Pants to the place from whence at first she flew;
We still have hopes our long vexations past
Again to return—and die at home at last.

Through the windows that presented so many joyous groups, could be seen the furtive glance of many pitying eyes cast on the wandering couple, whose beggarly aspect spoke of an interest more elevated than their wretchedness presented. The sympathizing expressions were so obvious that, if the Greenes had appealed to their hearts, the holy mantle of charity would at once have been thrown over their wants. But they refrained from that last resort—"the beggar's appeal."

These scenes transpired in 1819 in the suburbs of Chilicothe, which stands between two rivers. The entrance to the town was over a bridge, which was guarded by a Cerberus in the shape of a toll gatherer. To pass this inexorable watcher of taxation without his tribute would be quite as difficult as the ascent to Mahomet's paradise to all skeptics in his faith. The Greene's had not a cent to pay this fare. They related their poverty and destitution and begged to pass over free. All this proved fruitless. This old surly dog only growled and barked at all their entreaties to pass. Here was a non-plus to our travelers. As a last resort, Greene bethought him of a handsome pen-knife in his pocket, most dear to him as the gift of a friend. This was offered for 6¢ toll. It was readily taken by old avarice and the twain passed over this river Styx in all their mortal misery to immortal fame as subsequent events will relate.

Their transit across this stream was more dignified than that of the elder Kean's in one of his strolling peregrinations in England in 1805. This Roscius had made an engagement to appear at a town in Essex; but, on the day fixed for his appearance, he found himself in the county of Kent with the river Thames between him and the rest of the performers. What to do was the question. He arrived at the river banks without a *sou* in his pocket; and he disdained to entreat the grim, bluff Charon of the Thames for any favors that a few years afterwards, says Leigh Hunt, "he might have commanded the ferryman's services by the mere mention of his

*Theatrical Rambles of Mr. & Mrs. Greene*, Charles Durang

name: *Caesarum Vehis!*" So stripping himself, he tied his clothes in his dingy pocket handkerchief and, seizing the bundle with his teeth, plunged into the river and swam over. Unluckily, in the course of this natatorial passage, his head dipped so often in old Thames that by the time he reached the Essex side his clothes were completely saturated with water. Although Mr. Greene might have performed such an aquatic feat, Mrs. Greene could not have gone through such a water gymnastic.

We now arrive at a turning point in the Greenes' melancholy rambles in real life to reach fame's temple in the mimic scene. Shakespeare says, "all the world's a stage"; as Horace said before him, "all the world acts a play." Two lines which from time immemorial have been engraved over the arch of theatre prosceniums as moral maxims for the public eye and sense to rest upon. The first motto on the old Chestnut Street Theatre of Philadelphia was "the Eagle suffers little birds to sing," taken from Shakespeare's *Titus Andronicus*;[2] suggested, it is said, by the father of the late George M. Dallas, then, in 1793, a prominent member of the bar and a great patron of the drama.

This motto had reference to the then recent repealed laws against all stage dramatic exhibitions. Puppet shows, lectures on heads, etc., were tolerated by law on the same stage, but not the pure dramas of Shakespeare, Otway, Beaumont, Fletcher, Dryden, Addison, etc. Dramatic literature was legally prohibited, while Punch and Judy, rope tumbling and their correlatives were allowed. Could fanaticism go further? It is to be regretted by the liberal minded that the antagonists of the drama should blend its improprieties and abuses with the thing itself. It is granted from the highest sources of mental judgment that the drama is seated unalterably in the heart of man; and, if so, it should receive from the statesman, the philosophical teacher, the parent and the guardian, a fostering care to insure its moral teachings as blending instruction with amusement.

When the Greenes had wended their way into the center of the town, the snow continuing unabated, their worn out physical wants only increased. They looked earnestly

*Theatrical Rambles of Mr. & Mrs. Greene*, Charles Durang

about for some benevolent face among those who were hastily passing to and fro through the streets on business, to whom they might venture to address their sufferings. Thus, in doubt, that beneficent aspect, that angel of charity personified in any of the groups they passed wherein they could have made their condition known and solicited the favor of a shelter from the pitiless storm, did not appear to the vision of their anxious despair. The Good Samaritan was not tangible to them in any form and their hearts failed to address any of the passers by. It was now night, despair reigned in their hearts, but a sudden thought struck Greene's mind: "necessity has no law."

"Anne, do you walk here about for a few minutes. Walking can only keep you from freezing. I'll soon return."

And he made his quick exit. But he was very soon returned with a smile and succor, took his wife under his arm, and hurried her along with feeble steps. He conducted her to a large hotel kept by a Col. Madery, who proved to be a prince of hosts. His draggled-tailed, wretched, ragged wife started back with awe at entering so magnificent a house; but Greene, with assumed independence, took her arm and with a polished air introduced her to the host. His gay kind of hauteur, blended with an easy jaunty manner, won the chef of the hotel at once, which Mrs. Greene, with all the tact of the actress, seconded with infinite skill.

The ruse had the desired effect. They were immediately ushered into a snug parlor, carpeted, and easily furnished, with a cheerful fire and well lighted. A delicious supper of coffee, buckwheat cakes, eggs, sausages, boiled chicken, etc., was soon spread before their astonished sight and voracious appetite. To it they went "like French falconers." A mental grace preceded the attack of the eatables.

Greene, with kingly manner, dismissed the servant in attendance, waving his hand to him, "You may go. We'll wait upon ourselves."

The distressed Thespian couple now paused for a moment in wonder at this truly magical change in their affairs. It surpassed in reality any harlequin trick in a Ravel pantomime. The twain paused, looked at each other. The lady at length burst into a hysteric fit of laughter mingled with

## *Theatrical Rambles of Mr. & Mrs. Greene*, Charles Durang

tears. It was "joy, passing joy!" But reason regained its throne with appetite being thus feasted. No cloud intervened to shadow their present banquet but the consequences of the trick passed on the landlord upon a final settlement. But hunger satisfied and sweet "sleep that knits up the ravell'd sleeve of care" restored exhausted nature, while flattering dreams told of visions of future bliss.

The surprise of Greene's wife in their sudden transition from shelterless beggars to palatial accommodations led to the ardent inquiry, "How did you so quickly accomplish the change?"

"My dear, our case was desperate and desperate was the means to be used. The idea flashed upon my mind, suggesting at once the only expedient. I walked boldly into the hotel and up to the official acting behind the bar, and, *sans cérémonie*, ordered a bed and supper for a fatigued sick lady who has been traveling for twenty days on horseback through the western forests and prairies beyond the Mississippi. Our horses became lamed ere we reached the borders of Ohio. We relieved our animals by walking occasionally with them and were obliged at last to abandon them on the road with our luggage. The host of the hotel, possessing the heart of real benevolence and the most congenial manners, as clearly marked in his laughing jolly face, instantly believed the apparently unsophisticated tale. And, so here we are. Anne, my dear, I learned that confidence in my profession was the only road to success. In playing the blunt, honest Irishman before the gods of the gallery, I observed how plain, honest dealings will enlist the sympathies of men if you touch their heart strings with truth in manly appeal. Woman in misfortune ever touches the heart of the true man and readily brings forth the best and sweetest notes of its affections."

"But John," replied Mrs. Greene, "look at my shabby and ragged habiliments. Even by candle light they may have the false look that a misty sunset may cast o'er their texture, or the delusive tints that a silvery moonlight may charmingly tinge them withal, but, in the sun of broad daylight they must show the real aspect of shreds and patches. We shall be turned out, neck and heels."

## *Theatrical Rambles of Mr. & Mrs. Greene*, Charles Durang

"If so," said John, "I can only exclaim with Macbeth, 'The flighty purpose never is o'ertook, unless the deed go with it.' Let us dispatch our supper quickly so they shall not send us away hungry. But Anne, fear not. Here we are entrenched, defying all brute force, and if we are assailed I'll play the Gladiator, 'Let them thus come in, we are armed' in honest poverty.'[1] In Wellington's motto, 'Virtue is ever the companion of fortune.'"

They met, however, with no such ill luck, as the sequel will show. For many weeks previously they had not enjoyed one humble meal or night's rest. If the dress of this unfortunate couple was beggarly, the host and servants beheld at once that the lady and gentleman truly existed in their persons. Their manners and conversation attested that they had moved in a refined sphere of society and that the exigencies of the rugged journey through the wilderness sufficiently explained their ragged personal condition. Such were the natural impressions of the host and his attaches.

The actor and actress retired to rest, "perchance to dream," (there's the rub) not visions of "sheep hooks and daisies," but of a huge bill of hotel charges, albeit, not one cent to pay it withal. Sleep soon sealed their eyelids in the image of death, with their bodies entrenched in a fine bed of snowy sheets, pillows and curtains, with comfortable furniture to match.

Mr. Greene, refreshed but still in a state of anxiety, arose early. He ushered forth in quest of fortune. Silent and soft as the floating down he made his exit from the chamber, not wishing to disturb his wife's gentle slumbers. Late in the morning she soundly slept, unconscious of her husband's absence. On awaking, strange forebodings shook her mind at his prolonged stay, fearing that some accident or untoward event might have occurred to prevent his sooner return and that she alone would have to encounter the landlord's ire and probably insulting comments. While agitated with these reveries of forcible ejection from her present Elysium to a Cinderella fate, our noble comedian entered the apartment singing "The Boys of St. Patrick." Arrayed in a dashing full suit of broadcloth fashionable clothes, a new beaver, boots of a tasty pattern and patent leather of modern style, he

## Theatrical Rambles of Mr. & Mrs. Greene, Charles Durang

looked like one of our early Western Congressmen bound for Washington. Under his arm he bore a large-sized parcel of fancy articles of female gear.

The poor wife, perfectly astounded at his magical change of costume and manner, screamed out with ecstasy of surprise, "In the name of our patron saint, John, what have you done? Not guilty, I hope, of any wrong? Where did you get that splendid suit of clothes? Do tell and end my forebodings!"

"Well, dear Anne, when I sallied forth this morning in a state of despair in search of employment in some printing office, or any work that might give us temporary relief, I met an old friend who once was an actor with me in a provincial *corps*, and also a fellow typo. We had been as brothers in our vocations but were suddenly separated by circumstances and became ignorant of the whereabouts of either. Nearly the first man I met this morning as I left the hotel was my old companion. He greeted me warmly, an explanation took place, and he proved a friend indeed. This extraordinary event can better be imagined than described. But let us breakfast first and then I'll explain all this apparent mystery to your satisfaction. In the meantime I have taken time by the forelock and brought a bonnet and cloak, that you may usher forth and choose for yourself such clothing that may suit your taste."

The clothing being properly adjusted, the promised explanation followed. Mr. Greene, on meeting his quondam friend and actor, at once unburthened his peculiar fix to him without reserve; and, like Aladdin's genius, with pantomimic celerity, he changed Greene's beggarly garments into fashionable habits and his miserable lodgings heretofore into marble halls. Greene found his old Thespian chum keeping a large clothing bazaar, hence the metamorphose of dress. Money was generously put into the pocket of the coat to meet his present expenses, hence the cause of our miraculous change of scene from squalid misery to comparative prosperity.

The relief thus extended was not one of abject dependence, for the benevolent friend designed and placed in

## *Theatrical Rambles of Mr. & Mrs. Greene*, Charles Durang

operation a professional mode of honorable employment for the wandering pair. There happened to be a very fine amateur dramatic *corps* in the town who performed very often, composed of merchants, lawyers, and other literary young gentlemen. Of this association his friend was an active member (for reasons cogent, the name is omitted). He caused this company to be called together in relation to the Greenes. At this meeting he proposed to give performances twice a week, to be assisted by Mr. and Mrs. John Greene, regular professionals, in the leading parts. The theatre, lights, etc., were to be given gratis for one month or longer. After the dead expenses were deducted, such as door-keepers, music, scene-shifters, and printing, the receipts were to go to Mr. Greene and lady. Here was an intervening providence in their favor.

Mrs. Greene, young, handsome, and a fine figure, made (in theatrical parlance) quite a hit in her tragedy. An avalanche of friends poured fortune's favors into her lap. Like a meteor she shone, while presentations of valuable silks, velvets, satins, jewelry, ornaments, and other luxuries flowed unceasingly into her domicile. She had soon a queenly wardrobe. And thus, we have here an ocular demonstration of heaven's protective care of the virtuous poor, intellectually endowed, whose indomitable honesty in all their vicissitudes could never be tempted by the great evil spirit to do a criminal act.

It was at this time and place that Charles Webb, well-known to the Philadelphia public as a native and an excellent actor, made his first appearance in Valcour, in *The Point of Honor*.[3] His very musical voice, pathos and good judgment as a reader, and judicious declamation as an actor, made him an immense favorite with our audiences. However, a wayward destiny attended poor Charles. Strong-minded as an actor, he was weak-minded as a man. In the winter of 1851, while playing at Washington City, he was found drowned in the City Canal one morning, frozen stiff in an upright position. Whether this was the effect of design or accident it is not known.

## NOTES

*Theatrical Rambles of Mr. & Mrs. Greene*, Charles Durang

**NOTES**

[1] The passage was taken from Act II, scene 3, of Robert Montgomery Bird's *The Gladiator*.

[2] *Titus Andronicus*, Act IV, scene 4.

> The eagle suffers little birds to sing,
> And is not careful what they mean thereby,
> Knowing that with the shadow of his wing
> He can at pleasure stint their melody:
> Even so mayst thou the giddy son of Rome.

Alexander James Dallas, a Scotsman became a leading member of the Philadelphia Bar. He was appointed United States Attorney for Eastern Pennsylvania by Jefferson in 1801; and was instrumental for arranging a $16,000,000 war loan in 1812. He died in 1817. His son, George Mifflin Dallas, became Polk's Vice President. Dallas, TX, was named after him.

[3] *The Point of Honor*, a comedy by Charles Kemble.

*Theatrical Rambles of Mr. & Mrs. Greene*, Charles Durang

## VII.

BLANCHARD'S COMPANY — ROUGHING IT IN THE BACKWOODS — MIXED AUDIENCES — CURIOUS CURRENCY — ENTHUSIASM OF THE INDIANS — A LOVE AFFAIR — CHICAGO THEN AND NOW — WITH TURNBULL IN CANADA.

When Mr. and Mrs. John Greene left the amateurs of Chilicothe, it was with mutual and kindly feelings of friendship, for it had been a most happy, genial association. They joined the traveling company of Mr. William Blanchard (not the great Blanchard of London who made his appearance at the Bowery Theatre in New York in 1831, and was the father of Mrs. Hamblin), whose performers, with the exception of Mr. Woodruff, subsequently a well-known performer at the Bowery Theatre, were entirely composed of his own family.[1] Blanchard, enrolling the Greenes and two or three others of the tribe of Thespis, plumed himself on having a fine company. The campaign commenced by a tour through Ohio, a State then (1820) beginning to receive all the adornment of art and civilization, in addition to all its natural beauties. This company traveled through Ohio, and then ascended the Lake to Detroit in Michigan on the only steamboat then running in those regions, called *Walk-in-the-Water*.[2] Here they halted and performed like Thespis of Athens, erecting a stage over the wagon placed between two huge black oak trees, the branches forming a foliage proscenium. This was backed by a stockade fort used in the war of 1812. In this fort the company dressed. From thence they went to Malden, Mackinaw, and Green Bay;[3] a truly romantic circuit they made through this almost unknown region inhabited by the Indian tribes and trappers, with a sprinkling of emigrants; and where they

*Theatrical Rambles of Mr. & Mrs. Greene*, Charles Durang

assisted in a primitive way to plant civilization through the drama and a hand press which Blanchard brought with him and on which John Greene printed play bills the size of a card. Their orchestra consisted of two dashing, dandy darkies who always traveled with them. One of these sable musicians was quite an expert on the violin and an original character of comic eccentricity; and, what is more extraordinary, he was a Cockney Negro, born in London.

The steamboats in those days went no further up the lakes than Detroit. The manager was obliged to charter a small sloop to convey them to Mackinaw. On their arrival there they put up at a public house dignified with the title of hotel. Their theatre here was a long building made of logs, crossed and weather boarded with the bark of trees. The place had been used as a sheep-fold. When filled with people, as it was every night of their performances, the odor and the bad air arising from the ground was of the most offensive kind to delicate senses, yet was not thought of by these crowded audiences, who seemingly enjoyed themselves with continued shouts and laughter. They were composed of Canadian French, Indiana, and half breeds, roving Americans, and permanent emigrants.

The Indians, who enjoyed the entertainments, paid for their tickets in valuable skins, always as good as cash, for the trappers and skin agents paid in ready money for those articles of trade. They would often pay in silver medals, gold rings, and other ornaments of that kind, or barter their blankets for a chance to see the exhibition, being positively stage struck, probably instinctively receiving a spark of refinement from the spirit of Shakespeare. The manager that had furs with which to pay his company their salaries, as Mr. Blanchard had, and kept these valuable Indian certificates until he found a good market for their sale, made money, doubling his capital.

The next field of the company's operations was a place called Drummond's Island,[4] forty miles from Mackinaw, and, like all the other tours by land and water, was not accomplished without some stirring incidental event. The transit was to be accomplished in a boat of a frail build. They

*Theatrical Rambles of Mr. & Mrs. Greene*, Charles Durang

did not start from their moorings till late in the day. About nightfall they found themselves near a small island covered with beautiful verdure and magnificent trees. It was resolved to moor the boat and to go ashore, there to remain till morning's dawn. The only inhabitants of this isle were Indians, dwelling in good and well located wigwams. With their native hospitality they proffered their accommodations. This was accepted by some, while others of the company pitched their own tents on a pleasant knoll overhung with wild grape vines. They then partook of such refreshments as the red men gave them, and some *morceaux* of their own. The meal ended, they spread their buffalo robes and slept soundly. In the morning they set sail for their destined island where they were to unfurl their Thespian banner. This was at a British possession in Upper Canada, the headquarters of a British regiment.

Having safely arrived at this English post, the military officers—always gay and animated for tasteful sports, especially when quartered in remote corners of the world, as the Lakes of Upper Canada then were outside of all civilization—received this itinerant company of performers with open arms.

A large government ware room was given for the erection of their theatre. A stage and orchestra were arranged with front rows of seats and a back gallery for privates and their wives. The traveling press, under the care of Mr. Greene, threw off bills of the play in sounding phrases and puffing verbiage. The front seats were reserved for the nobility and gentry, consisting of the officers of the army and their ladies. The upper gallery was laid with pine boards across the beams, and joists under the roof. It was a strange sight to see the string of redcoats on these upper seats, puffing and blowing for air, and the Indians above them with their grave looks, not a smile visible upon their faces, while the elite of the army in the front offered a very charming sight of good humored, gentlemanly attention to the performances. Here the manager was favored with the band of the regiment, which enlivened the entertainments. During the performances the band played England's national anthem, "God Save the King," in which hymn the company, in com-

## *Theatrical Rambles of Mr. & Mrs. Greene*, Charles Durang

pliment to their patrons, joined with the audience. This is a sacred custom in all English theatres. Here the auditors displayed a courtesy with much good will and taste, in responding to the American comedians in a hearty strain of "Hail Columbia!" and merry "Yankee Doodle," and the Indian spectators commenced dancing with heartfelt delight.

The company's campaign had so far proved brilliant and interesting. They now steered their course for the village of Navarino,[5] at Green Bay, the paradise of these remote wilds at that day, 1820. The schooner, which was freighted with our first dramatic missionaries of the then far West, was named *The Fairy of the Lakes*. She was a perfect model of naval architecture, like a graceful naiad with her white robes, and her gallant mast surmounted with the American union flowing in fitful curves with the gentle breezes of Green Bay. Her beautiful hull floated like a swan into the secluded wooded cove of Navarino, as the enchanting silvery twilight of these regions cast a magical mist over all the glowing landscape. The schooner anchored under the shadows of the colossal forest trees, which were beautifully reflected in the transparent waters of the bay.

The officers of the army received the company with ecstasies; so indeed did all the gentlemen, agents, traders, and various residents there. The officers had their *soirees* on the river bank in large tents, or marques, during the hot weather, and tendered to the company every assistance. The barracks were converted into a temporary theatre. All the soldiers that were mechanics assisted in the work. Some of the officers assisted in the cast of the plays and a small band of musicians belonging to the army formed an orchestra. The theatre opened with the scenery that manager Blanchard traveled with. They had no study of part, no rehearsals.

The manager's daughter, Miss Blanchard, was a beautiful, accomplished, fascinating girl, of symmetrical form and expressive face. This beautiful girl captivated the heart of a young lieutenant of the United States Army, who was stationed at that post. They were discovered by the father at the back window of the barracks, playing the garden scene in *Romeo and Juliet*. Fathers have flinty hearts, so had man-

*Theatrical Rambles of Mr. & Mrs. Greene*, Charles Durang

ager Blanchard. He was an Englishman with all his country's prejudices in full blown selfishness, loathing the very idea of his daughter marrying an American of any degree; while her eldest brother carried this absurd feeling to such a ridiculous extent that he would rather have his sister marry a footman of an English nobleman than a Yankee officer.

The company having completed their Green Bay campaign, set sail out of it and traversed the waters of Lake Michigan to Chicago, in the State of Illinois, the commercial depot of the State, located on Lake Michigan at the mouth of a river of the same name. The rise and progress of this city from a mere swamp, occasionally occupied as a site for Indian wigwams, has been without a parallel in the world's history. The city of Chicago, at the time that our Thespians visited it, was a mere trading post for skins, where the trappers and traders met as a central market to buy and barter with the Indians for their goods. It was composed of a few mud huts, with the aborigines' encampments, a place of refuge for the worst of the Western peoples, where desperadoes plotted "treason, stratagems, and spoils." What is it now? One of the most splendid cities in the Union in palatial private mansions, in public buildings of architectural magnificence, in hotels vying in elegance and accommodation with those of New York, Boston, or Philadelphia, princely stores and gigantic warehouses; while forests of masts with their flowing sails interlaced with hundreds of steamboats, stud and dot the harbor, reminding the traveler of New York. The origin and building of this wondrous city partakes of the magical element. At the time this dramatic troupe visited Chicago—now some forty years ago—it had a wild, desolate appearance. It was the *ultima thule* of America. There were but two white families permanently inhabiting the present site of the great city of the Western regions besides the United States soldiers posted there in their log forts and quaint watch towers to observe the wily doings of the aborigines and to quell the riots and sudden forays made on our extreme frontiers. A few hundred dollars might have purchased the site of this city, now worth billions.

Manager Blanchard and his company saw at once that it was useless to try to perform there, and immediately re-

*Theatrical Rambles of Mr. & Mrs. Greene*, Charles Durang

turned to Mackinaw. The young Lieutenant Vallee followed his lady love, Miss Blanchard, with increased ardency; and at Mackinaw he wrung the slow consent of her parents to their union and the Lieutenant became a Benedict.

The company performed here for a time, then went to Detroit, and finally to Canada. Here they met a family of the name of Turnbull who were playing there. Blanchard was in want of another useful actress, and engaged one by the name of Thornton, wife of Jack Thornton, an Englishman who had been a subordinate in the Chestnut Street Theatre, Philadelphia. He was an oddity in his way. The new actress proved troublesome and really worthless. Captain Turnbull was quite an original. He was at this time lessee of the Montréal Theatre that stood over an old, oblong stone warehouse and had been fitted up by an English scene painter named Joseph Allport, a very good landscape painter who afterwards died in the West Indies.[6]

Turnbull made his first appearance in America at Boston in 1799. He was a small, lame man who attempted low comedy. From possessing a face strongly resembling the great John Bernard, he was led to play that actor's great parts in imitation, but there was nothing like a resemblance therein. However, he had literary pretensions and was the author of several noted melodramas; *The Wood Demon* was one which was very successful.[7]

## NOTES

[1] Odell lists a circus man, W. Blanchard, performing at a "minor theatre," Warren Street and Broadway in feats of legerdemain. His 1818 company included an Indian act and a tumbler. He later appeared with his family—a 14-year-old Master G. Blanchard, balancing artist, and a 12-year-old daughter—on the slack wire. The Blanchard Company was in Cincinnati in 1819 for a few nights at Mr. Dawson's school room on Water Street.

[2] In 1818, *Walk-in-the-Water* became the first steamship on the upper Great Lakes, making regular trips from Buffalo. The following year, a voyage was made to Mackinac and

*Theatrical Rambles of Mr. & Mrs. Greene*, Charles Durang

Green Bay. The ship was wrecked by a storm three years later.

[3] Delafield described Malden as a town of 175 to 200 houses, with a garrison at this time of 36 men. It was located across the river from Detroit, a few miles below what is now Windsor.

[4] Named after Sir Gordon Drummond, it was a rocky and barren British outpost, militarily strategic to the Straits of Mackinaw. At this time there was but a single street with some 15 houses and only two companies of British troops.

[5] Navarino was settled in 1819, now a part of the city of Green Bay.

[6] The scene painter Allport was manager of a company in Montréal in 1809 in which Charles Durang and Turnbull were members. J. O. Turnbull made his debut at the Haymarket Theatre, Boston, 1799. He first appeared at the Park, New York, October 25, 1801, in a subordinate position. More important, he fathered useful actresses in the Misses C. (Mrs. Pritchard) and Julia Turnbull.

[7] John Bernard, born in Portsmouth, England, 1756, was an old school actor, said to be the first with a metropolitan reputation to come to America, brought over by Wignell for the Philadelphia theatre. Eventually he returned to England and died destitute, November 29, 1828, at age 72. *The Wood Demon, or, The Clock Has Struck* was a melodrama by M. G. Lewis.

*Theatrical Rambles of Mr. & Mrs. Greene*, Charles Durang

## VIII.

MONTRÉAL THEATRE — AN INSULT REMEMBERED — JUST REPROOF — A RETURN TO THE STATES — MRS. DRAKE AND THE PRESIDENT — DRAMATIC READINGS IN NEW ENGLAND, ETC.

Blanchard next moved his company to Fort George, then Kingston, the Greenes continuing with him. Then it was arranged that they were to occupy the theatre with Turnbull. At that day a winter journey in Canada was not a small affair; it was nearly as great an effort as that of Napoléon crossing the Alps. They had to travel from Upper Canada to the lower province. For this snow exodus a train of seven sleighs was engaged to convey the company of performers with their baggage, an experienced driver and a principal guide to conduct the train being duly selected. The stout trotting, hardy Canadian ponies swiftly drew the sleighs at their heels. But great caution had to be observed. Part of the way they sleighed on the shore and the other on the frozen snow of the St. Lawrence River. All had to follow the leader in single file.

The company opened in Montréal. The business proved very bad. Money was excessively scarce, the times out of joint. In truth, the snow storm had rendered the streets impassable. The theatre doors, which stood twenty feet high from the level of the street, were literally blocked up to that height with mountains of snow. Montréal was truly a city buried up in ice and snow during this winter. The manager determined to return to the States, and thither they started bag and baggage.

*Theatrical Rambles of Mr. & Mrs. Greene*, Charles Durang

While on their journey a small white cloud arose in the sky, in shape resembling a clenched hand with the forefinger pointing in the direction they were going. All observed it.

Woodruff remarked, "It is a good omen. It points out our course and its destiny," and then in a whisper, added, "too good for such a roaring John Bull."

This was intended for Blanchard, who overheard it and secretly resolved to punish those who enjoyed the joke. When they stopped to bait their horses, he made a new arrangement with the travelers, putting all the English part of the company into the carioles or sleighs. Then he suddenly had the ponies hitched up and drove off, while by some contrivance he kept Woodruff and his coadjutors in a back room quaffing whiskey punch in great glee. When they had finished their hot potations of the lily dew, they found the only vehicles left them to get over the road into the United States were their own feet and legs, and so they had to foot it on the snow to the next stopping place.

The most of Blanchard's company were Yankees. At Little Town, state of New York, they played to very good houses. And after making a professional tour through the many towns in the north part of the state, they crossed Lake Champlain on the ice. The season was far advanced, which made that operation a dangerous experiment. When at about the middle of the lake, the guide sledge lost the proper track and came to a dead halt. Directly after, an awful and most alarming sound was heard, as if thunder were rolling in dreadful peals under their feet. It was evident the ice was giving way. The drivers at once crowded all the baggage into one sleight, hitched all the other horses to that one, and started off at full speed toward the Vermont shore, leaving the bipeds to follow as well as they could.

Thus nonplused, the actors and actresses, without being acquainted with the true and safe path or any means of its being pointed out to them, as night had overtaken them, wended their way through snow slush up to their knees. Almost frozen to death, hungry and broken down with fatigue of body and mental anguish, they reached Vermont perfect objects of misery.

## Theatrical Rambles of Mr. & Mrs. Greene, Charles Durang

After a few days rest, all assembled together and in Canadian carioles (or sleighs) crossed the St. Lawrence River to the village of La Prairie, and thence to St. Johns, eighteen miles from there, the first port of entry from the States. The tour through Canada was short and disagreeable. "The actress of all work," Mrs. Thornton, made herself very obnoxious; her behavior was intolerable and disagreeable. The company soon retraced its steps back to the states of New York and Vermont, till it finally reach New Hampshire, where the Greenes left the Blanchard association, directed their course to Boston, and entered into an engagement at Schaeffer's Washington Garden Theatre, a beautiful summer temple in Tremont street, opposite the lower part of the Boston Mall.[1] To the Greenes this was a blessed change from a theatrical pandemonium to the Elysium of a respectable theatre. The fashion of Boston supported this fresco establishment. The performers were first-class in their roles.

Mrs. A. Drake, the celebrated tragedienne, was a member of this company.[2] Her career as a leading dramatic star had placed her high on the scroll of fame. She was enthusiastic in her love of poetry. Her particular favorite was Lord Byron.

When the news of his death was received in America, her husband related it to her in the following manner, "Sad news, my dear."

"What is it? Any of the children sick?"

"No, worse than that."

"Any dead?"

"No."

"Oh, Alexander, do not keep me in this suspense. What is it?"

"Byron's dead!"

"Then there is no longer anything worth living for," was her mournful reply.

She was a most joyous, affable creature, full of riddles, good nature, and capital jokes. At the time R. M. Johnson was a candidate for President of the United States.[3] He was also a candidate for the hand of Mrs. Drake.

*Theatrical Rambles of Mr. & Mrs. Greene*, Charles Durang

A friend rallied her on the subject, when she replied, "Well, I will wait till I see how he fills the Presidential chair; then, if he wants my assistance to aid him in governing the United States, why you know I am a patriot and I will heroically resolve to sacrifice myself for my country's good." Johnson lost his election and was non-suited in his love cause.

During Mr. Forrest's engagement, Mrs. Greene was playing the Widow Melnotte in *The Lady of Lyons*. When she entered the cottage scene she saw the picture that Claude had to use in descanting on the beauties of Pauline lying on the ground where it had by accident fallen. She took it up and placed it on the easel. When Mr. Forrest entered after, and eloquently praising the charms of his mistress took the portrait as if to display her loveliness to the audience and his mother, the audience burst into one loud shout of laughter. Mr. Forrest, much disconcerted, looked at the portrait of that beauty he had been extolling, and lo! instead of the likeness of Pauline, it was Dennis Brulgruddery's sign of the "Red Cow," which had been painted at the back of it.

After the summer engagement at Boston was over, the Greenes joined a company of comedians on a tour through Vermont under the auspices of a gentleman. The company was good but the conductor was a very indifferent one, as no money was ever received from him by the performers. Not even the boarding bills were paid, as events painfully disclosed when the break up of the company came.

As Mr. and Mrs. Greene were about to take their leave, their trunks were detained. With well considered philosophy to be exercised in such exigencies, Greene put a few necessaries in a white and blue pocket handkerchief, and with an old umbrella over his shoulder, on the end of which dangled the bundle and a clean shirt, like the great Edmund Kean before him (with this reservation only, the tragedian had a child to carry with the bundle), did Mr. and Mrs. John Greene trudge it in sorrowful steps, till they reached Brattleboro in Vermont. Their purses contained after this hard march just $3.50 and a bundle of dress articles that a city pawn broker would hardly give 50¢ for.

### Theatrical Rambles of Mr. & Mrs. Greene, Charles Durang

John Greene nobly resolved to defy fate and extricate himself and wife from these terrific difficulties through the force of their talents and an appeal to public sympathies. They determined to give scenes from plays and recitations in the hall of the hotel, an exhibition that in these days is eulogized into "Readings of Shakespeare and other Poets." He accordingly issued an *affiche* of his purpose. Greene, being a professional printer, went to a printing office, stated his case in a "plain unvarnished tale," and asked permission of a brother typo to be allowed to set up his own bills. Being a member of the craft, it was cheerfully granted, and they assisted him in it. The bill was made out in the usual style, with a curt statement of his case at the top. The entertainments were for two nights only, to consist of soliloquies and scenes from *Hamlet, Macbeth, Richard III*, with comic recitations, "Johnny Gilpin's Journey to London," etc.[4] The entertainments were a success—a hit! They cleared enough to pay all their debts and to carry them to Burlington. Here was a sudden emancipation from dire distress.

Greene went to the bar before their exit and asked for his bill. The answer was, "It is paid, all settled."

A start by the comedian, "By whom?"

The answer, "No matter, all's right!"

Greene then took seats in the stage coach and handed over the cash.

The clerk said, "Sir, your places for self and wife are paid for."

Another ah! and a start. On the journey the driver was questioned as to the good, unknown friend, but the Jehu shook his head in ignorance. In vain did they try to find out their mysterious benefactor, but never did.

They arrived at Burlington with fifty dollars a piece in hand. Upon this hint did they act for some time, and went from town to town giving recitations and scenes from plays, clearing from forty to fifty dollars at each place. At one town there was a revival (as it was termed) in full force, and Greene bethought himself of an expedient to arouse excitement in his own behalf. Therefore, without ceremony he went among this assemblage and delivered his bills broad-

*Theatrical Rambles of Mr. & Mrs. Greene*, Charles Durang

cast. This had the desired effect. The backsliders must have been numerous in this society, for his exhibitions were filled night after night and the majority of the audiences were the individuals composing these thronged revivals. The ways of hypocritical sinners may be curious and very mysterious, but they clearly evinced good taste in listening to good poetry, well delivered, with a good moral.

The amiable Watts, the great psalm composer, says on dramatic literature, "It is granted that dramatic representation of the affairs of human life is by no means sinful in itself. I am inclined to think that valuable compositions might be made of this kind, such as might entertain an audience with innocent delight and profit."

At this period of their peregrinations from place to place, they were uniformly successful. In less than two months it took two large trunks to hold their increased wardrobe, and they had five hundred dollars in cash besides. Here was a change achieved by themselves, without the aid of scenery or a *dramatis personae.*

## NOTES

[1]Schaeffer's Washington Garden Theatre was a brick amphitheatre, opened in the summer of 1819 under the management of Mr. Bernard, originally for variety performances.
[2]Mrs. Alexander Drake, a native of Albany, as Miss Denny, coming from the Boston theatre, made her debut in New York at the Anthony Street Theatre, April 17, 1820. She rarely performed in that city but ranked high as a comedian in the West.
[3]Richard Kantor Johnson was Van Buren's running mate in 1836. With no majority in the Electoral College, Johnson became the only Vice-President in history to be selected by the Senate.
[4]"Johnny Gilpin's Journey to London" was probably the William Cowper poem, "The Diverting History of John Gilpin, Showing How He Went Farther Than He Intended, and Came Home Safe Again." Written in 1782, the piece became a popular monologue for actors after John Henderson used it

*Theatrical Rambles of Mr. & Mrs. Greene*, Charles Durang as part of a recitation program in 1785, making it celebrated throughout England.

*Theatrical Rambles of Mr. & Mrs. Greene*, Charles Durang

## IX.

A MINOR THEATRE—IN THE BALLET — OLD TIMES IN PHILADELPHIA — MRS. GREENE AT BALTIMORE — JAMES WALLACK — THEATRICALS IN MARYLAND — COFFEE AND CAKES FOR THE PLAYERS — THE GREAT RACE BETWEEN THE NORTH AND SOUTH — WOOD AND WARREN.

In 1821 the Greenes received an offer of an engagement from Philadelphia. A new minor theatre had been constructed in Prune street, between $5^{th}$ and $6^{th}$ Streets, by a Polish magician performer called Stanislaus, which was to commence operation in the fall of 1821.[1] The drama was there represented in all its various phases with a tolerably good company. Greene determined to accept the offer, although the terms and lines of business they were to perform were not definitely stated as is usual in contracts. Mrs. Greene opposed it with woman's foresight—they were doing very well as it was—but Greene willed it otherwise. He wanted to fret and strut his hour on the stage. She yielded and to the Quaker City they went forthwith and in due time reported themselves to the managerial department in Prune street.

The folly of going to that engagement without the salaries or lines being previously defined was soon made apparent to the novice comedian, John Greene. They left a good business at the North to accept this proffered situation, without any preliminary stipulations being even canvassed. The result was that being at the mercy of the manager they were obliged to submit. Having traveled 400 miles, they were without any engagement elsewhere. And the alternative of

## *Theatrical Rambles of Mr. & Mrs. Greene*, Charles Durang

traveling a great distance to procure another situation (for theatres at that time were few and far between), their means being exhausted, Mr. Greene had to accept such terms as the minor manager with his penurious foreign notions chose to give, which were $10 a week and simply utility business—that is, such parts as the stage manager thought proper to cast him in but no lines could he claim.

For Mrs. Greene no situation could be given at all, not even a super's place was vacant. Here was a dilemma! Necessity has no law and Greene had to accept. It paid their board, however, and kept the wolf from the door till they looked for something better.

The firm of Warren and Wood's fine theatre on Chestnut Street had been burnt down at the latter end of the season of 1820. The old Walnut Street Circus, at the corner of $9^{th}$ was then reconstructed into a theatre and was on the eve of opening for the winter season of 1820-21.[2] Mr. and Mrs. Greene applied to this management for situations while the company was then performing in Baltimore. The answer to this application requested them to await their arrival in Philadelphia in a few weeks and they would be happy to negotiate with Mr. and Mrs. Greene. The end of the matter was, Mrs. Greene only was engaged at the Walnut Street Theatre at $5 a week, to go on in groups, dances, etc., whenever required—a position that now receives the name of *corps de ballet*—and nearly sure to be employed every night of performance.

She now discovered, what many actresses have done, the expense of dress and labor of the position. They have to be their own mantua makers, unless it be a leading actress or a star whose large incomes of salaries and benefits from popularity and talents give them vast pecuniary advantage over the secondary and minor female performers, and must perforce do their own sewing on dresses consisting of every variety of costume, from the richness of the queen to the plainness of the peasant. This compels them to be eternally employed in the alteration of their dresses to suit the age of the characters they may represent, which requires some mental study as well as physical labor and the purchase of

*Theatrical Rambles of Mr. & Mrs. Greene*, Charles Durang

some new material suitable for the specific occasion, too often an inconvenient expense to the actress, yet in the line of her business indispensable. During this process there is often a new part to study and digest, first to learn the words, then to rehearse daily. Thus with work and study at home and rehearsals in the mornings and performances at night, the actresses during the season have their whole time absorbed in professional duties; and this under strict disciplinary rules of obedience to managerial casting of pieces, of attention to business, to being perfect in the language of their parts subject to arbitrary forfeits, and finally to a discharge at the will of the manager, from which the performers seldom have any appeal.

When Mrs. Greene took the engagement for $5 a week at the Walnut Street Theatre, it was her first object to make a little money go a great way. Her husband was by birth a Philadelphian and had relations there. Mr. and Mrs. Greene were engaged in different theatres. To economize as much as possible they took humble lodgings in Southwark, in Second Street, below Shippen Street.

Being in different theatres made it inconvenient. From Ninth and Walnut was a long and dreary walk to their boarding house; passing down Sixth street by the old prison wall and Potters Field, the present Washington Square, the sidewalks unpaved, poorly lighted with small oil lamps of two dim wicks, no street-passenger vehicles of any sort but the hackney coach at high prices, and not found at a stand. In those days these were rather dismal promenades for a lone woman. Sometimes she called at the Prune Street Theatre for her husband on her way home.

They both had philosophical minds and mutually consoled each other with the green-room tales of the two theatres, which are ever racy and humorous, or a retrospective glance at their past life, which ever gave food to cure the weariness of the mind. A theatre is always a place of stirring events and beguiling circumstances. They had passed through scenes enough and had hair-breadth escapes of a romantic nature in their sojourn among the savage tribes to philosophize upon. In those dreary midnight walks to her home she never met with any insult to her person or attack of foot-

## *Theatrical Rambles of Mr. & Mrs. Greene*, Charles Durang

pad, maugre there were no police patrols beyond those nightly guardians except "Charlies" who lustily called every hour of the night in a recitative tone, with a foreign accent, *viz.*: "Past 12 o'clock and a moonlight morning."

In the spring Mrs. Greene accompanied Messrs. Warren and Wood's company to Baltimore. This season (1821-22) at the Walnut Street Theatre was not a profitable one. Kean had exhausted curiosity the season before. The new theatre in Chestnut Street was in course of building, which opened in December. The Walnut Street house, altered as it was, did not meet fashion's sanction, although the company had received several additions to the stock force. Mr. and Mrs. Burke, Mr. and Mrs. H. Wallack, Mr. Nichols (a tenor vocalist), Mrs. Drake, and W. Pelby starred. *Damon and Pythias*[3] was the first acted this season in Philadelphia to good houses for eight nights. Mr. Wood was the Damon.

This management suffered reverses from unforeseen accidents and several untoward events this season. Mr. James Wallack, just arrived from England, was announced to appear as Hamlet. He was thrown from the mail stage while an his way from New York and severely fractured his leg, which rendered him for many months incapable of any professional exertions.[4] This deranged their business for the better part of the winter. Master William Forrest appeared this season in the revived play of *Mahomet*.[5] They brought out the water drama of *Undine*[6] with careful effects but it failed to pay. Many other novelties were produced without attracting.

On the coldest night of the winter, the orphan Asylum, near the new Catholic Cathedral at Logan Square, was burned down and twenty of its orphan pupils perished. A benefit was given at the Walnut Street Theatre, which netted $1,400 after deducting the sum of $360 for expenses.[7]

The Baltimore season ended on the 4$^{th}$ of July. The company, as usual, went to Washington D.C. The Greenes, who had made their winter engagement with Messrs. Warren and Wood for the new Chestnut Street, formed a temporary traveling scheme with Mr. and Mrs. Bignall, Mr. Lockwood, and some others. Their first essay was at Chestertown, on the eastern shore of Maryland, where they fitted up a large hall in

## Theatrical Rambles of Mr. & Mrs. Greene, Charles Durang

theatrical form, having obtained the loan of some small-sized scenery and wardrobe with necessary properties from Managers Warren and Wood.

They found the patronage beyond their most sanguine expectations. Some of the most prominent citizens took them by the hand. Two of them may be named especially as great friends of the drama, *viz.*, Judge Bailey and Dr. Muse, who used their personal influence to animate the dormant love for theatricals in their fellow townsmen, themselves sending presents to the performers. Their own servants waited daily upon their wants and comforts, arranging the theatre, sweeping it clean every day, carrying out the bills, etc. At the rehearsals and performances the servants served hot coffee and cakes and every variety of lunch and fruits in silver salvers. Those repasts were served up with luxurious taste and profuse hospitality.

The company also made a large sum of money. Their stay here was brief, as there was but one audience and that was sparse. Their next place of performance was at Princess Anne, where the encouragement was equally flattering. Thus through the Eastern section of Maryland did they successfully perambulate from town to town till it was time at the last of August to join Warren and Wood's company in their opening campaign at Baltimore.

This fall season continued till the new Chestnut Street was ready to open, which occurred on the 2$^{nd}$ of December, 1822, with *The School for Scandal.* Mr. and Mrs. Greene performed humble characters in it—Snake, Mr. John Greene; Maid, Mrs. Greene. From this subordinate position they soon rose to consequence and high favor.

When the autumn Baltimore season closed in the end of November, the new theatre was not yet completed to open in Philadelphia as arranged. A fortnight's recess was agreed upon per force. Mr. Thomas Burke, the father of the late Charles Burke,[8] proposed to a portion of the company so inclined to occupy that recess in performing a few nights at the Washington Theatre. The great race between Eclipse and Sir Charles was to come off there during that week, where all the fast men and women in the Union would be assembled, and all the world besides. The temptation was great, and the

*Theatrical Rambles of Mr. & Mrs. Greene*, Charles Durang

scheme readily embraced, for probably nothing since the foundation of our government created a greater furor than this celebrated race. It worked itself into a national excitement. Sectional feeling became delirious and raving on this subject of horse merits; and it seems as if it was one of the social remote causes that fanned the devilish flames of anarchy in our national councils and inharmonious sentiments amongst our people.

The jealous feeling of races and pride of sections of country are ever disturbing qualities. The Sayers and Heenan combat became a national emotion in which the better sort of people took as warm an interest as those of the rougher class. After the New York race of Eclipse and Henry, there was another of those frenzied sectional excitements.[9]

On the day of the great race at Washington, D.C., all attended the course as they did at Rome in the orgies before lent, from the polished elite of society to the white working men, the Negro with his loud laugh and catfish grin, and the more demure and simpering mulatto, and other distinctive shades of color. The field presented the aspect of some 30,000 human faces in contrasted colors as aforesaid, all amphitheatrically arranged on stands *à-la-échelon*, a magnificent view of curious masses of humanity to see two horses run under whip and spur.

The two contending steeds were the admiration of the assembled thousands as the grooms led them about the distant track. Their black eyes rolled in vivid flashes. The order to saddle and mount was announced from the judges' stand. Then the scene presented was one of a thrilling nature. All was animated expectations, backing ardent opinions with bets, and great chattering amongst the knowing ones.

"Hurrah! Eclipse!" "Eclipse is the word!" "I say so!" "Hurrah, Sir Charles, I bet!" "Done, done!" "I bet!"

The bugle sounded to horses; then the horses appeared, mounted by their riders in their fanciful jockey costumes, while the fiery plunging steeds led by the grooms could hardly be held, so mettlesome was their impetuosity to break forth from the starting post. Eclipse was a magnificently formed animal. He had great height and broad

## Theatrical Rambles of Mr. & Mrs. Greene, Charles Durang

set chest, body round and long, yet well knitted to his haunches, and shoulders literally strung with muscle. He kicked and snorted to get away from thralldom.

Sir Charles was all symmetry and more calm, not so strong of limb or muscle, evincing more of the light Arabian breed of figure, while his more stalwart rival looked of the heavy Norman race of speed and endurance. Yet Sir Charles had great spirit, but much docility. In their pawings, snortings, and restless curveting they seemed to realize Ovid's description of the horses of the sun; where Apollo instructs his son Phaeton to hold the reins and guide the steeds:

> Bring forth the steeds, the nimble hours obey,
> From their full racks the generous steeds retire,
> Dropping ambrosial foams, and snorting fire,
> Take this, at least, this last advice, my son;
> Keep a stiff rein, and move but gently on;
> The coursers of themselves will run too fast;
> Your art must be to moderate their haste.

And in this great race the respective riders seemed to have been so instructed, and skillfully obedient to it. It is needless to say Eclipse was the victor, and *Io Triumpho*! the South was defeated in its great champion. The vaunted Napoléon of the Turf lost his prestige, and the sectional feeling, always so delicate and chary, seemed wrought up to undue mortification. The journals of the day gave the history of the event.

To the theatre treasury it was a god-send; the houses were crowded from pit to dome. The play on the night of the race was not heard at all, nothing but the music. The shouts for Eclipse from the winners, the retorts from the losers, or cheers from the friends of Sir Charles could only be heard. It was a complete jubilee in Washington. And although the Southrons were defeated, still, good humor and social enjoyment prevailed between the parties at the *adieu*. There were no pugilistic scenes; the absurd prejudices of the North and South were joyfully quiescent. This dramatic episode of a night among the sporting world gave Mr. and Mrs. Greene

*Theatrical Rambles of Mr. & Mrs. Greene*, Charles Durang

a share of $124, the scheme being what is called a sharing one amongst the actors.

The company of sharers being members of the new Chestnut Street Company—which was on the eve of opening—thither they wended their way and opened with marked success.[10] Yet, its flattering auspices were soon overcast and soon experienced sad reverses. After the destruction of the theatre in the spring of 1820, its rebuilding was rather retarded by Messrs. Warren and Wood from policy. The two seasons at the Walnut Street in the occupancy of the old company were very unproductive. The theatre did not afford appropriate accommodations for the Chestnut Street audiences; and therefore they became impatient for its revival. The stockholders seemed anxious to reconstruct the old edifice and the managers expressed a desire that that course should be pursued. A subscription list was opened and filled up in two days. A lease was given to the old management on the most liberal terms. The then subscribers looked more to the fostering of enlightened amusements than speculative gain. The lease was given for ten years at a rent of $2,000 per annum, renewable for ten years more at the expiration of the first term in the event of either of the lessees being desirous to continue it.

About this time a proposition was made to Warren and Wood by Mr. Beekman, a junior proprietor of the Park Theatre, New York, for the Chestnut Street Company to play there from the 10th of September to March in New York, and from March to July in Philadelphia, making one company answer for the two cities. The object was to relieve the two cities of their length of seasons. But as Messrs. Warren and Wood had Baltimore to relieve theirs, and which yielded them large profits, Mr. Warren decidedly refused to enter into such an arrangement and the offer was declined.

The suggestion of Mr. Beekman emanated from a discontent between Stephen Price and the proprietors of the Park Theatre, which was subsequently adjusted.[11] In the course of events the old Chestnut street house lost its prestige. The Park became the metropolitan theatre of the United

*Theatrical Rambles of Mr. & Mrs. Greene*, Charles Durang

States, while the others throughout the land subsided into provincial institutions.

## NOTES

[1] The Prune Street Theatre, managed by Stanislaus Surin was the former Winter Trivoli. It had been converted into a theatre in the winter of 1820. The Winter Trivoli (or Columbian) Gardens, in Market Street, between 13th and 14th, was opened in 1819 for summer promenading. It was converted into a theatre the following year. The winter Trivoli, Prune Street, opened an October 25, 1820. The Prune Street Theatre was in its second season when Greene joined the company. That season opened September 24, 1821.

[2] Warren and Wood opened the Walnut Street Theatre on November 10, 1820.

[3] A tragedy by John Banim, introduced to the Philadelphia stage December 14, 1821, along with Wood as Damon; Henry Wallack, Pythias; John Greene, Nician; and Mrs. Greene, an attendant.

[4] The injury to James Wallack occurred on November 29. He was riding outside the mail post coach when the accident took place. This confined him to his room for months.

[5] Young William Forrest appeared in *Mahomet, the Impostor* as Zaphna; Wood, Mahomet; and Greene, Hercides; on February 2, 1822.

[6] *Undine; or, The Spirit of the Waters* was first produced in America at this time, January 1, 1822, with Mrs. Darley as Undin; Mrs. Greene, Angtha; Greene, the Rosicrucian Seer.

[7] The orphanage burned late in January of 1822. The benefit was performed January 28 with *The Voice of Nature*, *The Rendezvous*, and *The Forty Thieves*.

[8] Thomas Burke was born in England and came to America as a young man, first appearing on the stage at the Charleston Theatre. He married a Miss Thomas and, later, Mrs. Joseph Jefferson. He died in Baltimore, June 6, 1825. Charles Burke (1822-1854), a native Philadelphian, made his first appearance on the stage as Cora's child in *Pizarro* at the Chestnut Street Theatre. His early death was caused from consumption.

*Theatrical Rambles of Mr. & Mrs. Greene*, Charles Durang

[9]The match between Eclipse and Sir Charles was arranged through a challenge by James J. Harrison of Brunswick, Va., in a New York paper. On November 20, 1822, when the riders had mounted, a forfeit of $5,000 was paid by Harrison because Sir Charles had met with an accident. But the crowd would not be put off; so a match of four miles was decided for the purse of $19,500 a side. Sir Charles broke down after two miles and did not finish. The Sayers and Heenan boxing match for the championship of England, which occurred at Farnsborough, England, April 17, 1860, went forty-two rounds, ending with victory for Heenan, the American pugilist. The attending publicity created bitter feelings on both sides of the Atlantic. The inter-sectional match in 1823 at Union Course on Long Island between the Northern horse, Eclipse, and the southern horse, Sir Henry, was of significant interest. More than 50,000 spectators jammed the roads from New York throughout the day of the contest. Eclipse won two of the three heats. They never met again.

[10]The new Chestnut Street Theatre opened December 2, 1822, with an occasional address by Charles Sprague, Esq., of Boston, delivered by manager Wood. On the bill was *The School for Scandal*.

[11]Price had purchased an interest in the Park Theatre in 1808 from Cooper. He eventually became the sole lessee and managed the house for some thirty years, ably engaging distinguished artists from abroad.

*Theatrical Rambles of Mr. & Mrs. Greene*, Charles Durang

## X.

A LADY AS HAMLET — DEATH OF MRS. LAFOLLE — THE PLACIDES — MASTER EDWIN FORREST — JAMES H. CALDWELL — SOUTHERN THEATRES — THE RISE OF YOUNG FORREST, ETC.

The season of 1823-24 approaching its close, the stock company's benefits were given. Among others, Mrs. Battersby's benefit was to come off. That lady, quite a dashing, showy actress, chose Shakespeare's *Hamlet* for that occasion, and by way of novelty played the moody prince herself. She was rather too fat and stout of figure for male attire. She, however, dressed it in a black-bulged tunic of petticoat shape, which served to hide her extreme obesity; yet her pedals, encased in black silk hose, still showed their pillared huge rotundity.

The death of Mrs. Lafolle left the theatre without a suitable representative of the Queen Mother. She was an actress whose dignified mien made it ever a feature in this tragedy. In the dilemma, Mr. Wood cast about for a lady fitted to don her royal robes. At length he requested Mrs. Greene to assume its responsible functions. Her position in the theatre was as yet subordinate, and she at once shrank from the attempt.

She felt quite able to master the words, and said to him, "But, Mr. Wood, I have not a suitable dress. I have neither royal robes nor ornaments."

"Oh, never mind. You can fudge up something out of the ladies' wardrobe (there had been a ladies' wardrobe in this theatre, which was the only one on the continent that contained anything of the kind, although it was nearly destroyed) with what you have yourself, and Mrs. Battersby

*Theatrical Rambles of Mr. & Mrs. Greene*, Charles Durang

will loan you some jewels. She has enough to stock a jewelers shop."

Thus Mrs. Greene undertook and studied the Queen, letter perfect. At the rehearsal she never missed a word of the text, a quality that marked her after professional career. In the Queen she acquitted herself so well and so satisfactory to all parties that the manager thanked her for her careful rendition of so important a part. Her salary at this time was only $8 a week. Her success did not now advance her income but it produced a more pleasant influence and position for her in the theatre. She was promoted to better parts but still doing a great many disagreeable ones. She was also removed from the *corps de ballet* dressing room to one occasionally occupied by the stars and those fine actresses Mrs. Duff, Mrs. Darley, and Mrs. Joseph, who were ladies of high position and respectability. The etiquette of the Chestnut Street Theatre was proverbial throughout the theatrical world, where drawing room manners were ever required.

Mrs. Lafolle, the lady whose place Mrs. Greene had so suddenly been called to replace, died at the latter end of the season of 1823 in Sansom Street. She was a lady of most amiable qualities and excellent abilities as an actress. Her husband was a Frenchman, a capital violinist and leader of the orchestra. On the day of the funeral the weather was rather mild and pleasant for the season of the year. The entire company attended the obsequies to a cemetery in Southwark, where, it is regretted, no stone marks her last resting place. Her sons endeavored some years since to find out the spot, but her grave could not be certainly discovered. Improvements had been made, and since no mark had been made at the interment, all identification was lost.

The life of this actress deserves some record. In life she was beloved by all; in her death equally mourned. In her latter days she inclined to agreeable obesity, but her face was beautifully expressive of meekness, the most tender sensibilities, and intellectuality. As she looked, she acted. She was a daughter of Mrs. Pownall, better known as the once popular Mrs. Wrighten of Drury Lane Theatre, a singing actress and a

## Theatrical Rambles of Mr. & Mrs. Greene, Charles Durang

concert vocalist of great merit and a contemporary of David Garrick.

As Mrs. Pownall, she made her first appearance in America in 1794 at the Boston Theatre and afterwards joined Hallam's Company at the John Street Theatre, New York, and the old South Street, Philadelphia, where she died. She left her daughter, Miss Pownall, who became subsequently the wife of Alexander Placide, the renowned rope and pantomime artiste, who first arrived in New York about 1789 with his ]French wife, a fine dancer and pantomimist. There came with him a Frenchman known by the name of the "Little Devil," from his wonderful feats.[1] Hallam engaged Placide, his wife, and the "Little Devil" when they became very attractive with their pantomime, rope dancing, etc., at the John Street Theatre.

Mr. Placide repudiated his first wife from some just cause. He then became the successor of Mons. Sollée in the proprietorship of the Charleston, S.C., Theatre, at which time he married Miss Pownall, then a young rising actress of great talent and a very clever vocalist. The talent of this family is very remarkable, descending in brilliancy through a period of more than a century, as exemplified in the present Placide family, viz., Messrs. Henry and Thomas Placide, Mrs. William R. Blake, Miss Jane Placide, Mrs. W. Mann, Mrs. J. Wallack, Miss Alice Placide, etc. Mr. Placide held the lease of the Charleston, Norfolk, and Richmond Theatres till the latter was burnt down, which disaster took place on his benefit night, December 26, 1811. He died In New York in 1812. His widow afterwards became a member of the Philadelphia *corps*, where Mons, Lafolle was installed as leader of the orchestra. A mutual esteem arose between them and Mrs. Placide a second time entered the marriage state and became Mrs. Lafolle.

In those days burial business was not so skillfully managed by regular undertakers as at the present time. The body of Mrs. Lafolle was lowered into the grave by Mr. Burke, young Thomas Jefferson, John Jefferson, and John Greene.

## *Theatrical Rambles of Mr. & Mrs. Greene*, Charles Durang

As they left the cemetery Burke remarked to Thomas Jefferson, "Your time will come next, I shall follow you, and Greene will be the last."

"Peace! Raven, croak no more!" was Thomas Jefferson's exclamation.

Burke was prophetic. Thomas Jefferson died in less than a year, Burke in 1825, John Jefferson a few years later, and Greene was spared to his wife till 1860.

About this time Mrs. Riddle was an actress of note at the Prune Street Theatre, Philadelphia. At her benefit Master E. Forrest played Young Norval for the first time, he having volunteered. Some of the oldest actors who witnessed the performance were prophetically eloquent in praises of this young aspirant, and foretold his future fame. His performance was as sublime as his modesty was remarkable.

In the fall of 1824, Mr. and Mrs. Greene withdrew from the Chestnut Street Theatre with some regrets; but professional self interest in every sense dictates the changes. They saw but a meager chance for advancement in this honored company, where the business was occupied from season to season, where the audience was always content to dwell upon old faces with that pleasure that all look upon their old homes and old landmarks, where new faces did not efface the sacred memories of the old. The novice, or the young, of this company seldom could climb the ladder by looking upward; therefore he could "not look back on the low degrees by which he did ascend." This company was ever like a family association, as remarkable for that feeling as they were elevated in their respective roles, in talent, and moral conduct, an exemplary circle of brothers and sisters. The managers were truly the *patria potestas*, for each one and all that were connected with it could not but feel affection and respect, etc.

James H, Caldwell was playing star engagements in the Holliday Street Theatre, Baltimore, and at Washington, D.C. During the company's sojourn there he became acquainted with John Greene and took a fancy to him, both as a man and a promising actor of talent. He offered Mr. Greene and wife $30 per week for the New Orleans theatre.[2] The en-

*Theatrical Rambles of Mr. & Mrs. Greene*, Charles Durang

gagement was accepted and they commenced with Mr. Caldwell at Petersburg, Virginia, where the company were temporarily performing previous to the winter campaign at the Crescent City of the South. The following were among the actors and actresses of that company: Mr. R, Russell, George Farren, Edwin Forrest, Jackson Grey, Lemuel Smith (brother to the celebrated Sol Smith), Garner, Kelsey, Higgins, John Moore, Joseph Page, and McCafferty. This was a galaxy of talent; nor were the ladies inferior, as they were Miss Jane Placide, Mrs. Battersby, Mrs. Russell, Mrs. J. Rowe, Mrs. Higgins, Mrs. Waring (late from England), and little Marian Russell; the new members, Mr. and Mrs. Greene.

Mrs. Greene opened at Petersburg in Emma in the play of *The Birth Day*,[3] Edwin Forrest playing Bertram, a walking gentleman. He did his best in all parts cast to him, from half a length to a part of ten. He disclaimed no part or slighted any however humble, determined, as Mrs. Greene heard him say, to begin at the lower round of the ladder and to ascend, if possible, to its top through his own industry, energies, and the talent he might be possessed of. Nor did he indulge in any superciliousness, since so often ascribed to him, always playing well and carefully those characters entrusted to him.

We heard him say at one of his rehearsals of *William Tell*, in the Bowery Theatre, when he made his first appearance at that new theatre in 1826, that "if he ever rose to a first position in the profession he would prudently take care of his money"; and certainly he has done so with infinite prudence, as fortune crowns him with its riches. Nor can we say that he exhibits meanness with it. He is not uncharitable or stingy as the world in its malevolence says. He often loses his temper in business at the rehearsals, or may be too brusque at times; but those who know Forrest personally know that he is neither supercilious nor possessed of the least ridiculous pride; but is ever easy and familiar with his acquaintances, high and low. We can't say the same of many celebrated stars with whom we have had business intercourse, as to some of the old English stars, their hauteur was

## *Theatrical Rambles of Mr. & Mrs. Greene*, Charles Durang

unbearable and disgusting. We could name many of them, but let them repose in their retirement or graves in peace.

The company soon passed to Richmond where the nation's guest, Gen. Lafayette, then in his Southern tour, was daily looked for. The city was literally filled with strangers; therefore board and lodgings were almost impossible to obtain at any price. The first night of the company's arrival they reposed on the floor of a garret over a grocery store overrun with rats. The next day they procured board nearly a mile out of town. Here Mr. Greene was seized with a bilious fever, so severe that doubts were entertained for his life.

During this brief season at Richmond, Mr. Conway was announced for a few nights. On a Saturday night the admirable comedy of *The Provoked Husband*[4] was cast and put in the green room to be performed on the following Monday. Edwin Forrest was cast for the part of Mr. Manly, a very quiet and gentlemanly part of importance. Through some unfortunate means he failed to learn that he was cast in the part till Monday morning at rehearsal. He had never played it. The part is long and particular; therefore, too long to be studied in one day. He was dreadfully annoyed at this circumstance as he felt a pride in performing his duty. However, in this dilemma it was so arranged that he should read the part. He advanced to the audience on his first entrance at night and made a plain statement of facts. The apology was cheerfully received and he read the part with so much propriety, throwing so much acting tact into Manly as to veil the reading altogether and gained more applause than if the words had been carefully committed to memory. At this early day he was a great favorite with the Richmond public, they always receiving his efforts with cheers and with prophesies of his future elevation.

Conway's Lord Townly was a fine piece of acting. In two years after this, in 1824 at the Bowery Theatre, Forrest played on alternate nights with Conway, when the latter played to empty benches and the former to houses over crowded. In truth, hundreds were unable to get seats. Mr. Conway was so mortified at this result that he abruptly broke his engagement with Charles Gilfert.[6]

*Theatrical Rambles of Mr. & Mrs. Greene*, Charles Durang

The Richmond season ending, Mr. Caldwell left for New Orleans in a sailing vessel. The accommodations for passengers were confined, the cabin being so small the ladies occupied it alone; the gentlemen had bunks, etc., placed for them in midship. Besides the company, there were forty slaves. The total number of passengers of all grades was ninety-nine, without the vessels crew, which was increased before they reached the Mississippi delta to one hundred souls by the birth of a baby on board.

Manager Caldwell, was very fond of operatic performances. He intended to bring out the musical play of *John of Paris*[7] at the New Orleans theatre as soon after his arrival there as possible. He had a leader and the principal part of the orchestra on board with the performers. He had the music rehearsed on board daily if the weather permitted it. The airs, duets, and concerted music of this operatic piece are very charming, simple and pleasing to those unskilled in the science, yet very touching to all ears.

The company arrived safety in New Orleans in January. The Greenes engaged furnished lodgings in a house of antique aspect, of Spanish architecture, resting on the site where the Delta office now rears its sign of business, at the corner of Poydras and Fayette Streets. Poor John Greene had not recovered wholly from his Richmond sickness, and sea-sickness had increased his general debility. The sea had not resuscitated his physical prostration. A northern clime would have doubtless been more restorative to his constitution, which was naturally strong. He was borne on a litter from the vessel to his home, for at that day public vehicles were a novelty.

A great and radical change now marks the aspects and conveniences of New Orleans as it was in 1824. Now it appears a nonpareil city in contrast to its dirt and filth at that time. Then there were no pavements, the sidewalks were laid with boards, the streets knee-deep in mud. There was no approaching the Camp Street Theatre; each step of a pedestrian or horse sunk a foot deep into a slough of inextricable mire in bad weather.

Mr. Caldwell immortalized himself in causing a crossing to be laid of oyster shells leading to the theatre. This

## *Theatrical Rambles of Mr. & Mrs. Greene*, Charles Durang

was deemed a magnificent improvement and that section of the town received the name of "Shell Ward." Mules harnessed to the cotton drays would often be found hopelessly installed in the tenacious mud, immovable as a rock till a large team of extra mules was brought to extricate the mire-impounded carts or drays. Ladies visiting the theatre would often slip out of their overshoes and be compelled to call on some sable biped to assist her, *cavalier servant*, to tote her to the door. The actresses generally went to rehearsal in men's long boots, carrying their slippers in their pockets. It is jokingly mentioned that a British regiment ordered to charge up to the American lines at the great battle in 1815 stuck so fast in the Delta mud that they could not move a leg, and, so imbedded, were pretty well peppered by the Tennessee Riflemen.

The theatre opened with the comedy *The Soldier's Daughter*.[8] Mrs. Battersby was the Widow Chearly, and a very pretty lively widow she made. Mrs. Malfort, Mrs. Greene, Young Malfort, and Mr. Edwin Forrest also appeared.

At this time the doctor had given Mr. Greene up as a hopeless case, past all recovery. Here was a blow to the young hopes and prospects of Mrs. Greene. To sustain her husband while life remained was now her dutiful task, and to do this she was obliged to act night after night in whatever part the manager thought proper to cast her.

**NOTES**

[1]Paulo Redige, billed as the "Little Devil," first appeared at Sadlers Wells in 1781 along with Signor Placido (Alexander Placide Bussart), performing amazing feats on the tight-rope. He eventually was killed in a stage accident. Stagehands failed to catch him in a blanket on a dive through a window and in the fall he hit his head on a stage screw. Seilhamer states that the "Little Devil "that accompanied Placide to America was "a sort of make-believe Redige" by the name of Martine.

*Theatrical Rambles of Mr. & Mrs. Greene*, Charles Durang

²The Greene's first engagement with Caldwell was in 1825. Richard Russell was prompter. Durang is in error in listing Farren as a member of the company. According to Ireland, George Farren made his American debut in 1830 at the Bowery Theatre. He was a nephew of the English comedian, William Farren. Driven from the stage in 1834 over a disagreement with an actor named McKinney, he went west and did not re-appear on the New York stage until 1859. He died in 1861, age 53.

³There were versions of *The Birth Day* by both Thomas Dibdin and William Dunlap, translated and adapted from Kotzebue. Dunlap's piece was called *Fraternal Discord*.

⁴*The Provoked Husband*, a comedy by Colly Cibber, was first performed in this country by military actors in 1782.

⁵Forrest's first New York appearance occurred on June 23, 1826, at the Park Theatre for Woodhull's benefit of *Othello*. He followed with a series of roles for Gilfert at the Bowery Theatre, beginning the engagement with *Othello* on November 6, 1826. Before Gilfert took over the Bowery Theatre, Forrest had worked under his management at the Pearl Street Theatre in Albany. The Bowery debut was an unbelievable success—some eighty consecutive nights to large houses. This was followed by a starring tour of the country.

⁶Charles Gilfert (1797-1830) was born in Germany, the son of a music teacher, and came to America with his uncle, John H. Myers, in 1801. From his youth he was a violinist in the orchestra at the Park Theatre. He became the first lessee of the Bowery Theatre, 1826, but eventually went bankrupt.

⁷*John of Paris*, an opera by Pocock, was first performed in America in 1816.

⁸*The Soldier's Daughter* was a popular comedy by Cheery.

*Theatrical Rambles of Mr. & Mrs. Greene*, Charles Durang

## XI.

SEASON IN NEW ORLEANS — A FRIEND IN NEED — THEATRICAL PERFORMANCES — LITTLE MARIAN RUSSELL — TOM PLACIDE, FAILURE — STUCK IN THE MUD — FURIOUS TRAVELING — MRS. BLOXTON, ETC., ETC.

On one of these occasions when Mrs. Greene had done everything that lay in her power for her husband's relief during her necessary absence at the theatre, she took leave of his almost insensible form but with little hope of finding him alive on her return. She summoned all her energies to perform her part. The excitement of her heavy task of labor seemed for a while to deaden the recollection of her miseries and the gaieties of the theatre obliterated the sympathy of her associates. She went through her part with mechanical labor, but in the recesses of the acts her distresses asserted sway. Nature will break forth in despite of all things. In these pauses of the play she withdrew to a remote corner behind the scenes and there gave way to her grief. Young Forrest observed her distress and asked her the cause of her sorrows, not knowing that poor Greene was supposed to be so near his end. The sympathies so warmly expressed by Forrest only redoubled her anguish of heart. It sunk more deeply into its throes, as it was unexpected. Forrest's feelings were deeply wrought upon.

"Be comforted," said he; "he may get over this attack. The crisis of the disorder may have passed and he still lives. But should the worst occur, I beg of you, dear madam, to look upon me as your friend. Whatever pecuniary means should be found necessary to restore you to your friends, as far as my means extend, look to me."

*Theatrical Rambles of Mr. & Mrs. Greene*, Charles Durang

These words in season at once cheered up her depressed spirits. She returned to her home this night with renovated hope. She joyfully found the crisis of the fever passed and her husband, as it were, restored to life. Never did either of them forget the friendship so disinterestedly proffered from the young actor. Mr. Greene slowly recovered and resumed his situation in the company. In after days he to refer to this act of Forrest's with the warmest eulogies.

At this period Mr. Alexander Wilson and Mr. William Forrest engaged in the company. The melodrama of *The Cataract of the Ganges*[1] was brought out with success. Edwin Forrest played the minor part of Colonel Mordaunt, which looms in the piece more from situation than acting elements. His fine manly figure and youthful expression of features, dressed in a rich British uniform, when he appeared at the back of the stage, invariably brought down showers of applause before he uttered a word.

The first night he appeared in New York at the Park Theatre as Othello for Jacob Woodhull's benefit, ere he spoke a word he enlisted the admiration of the audience, as evoked from his remarkable handsome person.

Mr. Caldwell hit upon a novel excitement, performing *Pizarro* with a nightly change of the principal characters. The male principals were Caldwell, Wilson, and Edwin Forrest; the female characters, Elvira and Cora, Miss Jane Placide, Mrs. Battersby, and Mrs. Waring. Mr. Caldwell played Rolla the first night, Pizarro the second night, and Alonzo the third.

Edwin Forrest took Alonzo the first night and made quite a hit, in *Pizarro* the second night, and on the third night he capped the climax with Rolla, obtaining the verdict in his favor in the these three parts of the three degrees of adverbial comparison—well, better, and best. His Rolla was superlative and astonished the Orleanists as well as the oldest actors among this troupe, who threw all professional prejudice and jealousy asides, a rare thing for ancients of the stage to do.

The palm of victory was awarded to Miss Placide in Elvira over Mesdames Waring and Battersby. She possessed splendid talents. It is a pity she was so short-lived, dying ere

*Theatrical Rambles of Mr. & Mrs. Greene*, Charles Durang

she had reached the meridian of her glory, while Forrest's countrymen have crowned him with laurels perennial.

The season at New Orleans was far advanced when the benefits were commenced. Forrest selected for his benefit *King Lear*, the first time of his performance in that character. That day may be remembered by all who were there for the fall of one of those cataract rains so common to New Orleans and so seldom seen elsewhere except in the tropics. It poured in torrents on the day of Forrest's benefit, a perfect Niagara deluge! The streets were for a few hours almost impassable; and not withstanding the vast popularity of the young actor, and a strong desire universally expressed to see this new role, the house proved very poor.

Mr. Richard Russell's young daughter, Marian Russell, began to be very attractive as Little Pickle, *Tom Thumb*, *Babes in the Woods*,[2] etc., her brother Richard playing the opposite parts with cleverness, although so young he could not speak very plain. When petite Marian was playing *The Spoiled Child*, her mother was standing at the wings during the affecting scene where he takes leave of his father and aunt. The child sang with much feeling the parting song, took out a tiny pocket handkerchief, crying in the most natural manner, and sobbed till the tears were seen coursing down her cheeks, while she wiped the drops away with her delicate little fabric. This might be said to be nature's flowing in reality.

"That idea has emanated from herself," her mother exultantly exclaimed. "I never taught her that!"

Marian Russell has become one of the most popular American actresses on the stage, remarkable for great spirit and effective acting. She married Mr. George Farren, himself a sterling actor of merit, now deceased. Mrs. Farren has recently introduced to the stage a very beautiful and accomplished daughter, Miss Fanny Fitz Farren, who as a light comedy actress bids fair to be as popular and successful as her talented mother has proved in the melodramatic line.[3]

Thomas Placide, then a thin stripling of a lad, made his first appearance at the New Orleans theatre as the Bleeding Captain in *Macbeth*, and truly he made a signal failure.

*Theatrical Rambles of Mr. & Mrs. Greene*, Charles Durang

The blank verse of the wounded officer was so choked up with stage fright that he could not give it utterance. From the painful disturbance of his mind, his tongue came to a dead halt. He seemed "unseamed from the nave to the chaps" in power of speech. The turgid tongue of tragedy was not his forte. All celebrated comic actors commence their trade with the serious muse or did so in former days, and the highest talent in the profession has ever, it is said, commenced its career in signal failure. Thomas Placide is now one of our best comedians.

The season came to a close and Mr. Alexander Wilson,[4] once a sea captain, a merchant, an actor, an aspiring star, and lastly a manager of various theatres, organized this second company of itinerants, to which scheme Mr. and Mrs. Greene attached themselves. The company was notified to send their baggage on board the steamboat *La Belle Creole*, then lying at the levee, the evening before the day of departure. It was necessary for the passengers to embark immediately as she would start by the dawn of the next morning.

The commander of the rather crack craft was Capt. Jackson. Like his frail and rickety steamer, he was rather vaporish and oblivious, but yet of a jolly turn. He had all the characteristics of a long-shore Mississippian. The recent rains had caused all the rivers in the state to rise greatly and a perfect inundation of the bayous and swamps was the consequence. The floods had caused a crevice in the levee before the city, so that there was a great difficulty in getting the lady passengers on board. They had to walk the plank with the balanced nicety of a tight-rope dancer. However, the gallant Capt. Jackson cleverly acted as the balance pole. Some of the lady actresses played off some of their melodramatic starts, which upset the frail plank bridge, thereby giving the poor Negro (who stood as a pier at the one end to keep it steady) an unexpected bath. The Captain saved himself and the lady by a sudden spring on deck with the fair one in his arms.

The company consisted of William Forrest, Moses Scott, who was a gay young Irishman, John Greene, Wilson the manager, etc. The ladies were Mrs. Wilson, Mrs. Waring, Mrs. Bloxton, Mrs. Greene, Rosina Seymour, etc.[5] Away they steamed up the river, visiting many of the tributaries of

## *Theatrical Rambles of Mr. & Mrs. Greene,* Charles Durang

the Mississippi and their towns, which were rising like crops of mushrooms in all directions. Many of them are now large and elegant cities.

In ascending the river, the water in some places became so shallow that the beautiful *Creole* put her foot, rather than her keel, so deep in the mud that she could not extricate it; and she became a river fixture, looking like a floating beacon with its expiring curling smoke from its extinguished light. She was fast anchored in the mud till another rise in the river could float her off. The cargo of biped livestock now became inpatient of this stay of execution forward. They assembled in convention on the deck to inquire what was to be done in this dilemma.

At a distance through the mist of the morning they perceived a boat, or something like it, wooding up. The thought occurred that they could reach her and so avail themselves of her upward progress. It was at least a mile distant; and the monotonous scenery around them, with the fatal delay in reaching their destination, inspired the effort of a walk upon the swampy, alluvial soil, lined with dense canebrakes and stumps of trees.

The stampede became general. The posse of all sexes and ages advanced toward the boat. Their exodus was very amusing indeed. This Thespian company, like a Grecian Phalanx, with one accord and vigorous purpose took their luggage, from the heavy trunks to the bundles and small parcels, to the watery land. The males toted some of their trunks, the females and children the bundles and bandboxes. Away they perambulated, pell-mell through the canebrakes, over shoe tops, wading through the swampy soil.

Thus the assembled crowd waded through the canebrakes of Tennessee, alternately stumbling, falling, crying, laughing, and the men sometimes swearing a little it must be confessed. They reached the spot where the boat was but she had just departed to the despair of all. The boat was yet in sight, in hailing distance. A general yell was given in true Indian style. They shouted. They all hailed the upward bound boat. But in vain. It was all of no use. The commander heard them not, steamed away faster, and they were left to plod

## *Theatrical Rambles of Mr. & Mrs. Greene*, Charles Durang

their weary and fatigued bodies and disappointed hopes through the devious and miry river paths back to the *La Belle Créole*, which they had quitted in disgust.

As humble penitents they returned to the *Creole* which was hopelessly ground. Their last and only expedient of progress offered itself in a flat bottomed boat which was going up the stream, propelled in the primitive mode of oars and setting poles shod with an iron sharp point, like a ferule at the bottom of it and a shoulder piece for the man's shoulder for it to rest against, and thus by main physical power shove the boat along, a very tedious and wearisome process of ascending the western rivers. As a last resort the company embraced this slow, miserable water conveyance. In this snail-like ascension of the river they would relive the tedium by walking on the river's bank and then resting again on the boat's gunwales.

Mrs. Bloxton was formerly Mrs. Seymour, and was for many years a member of the Chestnut Street Theatre. She was a smart, well dressed, dumpy little woman with a handsome, rosy English face, light flowing curls, with bright blue eyes. She was a useful actress with not much education except that learning which she acquired during a long career on the stage. And where intellect exists it is a very good and facile school to acquire correct language in. Her voice was an extensive soprano of great power, but no cultivation at all. For years she occupied a fair, nay, a popular reputation as a singer. Of course the merits of vocalism were then but little understood, so that Mrs. Seymour's "Soldier tired of war's alarms" was long esteemed a bravura of excellence among our musical amateurs. She was a character in her way. Being uneducated, her verbal blunders furnished much green room chit-chat fun. She always judged the merits of her parts by their length. Having heard the word medical used, she caught the sound and said short parts were always medical.

Many performers of short memories have the practice of writing on a small piece of paper the first words or line, placing it under the cuff of their garment, and thus slyly refer to it, unheeded by the audience. Mrs. Seymour's memory was so treacherous that she found it almost impossible to remember the first word of the verses of songs. She therefore

## *Theatrical Rambles of Mr. & Mrs. Greene*, Charles Durang

resolved to write on the palm of her kid glove the first words of the first line. A talented person may have a bad memory and the world has no right to lose the use of that talent if any remedy can be applied for the expedient to make it available. But her most inexcusable fault was her ignorant perversion of the text, which too often resulted in ignorant blunders of phraseology and pronunciation. In the musical farce of *The Agreeable Surprise*,[6] instead of saying as Laura, "Eugene's virtues have made me a proselyte," she quite innocently exclaimed, "Eugene's virtues have made me a prostitute."

Her husband, "Count" Seymour, as he was called in joke, abounded in similar blunders on the stage.[7] He was a Cockney and fully indulged in all aspirations and antiaspirations of the "H." In tragedy he was once playing the officer of a guard who was ordered to cut off some captive rebel's head and then to conceal it. The return of this execution should have been, "I severed his head from his body, and in an obscure spot disposed of it." He delivered the sentence thus, "I severed 'is 'ead from 'is body hand hin a nobsere corner hi disclosed hit."

Count Seymour died about 1815 and his widow soon after married a silly pated young dandy of rather a good face and figure, fond of fashionable dress and paste jewelry. His name was Bloxton. He helped to make her unhappy by spending what she had saved up and by his gallantries. He died and she left the Philadelphia theatre and went south, where she died.

## NOTES

[1]*Cataract of the Ganges*, a melodrama by W. T. Moncrieff, was a favorite piece with equestran performers.

[2]Little Pickle was a character in the farce *The Spoiled Child*, by Isaac Bickerstaff. *Tom Thumb* was probably from the adaptation of the play by Fielding into a burletta by O'Hara. *Babes in the Woods* was a musical interlude by Thomas Morton.

[3]George Percy Farren, an Irish actor, first appeared in America at the Bowery Theatre. He died in 1861. Fanny Fitz

*Theatrical Rambles of Mr. & Mrs. Greene*, Charles Durang

Farren made her debut at the Walnut Street Theatre, Philadelphia, in 1859. She married a scenic artist, Gaspard Maeder.

[4]Alexander Wilson first appeared at the Park Theatre in 1817 as Rolla in *Pizarro*. He later managed the Bowery and the National Theatres. Sometime around 1840 he retired to a farm in New York state.

[5]Mrs. Bloxton (formerly Mrs. Seymour) first appeared in America at the John Street Theatre, New York, in 1896. Aside from singing roles, she generally portrayed chambermaids and rustics. Rosina Seymour was probably her daughter. There was a Miss Seymour with Ludlow's Company in 1819 whom he hired from the Cincinnati theatre. She married J. S. Rowe.

[6]*The Agreeable Surprise* was a popular musical farce by John O'Keeffe.

[7]Seymour's stage blunders are accounted by Wood, who states that this kind of thing occurred "in the palmy days of 'old Drury'" before there were sufficient first-rate actors in the American theatre. Mrs. Bloxton died in Natchez in 1825.

*Theatrical Rambles of Mr. & Mrs. Greene*, Charles Durang

## XII.

UP THE RIVER — REBELLION — ALABAMA — PAINFUL SCENE FROM THE PAST — A "GREAT" EXPLOSION, AND FUNNY EFFECT — THE EDMUND KEAN CONTROVERSY.

  The new water conveyance of the flat bottomed boat was not of a progressive nature. With Herculean toil and labor they ascended the river, always anchoring at night by making fast to one of those large primeval forest trees, whose mystic branches overshadow the turbid waters. Day after day did they float with the current and at night anchored on some shore as lonely as it was ere Columbus discovered America.
  At last they reached Florence, below the muscle shoals at the head of steamboat navigation on the Tennessee River, where the company sojourned a month, playing to very good houses. They then visited Tuscumbia for a like period with the same success. These were new towns, containing from 1,000 to 1,200 persons. They then moved on to Cortland, another new place. The company had become very discontented with Wilson's management, or rather mismanagement. The salaries of the troupe were irregularly paid, the sufferings of the company had been great, and they all decided to return once more to civilization and social ease.
  John Greene, who had mildly remonstrated with Wilson upon their privations and sufferings, was only snubbed and condemned. All were discontented. Rebellion lay in their way and John Greene as a leader sounded the tocsin of revolt and the company became at once disintegrated, dissolved. The rebellious subjects packed up bag and baggage for a start, while manager Wilson swore lustily that they must not

## *Theatrical Rambles of Mr. & Mrs. Greene*, Charles Durang

dare to leave the place, as they were articled to him for one year and he would arrest them all if they attempted to go. But they had taken time by the forelock. John Greene had engaged seats for Huntsville in the line of stages. The stage driver they had suborned and he was a faithful ally. William Forrest and Scott had the trunks all lashed to the basket behind the coach. Mr. and Mrs. Greene, W. Forrest, Scott, and others took their seats and the Jehu, with reins and whip, took his seat and flourished his scepter lash, when down came Wilson with a constable and a posse to arrest the company. The horses' heads were seized by the bridle reins, but the driver, who had received his instructions and was a resolute, strapping fellow drew a pistol from his pocket, presenting it at the constable and his followers, exclaiming at the same time, "This is the United States mail and the first man who interferes to stop its progress will receive a bullet through his head. Gee up!"

And whipping the steeds, they reared, plunged, and dashed off at full speed with the stage coach at their heels, while the manager and legal authorities stared and railed with astonishment and the crowd, hurrahing and laughing with the absconding actors, enjoyed the joke and their triumph.

At Huntsville they found Mr. Ludlow, the manager of the Mobile Theatre, with whom they entered into engagements. Manager Wilson soon followed and again assumed his legal attempts and personal threats. John Greene and Mr. Wilson became quite belligerent and exchanged sharp war shots at each other. Wilson, getting the worst of the combat, returned to his meager company, defeated and dispirited.

Mr. and Mrs. Greene left for Blunt Springs, where Mr. Wells met them with a carriage and horses to convey them to Tuscaloosa, the capital of the state, in a rich district and on a fine site. Here Mrs. Greene and Mrs. Noah met for the first time and were greatly pleased with each other. The stopping place was at Canawba, where they gave entertainments, and at all the small villages prior to their starting for Mobile.[1]

The company's next transportation was to Montgomery, at the head of the Alabama, a thriving town, then containing about a thousand inhabitants. Their company was in-

*Theatrical Rambles of Mr. & Mrs. Greene*, Charles Durang

creased in strength by the addition of Mrs. Vos and her talented daughter Mary, afterwards Mrs. Stuart, who are both dead now. The manager did extremely well here, full houses every night.[2]

A most painful scene of an ill-spent, wasted life was witnessed by the company, the more so as it was that of a poor actor. One evening as the sun was about setting in one of those golden delineations, gloriously tinted in rosette and purple hues, common to the southern horizon, a boy approached John Greene and with a mysterious aspect and timidly called him aside saying, "There is a man not far off who seems almost crazy. He desires to speak with you upon urgent business, and if ye please to go I'll show you the way."

Says Greene, "Where is he?"

"Why, sir, out in the woods there," replied the boy.

"What kind of looking person is he?" asked Greene.

"A very poor and shabby-looking man."

This struck our friend John with some surprise. At once the case was suggestive of some distressed actor, like a wandering minstrel seeking bread. To such calls John had "a heart open as day to melting charity." Thus impressed, he followed the young messenger with alacrity to the drooping willow grove, where in the shades of evening he beheld buried in a thick shrubbery the miserable figure of an emaciated man reclining on a fallen, rotten tree. As his red sunken eyes turned towards Greene, suffused with tears, and stretching out his withered hand he tremblingly spoke in faltering accents, "Ah! Greene, pity the sorrows of a poor, decrepit, beggared man who once with you proudly trod the stage in many a moral dramatic scene. Oh! by that friendship that once subsisted between us, for humanity's sake, as one of God's wayward and unthoughtful creatures, give my cares and poverty relief and heaven will bless your life!"

Greene, starting with astonishment, at once recognizing poor Jack Thornton but his emotions stifled all expression of voice. When he recovered he warmly shook his hand.

"Come, my old friend, in me you shall find a brother. Come to my lodgings. There you will find my wife, whose heart will beat like mine to restore your lost energies and

*Theatrical Rambles of Mr. & Mrs. Greene*, Charles Durang

spirits, to make you what you were once, a man of mind and nobleness."

"No, John!" said Thornton. "In this shabby plight, all covered with filth, I cannot go before any lady, even though she should be my dearest friend. I have fallen, John, lost all sense of manly propriety, forgot the dignity that belongs to man through that bestial love of drink and at last have met the drunkard's doom!"

Greene respected his scruples and his lamentations for the shame he had incurred; but pressing his hand again, he led him like a child to his home, where Mrs. Greene, stricken with astonishment and grief, received him as a mother would her prodigal son. Board and clean clothes were procured immediately and he was then introduced to the manager, whose stage company was filled at that time. But the high eulogies passed on his honest and honorable character by all those who had formerly known him so well, prepossessed the manager, Mr. Ludlow, in his favor and he gave Jack Thornton the office of treasurer, wherein for some time he acquitted himself with scrupulous faith, industry, and unimpeached honesty.

Poor Jack had only one fault, but it was one of such fearful magnitude that love of all phases, the affections of the husband, filial sentiments, lofty friendship, ambition of profession and fame, the prayers of virtue, the strongest pleas of religion, and a blessed sense of redemption hereafter cannot save it from its fatal vortex. The brightest intellectual hopes of the world have been wrecked on this rock and shoal of drunkenness.

For a length of time poor Jack pursued the even tenor of his responsible office with integrity, accuracy and satisfaction to his employer, allowing no temptation to induce a friendly hobnob with an "auld acquaintance." The social "just one glass" passed not his liquor hermetically-sealed lips to bathe with balmy drops his drooping spirits. At last, however, he took the fatal cup of friendship as a parting token and fell, like fallen stars, to rise no more! He rapidly descended to the lowest degradation and died the death of a drunkard! The whole company felt compassion for his error and united in paying his remains funeral honors as an appro-

*Theatrical Rambles of Mr. & Mrs. Greene*, Charles Durang

priate respect due to honesty, goodness of heart and respectabilities.

The funeral service to the dead was read over his grave by Samuel Jones, with good accent and good discretion. After Mr. Jones had read the service, his sole eulogy of the deceased was given in a very brief but significant quotation from Shakespeare, *viz.*, "Alas! poor Yorick!"

Samuel Jones survived his contemporaries of that day in Alabama. He has long since retired from the stage, and now resides in Philadelphia, engaged in the civil relations of life.[3] Young Placide, who had been with the company before, joined them again, much improved in his acting, but still playing the line called the "walking gentleman."

The company now opened the regular season at Mobile with Cherry's lively comedy of the *Soldier's Daughter*. It went merrily, as it always does, if only tolerably cast. But in the part of the Widow Cheerly the charming little Sally Riddle (afterwards Mrs. Harry Smith)[4] had made so strong an impression that the audience were not prepared to receive any substitute for her. Therefore, Mrs. Greene, who was representative of the merry widow, felt the coldness of the audience towards her efforts; yet she was subsequently well received and awarded that cordial support which caused her to remember Mobile with pleasure, although she never eradicated the impressions that Miss Riddle had so firmly planted there.

During the performance of the operatic drama of the *Devil's Bridge*[5] to a fine house, a very funny incident occurred. This piece concludes with a tremendous explosion, blowing up the bridge with all the terrific effects of such representations. These conflagrations are generally attended with great alarm, especially to the lady portion of the audience; and on this occasion a large assemblage of the fair was present. Ere the scene came on, the manager forestalled this alarm by the expedient of addressing the sex with the information that they need not be alarmed in the least at the dreadful explosion of the bridge, as the fire machinery had been carefully arranged by the artist. Although it would be awfully effective, not a person could be hurt. When the grand fire

*Theatrical Rambles of Mr. & Mrs. Greene*, Charles Durang

finale came, the quick-match and powder was touched by the property man, but it only fizzled, and puff! puff! came the smoke, but no flash or bang. Alas! no loud reports, but smoke! smoke! This, after the solemn warning given, appeared so ridiculous that the audience became convulsed with laughter; and finding that the blaze was determined not to appear, the curtain was lowered amid cheers and cries of, "That was Dick Curry's powder, warranted not to explode."

The Dick Curry referred to was a merchant, a very rich man, a great patron of the drama, seated on the front seat of the center box. No one enjoyed the joke more than the vendor of the supposed damaged powder that marred the awful catastrophe of the *Devil's Bridge*.

On the very night of the failure of this imitation fire, one of reality occurred in Mobile. An awful conflagration of ware and store house took place in which great quantities of gun powder were stored. The powder caught and a terrific explosion was the consequence. One store after another went, wherein a number of persons were killed, most of them firemen. The destruction was lamentable and wide spread. The public was not warned here of this impending calamity! as in the evening before at the theatre.

Mrs. Greene completed her winter engagement here with a large complimentary benefit. The house was crammed to a surfeit with the elite of Mobile. The season being closed, the Greenes sailed for New York in the brig *Moro*, Captain Connell; and after perils past, they anchored one lovely morning under the beautiful shadows of Staten Island, where they were quarantined two days. It was like going into paradise, entering New York harbor on a fine summer's morning after a storm of several days and being short of water and eatables.

On their arrival in New York, no engagement offering there, they took up their line of march for Philadelphia and received an engagement in the company of the Chestnut Street Theatre. The company had prematurely arrived from Baltimore in consequence of the great Edmund Kean riot that closed up the theatre there in June, 1826.

## *Theatrical Rambles of Mr. & Mrs. Greene*, Charles Durang

He was announced at the Holliday Street Theatre for *Richard III*. A riot was anticipated by all, but heedless of those premonitory public impulses of senseless passion, the managers announced the tragedian's appearance, although a riotous whirlwind seemed to blow from every quarter of the Baltimore atmosphere, the origin of the feeling existing as far back as his hasty exit from Boston in 1821.

The moment he appeared as Richard III on this last occasion in Baltimore, the assault of hisses and mock applause began. There were lulls in the tempest and some scenes of the acts passed in dread silence. During the early part of the evening, the friends of Kean displayed two placards in front of the two stage boxes, one inscribed, "Let the friends of Kean be silent;" the other, "Kean forever." It would have been well had they obeyed the request of the former motto. Kean's friends did not do so but added fuel to the flames by seizing and turning out those in arms against Kean. Thrust thus out of the theatre, they harangued the outside mob. The crowd became incensed beyond all reason and stormed the exterior with stones, breaking windows. And at this crisis, when the missiles of all sorts fell fast and thick as hailstones, Mr. Montgomery, the Mayor of the city, at much personnel risk and commendable courage, interposed his authority and in this wise addressed the infuriated mob, "That the assailants shall not enter the theatre but over my body," etc.

This firm stand of the mayor gave a pause to the onslaught, while the storm within took also similar pauses. But at length the crash came and the friends of Kean by stratagem got him out safely through the private yard on Gay Street. Every carriage was searched. It was not until they were assured that the object of their vengeance was not within their reach that they dispersed, a band remaining on the ground till daylight.

Mr. Wemyss, one of the performers and a friend of Kean's, was called upon by Col. Benjamin Edes, a printer of Baltimore and a popular man, begging him to get Kean out of Baltimore.

*Theatrical Rambles of Mr. & Mrs. Greene*, Charles Durang

"For," said he, "if he attempts to play again he will assuredly be tarred and feathered!"

He was then smuggled to Philadelphia via the steamboat; where he was received with open arms an extraordinary reaction having taken place in public sentiment in his case, they deeming him unjustly used.

The Chestnut Street Theatre re-opened on the 12th of June and Kean appeared as Richard III with great applause,[6] to quote from out friend Wemyss, "with the tide of popular favor as strong in his behalf as it had ever been in his proudest days of success; and although he did shed tears at the idea of playing Shylock for a quarter of a dollar, all he received, his terms being to share the receipts with the management, after deducting $200 each night. Let that night, when he only received 25 cents for his unequaled acting of the "Jew that Shakespeare drew," be buried in oblivion. His engagement continued attractive. The last night he played in Philadelphia was on the 26th of June, 1826, when he appeared as Cardinal Wolsey in *Henry VIII*, and Sylvester Daggerwood[7] for his benefit, ending the whole in one of his mad freaks of throwing a "Flip flap" and a "Fore spring" *à la cirque*.

He then retired to a small cottage on the banks of the Hudson, where he sojourned with the old actor John Forrester Foote.[8] That such should have been the closing engagement of the wizard of the Shakespearean drama is to be regretted. Art and nature were with Kean convertible terms; one decorated the other and seemed twine at a birth. His performances were sublime but always wreathed with feeling and touching pathos. The old and young, men and women, fell prostrate to his powers, and like a magic wand it swayed the public will. Kean's genius ruled with a tyrant's power but none felt ruled as slaves, they only saw the passion of the artiste through the beauties of nature.

## NOTES

[1]Florence, Huntsville, Cortland, and Tuscumbia are all towns in northern Alabama along the Tennessee River. Blunt Springs is probably Blount Springs, south of the river toward west-central Alabama, where Tuscaloosa is located. Accord-

*Theatrical Rambles of Mr. & Mrs. Greene*, Charles Durang

ing to Ludlow, the Mobile season opened December 28, 1826; but he must mean 1825.

[2] Mrs. [Vos] Stuart (1815-1854), a highly respected actress in the Southwest, made her debut at the Park Theatre in 1835. She died at Rose Hill, near Mobile, AL.

[3] Samuel P. Jones, a native Philadelphian, was a bookbinder turned actor. Durang called him "an imposing and noble-looking man with a commanding and impressive countenance of the J. R. Scott contour." He had an amazing memory, "capable of committing an entire newspaper at first reading." Sam had acted everywhere, according to Durang, "Where a theatre could be found, there was Sam holding forth."

[4] Sally Riddle, whose real name was Sarah Lapsley Riddle, was born in Philadelphia and made her debut at the Walnut Street Theatre there in 1823. She was the sister of Eliza Riddle. W. H. Smith, her husband, had changed his name from William Henry Sedley. He was one of the better stock actors of the Boston and Philadelphia theatres.

[5] *The Devil's Bridge*, an opera by Henry R. Bishop, was first performed in 1815. There was another operatic piece with this title by S. J. Arnold.

[6] After the unpleasantness at Baltimore cut the season short, the company returned to the Chestnut Street Theatre and opened with Kean's *Richard III* on June 12, 1826. Announced for seven performances, public interest stretched Kean's engagement into twelve.

[7] Sylvester Daggerwood was a character from Colman's *New Hay at the Old Market*.

[8] John Forrester Foote, a scholarly Londoner, first appeared in America at the Broadway Circus, NYC, November 4, 1822. Misfortune placed this excellent portrayer of old men as an inmate in the almshouse, attributed to "one unhappy failing." He returned to England around 1845 where he supposedly came into a sizable fortune.

*Theatrical Rambles of Mr. & Mrs. Greene*, Charles Durang

## XIII.

AN INSULT REMEMBERED — JUST REPROOF — MR. WM. C. MACREADY — MR. AND MRS. GEORGE BARRETT — THE BOY IN *WILLIAM TELL* — NATIVE TALENT — FRESH ARRIVALS — MISS LATIMER — GEN. SANDFORD AND HIS GREAT AMPHITHEATRE — PHILLIPS, THE VOCALIST, ETC.

Mr. and Mrs. Greene struggled hard for many years in the old Chestnut Street Company to get up the ladder of fame; but the ascent was slow in the early days of the stage with us. Native talent had a hard road to travel. It was not thought worthy of cultivation. Dramatic talent was imported from abroad like other manufactures. It was under the management of Joseph Cowell that John Greene's laurels sprouted and flowered broadcast. Mr. Cowell was engaged by Mr. Warren as stage manager for the season of 1826 and 1827.[1] The Greenes were engaged in very subordinate situations. Mr. Greene was cast for the Irishman in *Rosina*.[2] His fine, rich brogue and quaint, natural manner of personating Paddy took managers and audience by surprise and led to his being cast in the part of O'Dedimus in the comedy of *Man and Wife*.[3]

The piece was put up for Miss Kelly,[4] but the success of John Greene in the Irishman was so great that the play of *John Bull* was cast, principally for the purpose of introducing Greene as Dennis Brulgruddery. The piece was well cast and put up on the off nights of the stars to crowded houses and for several benefits, Greene's among the number, which was filled to overflowing. Even those who had asserted that

*Theatrical Rambles of Mr. & Mrs. Greene*, Charles Durang

Greene could only be trusted with a few lines were ashamed at their own want of judgment. Mr. and Mrs. Greene were much improved by practice, and at length were placed in a position which their talent deserved. By this chance Mr. Greene arose very suddenly.

In 1821, John Greene, then being a humble member of the company, was rehearsing the part of Chatillon, the French ambassador, a short but particular worded one in *King John*. The play opens with Chatillon's mission to this monarch seated on his throne. Chatillon's speech is filled with the French names of places, *viz.*, Poitiers, Angers, Touraine, Mayenne. These Greene pronounced unwittingly in pure English, being ignorant of the French pronunciation of those French districts. Cooper was the Faulconbridge and Mr. Wood, King John. The former gentleman had a very correct ear for French, as he spoke it very well, but was of a most captious, haughty disposition at rehearsals, especially towards the actors, if they should through any mischance vary from Walker's standard of orthography, the then guide of the London and American stage. As soon as Greene had concluded Chatillon's speech, with his hauteur of manner, not deigning to look or even speak with civility to the delinquent, he addressed the prompter, Mr. Lopez, "Sir, tell that man that he has not read one word of his speech correctly" respecting the French words.

Greene was now quietly spoken to by Mr. Wood, with the request that he would repeat his speech to correct it. But Greene felt so indignant at the gross insult that he refused to do so. Wood then read the words to him and the rehearsal passed off without any further difficulty. Greene played the part at night, conforming as best he could to the corrections, but burning with restless revenge towards Mr. Cooper.

A great deal of this tyrannous manner of Mr. Cooper was foolishly assumed; no doubt thinking, in keeping aloof from the familiar association of the stock actors, that it gave him an artificial position above them that would operate to his advantage. From these absurd assumptions of

*Theatrical Rambles of Mr. & Mrs. Greene*, Charles Durang

caste, he was named "King Tom" by the performers. They generally disliked having anything to do with him.

This course of Cooper and a few other of the star people deserves the denunciation of the profession, as futile nonsense deserving the contempt of the respectable and the intelligent. It was a pity in Cooper, who was really at heart a very good man, of gentlemanly, correct principles at all other times, of very companionable and amiable qualities.

After the occurrence, Cooper and Greene met no more until 1827, when the poor Chatillon had become an actor of great promise. Such was now his position as to challenge the respect of the gentlemen of his profession. One of the company, who was on terms of intimacy with Mr. Cooper, contrived to introduce Mr. Greene to Mr. Cooper, being both on the stage together during rehearsal.

To this Mr. Greene made this replication, "No need of that formal ceremony. I know Mr. Cooper well. Some years ago we had a business introduction on the stage at a rehearsal of *King John*. I was then a young aspirant in the profession, deeply imbued with ambitious views, yet willing and anxious to perform my duty to the best of my abilities. But in committing some pardonable novitiate errors in reading, that gentleman exercised a paltry, cowardly power from his position to grossly insult my feelings as a man. That insult, so mean and unprovoked, I can neither forget nor forgive!"

"Why not have resented it at the time? That would have been a more manly course than to have nursed malice so long for a mere expression of words thoughtlessly spoken in the excitement of the moment," Mr. Cooper replied.

"Because, sir, I was then a mere dependent novice, an engaged actor. To have offended the manager, as I should have done by resenting the insult so sore to my feelings, would have subjected me to an instant discharge from the theatre. This, with no means beyond my small weekly salary would have thrown me out of all employment in the city. I would have had to seek an engagement in another theatre. I might have had to travel from 200 to 300 miles in the winter season, and it would have been doubtful whether I could procure one. The scene is now changed. I am now in the receipt

## *Theatrical Rambles of Mr. & Mrs. Greene*, Charles Durang

of $30 a week. I have earned a reputation and am no longer a subject to be trampled upon by an imperial star! I desire no further acquaintance with the tragedian."

Exit Greene. They often met after this in their various peregrinations throughout the Union, but for a long time they did not exchange a social word.

Mr. William C. Macready made his first appearance in America this season.[5] The excitement in Philadelphia was so tremendous that the theatre was nightly besieged by thousands. He opened in *Macbeth*, Mrs. Wood as Lady Macbeth. All the contemporaries of Mr. Macready are aware of his fastidious and teasing instructions to the players when engaged in scenes with him. They amounted to a complete bore and often defeated the object desired, as the tuition of the business perfectly confounded the performers.

Mrs. Wood, who was the leading lady in tragedy, was, of course, cast to act with this tragic hero; but insuperable difficulties soon arose between them. Mr. Macready would teach Mrs. Wood and she as zealously would decline the instructions, so that she seldom acted with him. This gradually threw Mrs. Greene into the supporting female parts with the tragedian. It was a fortunate event for Mrs. Greene, whose pliability of disposition made her teachable and of course acceptable to the fastidious requirements of the crooked ideas of Mr. Macready, who, although of an eccentric mind, was truly an intellectual actor and a man of genius *par excellence*.

On these opportunities of acting with him she availed herself with pleasing alacrity of all this tragedian's able instructions. She improved prodigiously and made herself a veteraness before she had passed her novitiate. It was the base whereon she established her tragic reputation in after days. She now, as 'twere, stepped into Mrs. Wood's slippers for the nonce. A biographer of Mrs. Greene, in her reminiscences, rather exaggerates her legitimate claims to superexcellence. Mrs. Greene was a very clever tragic actress. When Macready played Coriolanus, Mrs. Greene was cast to Volumnia and played the part well and carefully. She threw into it all the passion of the noble Roman mother. Her majes-

*Theatrical Rambles of Mr. & Mrs. Greene*, Charles Durang

tic figure, her well-toned voice, vigorous expression of high-toned mien, and maternal love that overcame her patriotic sentiments to save her son, were most truthfully delineated. Mr. Macready sincerely complimented Mrs. Greene on her able rendition of it.[6]

Mr. and Mrs. George Barrett were at this house at the opening of the season. Mr. George Horton Barrett had received, from his dashing, polished manners, his elegance of dress and address, extreme amenity of deportment, and vivid expression, the appropriate cognomen of "Gentlemanly George," an appellation bestowed on George IV originally. He was one of the best, genteel comedians ever attached to the American stage, as his mother was one of the first and most finished tragic actresses of our early stage. Her expressive face and musical voice, added to an exquisite feeling of the pathetic in Lady Randolph, Mrs. Beverly, Lady St. Valori, and other parts of tenderness have rarely been equaled and never surpassed on our boards. She belonged to a class of female performers whose merits, both private and public, filled the memories of their admirers many years after her death.[7]

For many years Mr. Barrett graced the stage with the versatility of his talent. In 1847 he crossed the Atlantic to engage performers for Col. Mann's new theatre, then erecting in Broadway, New York, he being his acting and stage manager.[8] While he was in London he acted Puff in *The Critic* at Drury Lane Theatre.

George Barrett was born in Exeter, England, in 1794. His parents soon after immigrated to America, where they lived long and honored and died. George not long since paid the great debt of nature himself. His daughter, Georgiana Barrett, was married to Mr. Philip Warren.

When Mr. Macready produced *William Tell* at the Chestnut Street Theatre, a female being cast as Albert, he objected to it and sent to New York for the boy, Master William Wheatley, who played it at the Park with him.[9] And well did this juvenile histrion enact the youthful hero of the Swiss Cantons. A few years have past and that boy is now a talented manager of one of our first theatres.

*Theatrical Rambles of Mr. & Mrs. Greene*, Charles Durang

Mr. Booth followed Mr. Macready with tolerable success, producing the tragedy of *Sylla* with effect. Mrs. E. Knight, the vocalist, shone prominent for some nights[10] and Jefferson and Cowell held forth as the two Dromios. Although they clearly looked unlike each other, they gave the piece a run for several nights by their good acting. It was played with the music but it did not seem to impart the zest anticipated by this harmonious addenda.

Mr. Macready returned for a second engagement, during which he enacted Henry V., also Henry VIII. The *Fatal Dowry*[11] was given with great acting effects. Macready's Romont was truly a fine piece of acting, quite equal and as appalling as his *Werner*.[12] These performances were announced as positively the last time Mr. Macready would ever appear in Philadelphia.

With all the apparent success that attended Mr. Warren's course after the retirement of Mr. Wood from the establishment, his fortunes seemed declining. Mr. Cowell seceded from the stage management and made arrangements to open the Walnut Street Theatre. It would be a curious investigation to ascertain how often that house has been cut and carved into something new since its original walls had been up in 1809.

Cowell offered the Greenes very liberal terms to join his company, which they readily accepted.[13] But the theatre not being quite completed at the time proposed for opening, Mr. and Mrs. Greene made a trip to New York and played a short time at the Broadway Amphitheatre, afterwards Tattersals. Between fishing and boating in the beautiful waters surrounding New York, they passed a pleasant summer.

About 1827, actors began to be manufactured of native material by the gross. The brilliant rise and progress of Mr. Edwin Forrest induced many fine figured and athletic young men to follow at a distance in his career. But with them the poet's line was painfully true, that "distance lends enchantment to the view." Forrest's success was great and deserved, gained by hard study, and his name will be ever luminous in the reflected luster of his country's dramatic annals. Forrest's followers found that something more

*Theatrical Rambles of Mr. & Mrs. Greene*, Charles Durang

potent was needed than faint imitations of his genius and talent and hit upon the expedient of appeals through the medium of "Native talent!" running through every note of the national emotional chromatic scale to awaken by tender strokes of art the public feeling of native admiration! But Forrest's rising sunbeams evaporated the surrounding mists of their aspirations like dissolving views, leaving not a rack behind.

In this category, Mr. Pelby was the first who so invested "native talent" as capital.[14] And thus his dramatic speculations were not without some prestige; albeit he encountered much difficulty in overcoming foreign impressions of acting requisites. He possessed a figure short and clumsy, devoid of symmetry, his face with rather regular features, yet without expression, a quality which is the lighthouse to the actor's functions. Without it the performer is a blank representative.

Another was John Jay Adams, a tobacconist of New York and also a *littérateur* in trade. He contributed pretty poetry and romances to the Sunday papers. He occasionally starred it on the Park boards to remind the public that tragedy still lived in his person. But his dramatic personations, it would seem, have not perpetuated his name to posterity. He received his dramatic readings from the clever actor, Pritchard, of the old Park days, when legitimate acting possessed a local habitation and a name. Mr. Pritchard had acquired fame as Pescara in *The Apostate*, and recited with much feeling a monody on the death of General Montgomery on the removal of that revolutionary patriot's bones from Québec to St. Paul's Cemetery, on Broadway, New York, where the promenader's eye may catch a view of his monument. This address Pritchard delivered with much excellence on the night of the day of the impressive obsequies, nearly half a century after his death. There were many surviving revolutionary officers marching in the mournful but interesting funeral cortege.[15]

At the closing of the Park Theatre in 1818, when a performance was given for the benefit of the old theatrical fund of that theatre, Mr. Thomas A. Cooper played the Duke Aranza and Mrs. Holman (nee Miss Latimer and late Mrs.

*Theatrical Rambles of Mr. & Mrs. Greene*, Charles Durang

General C. W. Sandford) made her first appearance on the New York stage and sang with great applause "The Soldier Tired of Wars Alarms" and the celebrated "Echo Song." Mrs. General Sandford died in New York, August, 29, 1859.

After the War of 1812, Mr. George Holman became the lessee of the Charleston, S.C., theatre, which had been lying fallow after the death of Mr. Alexander Placide till the fall of 1815. After Mr. Holman's first season at the Palmetto City, he went to England to recruit his company, returning in the autumn with large reinforcements, among whom was the celebrated James H. Caldwell, as his principal leading man, and Miss Latimer, a fine rosy cheeked, lady-like young girl, with very pretty features, small figure, with every personal and mental quality fit to adorn any position in which she would be placed. She was a vocalist of power and execution, having a very flexible and extensive soprano organ which had received due cultivation. With her came Mr. Nichols, a tenor, and a young man of talent as a musician and vocalist. During the latter part of the Charleston season, Mr. Holman married Miss Latimer; and at the close of the season sought a more salubrious clime during the summer and sojourned at Rockaway, Long Island, New York. Here Mr. Holman died suddenly of apoplexy on the 24th of August, 1817. He had grown to be a very plethoric figure from having been a very slender and symmetrical one. At his death he was 53 years of age, having been born in 1764.

Miss Latimer's first appearance after his death was announced and her reception was brilliant. Her abilities deserved no less an homage; her songs of "The Soldier Tired" and the "Echo Song" astonished and entranced the audience.[16] They were masterly performances of the voice and sold most impressively, as at that day but little good singing had been heard. The recollection of Mrs. Oldmixon's powers had passed away.[17] Therefore it may be said Mrs. Burke was the only female of vocal ability then before the public, and although she possessed an extraordinary natural voice, it lacked the great element of an opera singer, *viz.*, cultivation.

Of the male gender, we had the celebrated Incledon, who made his first American salutation on the 20th of Octo-

*Theatrical Rambles of Mr. & Mrs. Greene*, Charles Durang

ber, 1817, as Hawthorn in *Love in a Village*. His song of "The Storm" was truly a masterly and astonishing performance, and most graphically, in voice music, delineated the horrors of a tempest. Indeed, besides the wonderful effects of his sea ditties, the impressiveness of his sacred music, as heard in our Lent oratorios, remained for years upon the senses of his hearers. Yet Incledon was not a cultivated singer. He bade us farewell in August, 1818, and died in England in 1826, aged 69. He was a hearty, bluff-looking John Bull with all his brusque characteristics.[18]

In March, 1819, Mrs. Holman married Mr. Isaac Clawson, an amateur star who had illustrated Hamlet agreeable to his own ideas in our theatre, and he received thereby approbation. He filled a brief space in theatrical records. His course was eccentric and wayward, but his name was never known in our stage records. It was an unhappy union and he died soon after. He was, however, a person of gentlemanly habits and polished manners.[19]

In 1824 she became the wife of Mr. Charles Sandford, a distinguished member of the New York bar and subsequently a leading general officer in the military of New York.

Mr. Sandford was a great patron of the theatrical profession and became the proprietor of the magnificent amphitheatre known as the Lafayette Circus, which had an immense stage for horse melodramas. Mr. Sandford erected this grand military scenic establishment within a pistol shot of Price and Simpson's overwhelmed circus. General Sandford procured all the horses that were to be purchased, from a long tail to a short tail, and many curiously marked ones, which unfortunately did not long retain their strange coats. A little water washed off many of the devices that had been painted thereon, leaving them plain white beasts. He engaged Mr. Tatnall and some of Price and Simpson's riders, and some boys whose talent for gymnastics had not been developed, but which afterwards proved superior to any thing produced in Europe. His stage manager, Mr. Watkins Burroughs, was from the Surrey and Adelphi Theatres, and he had a large theatrical company.

## *Theatrical Rambles of Mr. & Mrs. Greene*, Charles Durang

The houses were immense and so were the expenses. He closed up Price and Simpson's establishment, though the proprietor was ultimately reduced to bankruptcy. The place closed and in a year after the amphitheatre was burned down, never to be built again.

Be it as it may, the horse dramas were most magnificently put upon the stage by Mr. Burroughs. The stage could be extended 200 feet in length and it was at least 80 feet or more in width. Their processions were truly imposing, as they approached reality more than anything before or since produced in America, nor have they been equaled in grandeur.[20]

Mrs. Sandford resumed her profession under her husband's management in October, 1826, and last performed at the Park Theatre, in the season of 1829.

At the close of Incledon's engagement, a highly accomplished opera singer appeared in the person of Mr. T. Phillips, who at once attained the highest summit of popular favor.[21] His personal appearance was truly imposing. With most respectable powers as an actor, his voice was unrivaled in softness and sweetness of tone, with all that distinctness of articulation that feeling and delicacy of expression that form the charm of the real Italian school, that method and simplicity that marks the genius of the lyric artiste. The Count Belino, wherein he first appeared, became his most popular character; then was followed by Young Meadows, in *Love in a Village*, Prince Orlando in *The Cabinet*, Carlos in *The Duenna*, and the Seraskier in the *Devil's Bridge*, which had been played entirely emasculated of its music, which is the only charm of the drama.[22] The Count being performed thus by Messrs. Wood, H. Wallack, etc., when the music was first heard through Phillips, the ecstasies of the public exceeded all bounds. Many play-goers, now overshadowed by age, must remember the sweet song of "Eveleen's Bower" as feelingly given by T. Phillips. Yet its moral has often been thought objectionable, or, rather, as inculcating and palliating the subjects of vicious principles through the charms of poetry and music.

*Theatrical Rambles of Mr. & Mrs. Greene*, Charles Durang

In the same year, Mr. John Duff, who had left the Chestnut Street Theatre for the Boston engagement, returned for a few nights to Philadelphia, and most successfully starred it to large receipts, playing Count Belino and singing all the music, imitating the style and manner of Mr. T. Phillips to a charm. His success was great. He made, in this operatic experiment as a star, some $5,000. I have heard him often afterwards comment on the occasion with much astonishment, having no claims to the position of a singing actor, excepting, indeed, a gloriously natural musical voice and the dashing, showy attributes of an excellent actor.

## NOTES

[1] The Chestnut Street season began December 4, 1826, with *The Stranger* under Warren's sole management.

[2] *Rosina; or, The Reapers*, a comic opera by Mrs. Brooke, had already received numerous performances in this country.

[3] *Man and Wife*, was a comedy by S. J. Arnold.

[4] Miss Lydia Kelly's engagement was for eight nights beginning December 5. She was born in London in 1795. Her first American appearance was at the Chatham Theatre, NYC, in September, 1824. Her masculine appearance was set off by elegant costumes. Ireland suggests that her acting was course but spirited and effective. After amassing a small fortune as an actress, she returned to England (around 1832) and retired. Greene's Brulgruddery did not come until the end of the season. Its success merited some four or five performances.

[5] The famous English actor, Macready, opened his engagement at the Chestnut Street Theatre on January 10, 1827, as part of a two year visit to the country. Mrs. Greene is listed as a member of the Chorus.

[6] Macready took his benefit of *Coriolanus* on January 24.

[7] Although born in England, George Horton Barrett (1794-1860) came to America as a child and became one of the best light comedians on the stage. Mrs. George Barrett (nee Miss Henry) was considered by Stone to have been one of the country's most beautiful actresses. Mrs. Giles Barrett, George's mother, was highly esteemed in tragedy. She died

*Theatrical Rambles of Mr. & Mrs. Greene*, Charles Durang

in Boston in 1832. Lady Randolph is a character in Home's tragedy *Douglas*, Mrs. Beverly in Edward Moore's *The Gamesters*, and Lady St. Valori in Cumberland's *Carmelite; or, The Knights of the Cross*.

[8]Col. Mann's New Theatre (the Old Broadway Theatre) was started by Thomas Hamblin, until he suffered a $100,000 loss from the burning of his Bowery Theatre. Col. Alvah Mann resumed the erection of the building with the assistance of a Mr. Raymond. The theatre, located on the east side of Broadway, between Pearl and Anthony Streets, opened its doors on September 27, 1847.

[9]Master William Wheatley appeared as Albert in Macready's *William Tell* at the Park Theatre on October 13, 1826.

[10]*Sylla*, a tragedy written by "a gentleman of New York," was adapted from the French version by Jouy. Mrs. Edward Knight (nee Miss Mary Ann Povey, 1804-1861) first appeared in this country on November 30, 1826. A vocalist of the English school, as an actress in comic operas, Ireland judged her to be superior to any contemporary star.

[11]*The Fatal Dowry*, was a tragedy by Philip Massinger.

[12]*Werner*, Lord Byron's tragedy, was popularized by Macready in America, where he performed it first at the Park Theatre on October 4, 1843.

[13]Cowell opened his Broadway Circus on May 9, 1827; but lack of success caused the establishment to close on the 25th of May. It is uncertain just how many performances the Greenes rendered for Cowell in New York. John Greene appeared in Placide's benefit as Dennis Brulgruddery at the Park on May 19. Cowell and Simpson opened the Walnut Street Theatre to equestrian entertainment during the summer of 1827, taking the Greenes, Mestayer and family, Porter, and others from Warren's company and causing the latter to write in his diary, "The departures of these I regret not, except Greene and wife. She is eminently useful and he valuable for low Irishmen—not good for much else."

[14]The Boston born William Pelby (1793-1850) made his debut in Philadelphia on November 26, 1821, at the Walnut Street Theatre as Macbeth. In 1827 he was manager of the

*Theatrical Rambles of Mr. & Mrs. Greene*, Charles Durang

Tremont Theatre, Boston, and later built the Warren Theatre there.

[15] When John Jay Adams was manager of the City Theatre, New York, in 1837, Cowell was stage manager. On July 30th of that year Mrs. Greene performed the Queen to Adams' Hamlet, with John Greene doing Murtoch Delany in the afterpiece. *The Apostate* was tragedy by R. S. Shiel. Pritchard's tribute to Montgomery occurred at the Park Theatre, July 8. 1818, at the benefit for the Theatrical Fund.

[16] Miss Latimer, whom Ireland considered one of the most charming singers ever presented on the stage, made her first New York appearance on the same evening as Pritchard's above recitation. "The Soldier Tired of War's Alarms" was composed by Arne; the "Echo Song" by Bishop.

[17] Mrs. Oldmixon (formerly Mrs. George) was a singing actress at the Haymarket and Drury Lane before coming to America. She was connected with the Philadelphia and New York theatres, where from 1797 to 1814 she was considered the leading vocalist. Without youth or beauty, she was skillful as a comic actress, chambermaids and country girls being her specialty.

[18] Charles Incledon (1757-1826) was in his day the most famous English vocalist in America. He made his first appearance in this country in 1817 when he was past his prime, overweight, unkempt, weak as an actor. However, Ireland writes that his rendition of "The Storm" was a masterly and astonishing performance. "His style was so expressive of the horrors of the tempest, and the confusion and despair of the sufferers, that, independent of the amazement excited by the vast power and flexibility of voice he displayed in the difficult undertaking, the effect upon the audience was always as strong as any expression produced by the finest piece of acting." *Love in a Village*, was a comic opera by Bickerstaff.

[19] Isaac Starr Clawson, better known for his poetry, came from a prominent New York family. His enactment of Hamlet occurred at the Park Theatre, June 18, 1823. Dissipation ultimately led to suicide in London in 1834.

[20] The Lafayette Circus (or Amphitheatre) was situated on the west side of Laurens Street and just north of Canal Street. It first opened for business on July 4, 1825, with Burroughs

*Theatrical Rambles of Mr. & Mrs. Greene*, Charles Durang

as acting manager, Dinneford stage manager, and James Hunter ring master. The structure was re-opened without circus performances a year later. It was rebuilt for the 1827-28 season by Sandford, the point during which the Greenes were in residence and with Burroughs functioning as stage manager.

[21]Mr. T. Phillips was a vocalist of high repute and had considerable merit as an actor. The made two visits to America, the last being in 1823. He met his end in a railroad accident in 1841.

[22]Count Belino was a character from Bishop's melodramatic opera, *The Devil's Bridge*. *The Cabinet* was an opera by T. J. Dibdin; *The Duenna*, one by Sheridan.

*Theatrical Rambles of Mr. & Mrs. Greene*, Charles Durang

## XIV.

IMPORTATIONS — COMPETITION FROM WEMYSS — COOPER'S FAREWELL — RECONCILIATION — WILMINGTON TOO GOOD — STARS AT BALTIMORE.

After Cowell's secession from the Warren dynasty, Francis C. Wemyss became the managerial Magnus Apollo of the old house, and during the summer recess both of the Philadelphia managements sent agents to England to recruit their companies, with large bounties offered to enlist for America. Simpson and Cowell had taken the Walnut Street Theatre.

John Hallam,[1] a friend and actor of Cowell's had a desire to visit his native country again to marry a lady to whom he had been betrothed. Having feathered himself well with some American eagles, thither he went to consummate connubially his lover's vows. In addition to which ceremonies, Cowell commissioned him to engage any talented performers he might meet with and would likely suit him. All these things he faithfully fulfilled, returning in the fall of 1827 with a number of new faces of both sexes, *viz.*, William Henry Smith (his real name being Sedley), Mr. and Mrs. Hallam, Mr. and Mrs. Mitchell, Mr. Grierson, Mr. Sefton, Miss Wells, Miss Stannard, Mrs. Kinlock, and her little girl, Miss Lane.[2] They arrived at New York in the ship *Britannia*.

By Cowell's order they were directed to put up at a fashionable restaurant in Park Row kept by a *bon vivant*, Charles Irish. Their bill while there reminds one of the Falstaff's bill of items: Item—sack, 2 gallons, 5s 8d; item—anchovies and sack after supper, 2s 6d; item—bread, ½d. This was supposed to have happened in the reign of Henry

## *Theatrical Rambles of Mr. & Mrs. Greene*, Charles Durang

IV. The following did happen during the reign of Cowell and Simpson. Mr. John Hallam to Charles Irish: one day's lodgings for self and party, $18.50; refreshments, $56.00. Hallam was a fine, jolly specimen of the John Bull, and, of course, he took care that the representatives of the British drama should be properly honored on this their first appearance on American ground.

As soon as Hallam's mission was known, Mr. Warren dispatched Mr. Wemyss on a similar errand; but whereas Hallam was limited to give only three guineas a week as the highest salary, Wemyss had to pay much more, of course, as he had to select persons who by talents or circumstances had achieved some kind of reputation in England. Cowell's had never been heard of out of their own little circle, with the exception of his principal man, Grierson, and Hallam prided himself on being the original Duke of Wellington in the *Battle of Waterloo*.

When these recruits arrived at New York, Cowell was in successful operation in Philadelphia. Grierson opened in Rolla and made no impression; Mrs. Mitchell was also introduced as Cora.[3] This lady had a pretty face but a broad Lincolnshire dialect, certainly not understood in tragedy by an American audience. Cowell doubled her salary on condition that she would play the old women, which offer she very sensibly accepted and made quite a hit in them. Pretty women always require to be well paid for making themselves ugly. Grierson was a tall, stalwart figure, with rather a small round face for 6 feet 2; and, unfortunately, very near-sighted, so that when he had to seize Coral's child from the Spanish soldier (Charles Lee being a very small man) who held the child in his arms, Grierson, instead of catching hold of the child, seized Charley Lee[4] by the nape of the neck and bore both off at once triumphantly! his sword shedding fire as he struck their Castilian sabers. The laughter of the audience was prodigious.

Mr. W. H. Smith became an immense favorite. He was a handsome fellow and, as a general actor, not surpassed on our boards. John Sefton at that time was a very thin, spare actor, and excellent in little bits, as they say in stage par-

*Theatrical Rambles of Mr. & Mrs. Greene*, Charles Durang

lance. His fame was not made till some years after, when, as Jemmy Twitcher in the *Golden Farmer*,[5] he therein made a perennial reputation. The equestrian company that had occupied the theatre before it was altered were sent to a circus temporarily erected in Wilmington, Delaware.

*Ad interim*, Wemyss returned from England with a large host of histrions and stars, from whom too much was expected, and hence a sad failure in the perspective. On the night that Miss Emery, Southwell, and Samuel Chapman were announced for Belvidera, Jaffier, and Pierre,[6] in *Venice Preserved* at Old Drury, Cowell announced Mr. and Mrs. Hamblin and Mr. W. H. Smith in the same parts at the Walnut Street Theatre. So it went, tit for tat, and some how or other it turned out that Cowell's half-priced actors proved as great, or greater, favorites than Wemyss' full-priced articles. With the aid of Walker's beautiful scenery, the *Sleeping Beauty* and the burletta of *Don Giovanni*, gotten up in splendid style by Mr. Cowell, had a very successful run.[7]

The great American star, Mr. Thomas A. Cooper, played a farewell engagement at the Walnut Street Theatre prior to his departure for London, whither he was going to play an engagement at Drury Lane Theatre, then under the management of Stephen Price. On October 31st, 1827, Mr. Cooper performed Macbeth for his farewell benefit, after which he delivered a brief address from a written paper. It would seem that Mr. Cooper was not happy in public speaking apart from a studied character. He reduced his thoughts to writing, as he could not trust them even by study to his memory. He evinced a great deal of feeling on this *adieu* occasion—probably a last farewell to those before whom he had so long labored and been crowned with fame. It was leaving home upon a doubtful trial, and which proved in the end a mortifying one, most unjustly inflicted, amounting to a national discourtesy. He preceded the address with an apology for placing it on paper, but in the simple reading he became embarrassed. Either his feelings veiled his eyesight, or the matter being in his own writing (he naturally wrote a cramped hand), and the manuscript being written on both sides of a sheet of foolscap that became transparent as he held it before the footlights, caused confusion, added to

*Theatrical Rambles of Mr. & Mrs. Greene*, Charles Durang

which his aroused sympathies made the writing perfectly illegible to his eyes; and not resorting to glasses, which he used at that time occasionally—being in the fifty-first year of his age—failing to make out his own manuscript, he gave it up and substituted a few extemporaneous words emanating from the heart, arising out of his own thoughts. As they were genuine, the audience sympathized with them, and honest tears were seen to flow from all.

When he retired to his dressing room, Cowell said to Greene, "I should like to see you and the veteran Cooper reconciled before he leaves us. He has his foibles, his infirmities of temper, but he is a noble gentleman of integrity and honor. You are younger than he, John Greene; it is for you to make the first advances."

Greene, who truly owed him no malice, and having had his manly say out, immediately entered the star's dressing room and tendered his hand to Cooper.

"Sir," said Greene, "I would not like to part in anger with you. Let bygones be bygones. We both may have been to blame. Here is my hand. Let us part friends."

Cooper grasped his hand cordially, mutual explanations followed, and they remained true friends till Cooper's death in April, 1849, which took place in Bristol, Pa.

When the season closed at the Walnut Street Theatre[8] the company went to Baltimore, where Simpson sent Cowell all the Park Theatre stars. This was a death blow to Warren's management, for he had to encounter their loss in attracting the audiences and depriving him of all the novelties. It was an unlooked-for stroke against him, and eventually caused his failure.

Previous to their Baltimore visit, the Greenes had formed a scheme with Mr. and Mrs. Mitchell, Miss Stannard, Miss Sarah Wells, Mr. Wells,[9] John Sefton, and Grierson, to go to Wilmington, Del.; but they were sorely nonplused. Neither the stage nor Shakespeare were scarcely tolerated at this saintly town. They were considered in the light of vagabonds, as the English laws had or have it. The theatre—lest it should demoralize the people in the town—was like an unclean beast, driven beyond the boundaries of the borough. The ac-

## *Theatrical Rambles of Mr. & Mrs. Greene*, Charles Durang

tors had a vehicle that conveyed them from their lodgings in the place to the theatre in the country, which they called "the Royal Boroughline Stage." They only cleared their expenses at this town.

The Walnut was opened for a season,[10] and then Cowell opened his great Baltimore campaign, as we have noticed, when the stars crowded the houses nightly. At Wilmington a funny incident occurred when the *corps* was performing *Pizarro*. During the Temple of the Sun scene, where a solemn Peruvian sacrifice takes place, the altar, the place of worship, is made to receive a ball of fire in token of the "power supreme's" approbation of their appeal to its protection. In their hymn of invocation, the fire of Heaven descends on the altar. Then the sacred music very effectively changes to a vivid measure, or time, thus: "Give praise, give praise, Our prayer is heard," etc. As this presto movement commenced, the entire altar took fire. It was composed of pasteboard painted in imitation of Lapis Lazuli stone, with a dazzling sun in the center. Behind was strewed with cotton saturated with turpentine to give effect to the fire. But the ball caught in its passage down the wire to some of the combustibles on the altar, and the whole structure was in a blaze. Rolla, Alonzo, and all on the stage exerted themselves to extinguish the flames, which had now scattered over the stage. The dress of one of the virgins took fire, and it being composed of light material, the poor female was in danger of being burnt to a cinder, but for the presence of mind displayed by Mr. Wisdom, the master carpenter of the theatre, who snatched up an old green baize curtain that had been laying behind the scenes, and, throwing it around her, rolled himself with the burning girl in it to almost suffocation, and so squelched the flames. The lady escaped death but was badly burned, and Wisdom himself was dreadfully scorched in the face and hands. It was a valiant and noble act in him.

Rolla was to address the Peruvian army before the sacred invocation, appealing in a stirring speech to their patriotism. There were no supernumeraries to be had in the town, consequently there were no soldiers to address. Imagination is very creative, so the audience had the liberty to fancy the six virgins on each side of the altar as Amazonians. Poetry

*Theatrical Rambles of Mr. & Mrs. Greene*, Charles Durang

admits of such things in the classics, but, Rolla imagined his "Brave associates, partners of my toil," etc., as outsiders to the *dramatis personae*, and addressed them as if off the stage.

After the Wilmington season the company went to Baltimore where there was a perfect milky way of stars; among them Macready, Forrest, Hackett, Miss Kelly, Mrs. E. Knight, Mrs. Austin Clara Fisher.[11] The houses were dense with crowds to witness the performances of such a galaxy of talent. Clara Fisher was the great star. Everything was Clara Fisher—boats, horses, bonnets, everything was called after her.

## NOTES

[1] John Hallam was born in Yorkshire, England. He was an unsophisticated provincial actor, best as a rustic comedian or in sailor roles. There was no polish in his manner, and he was plain and simple of dress.

[2] Thomas Grierson was a diligent workman and gentlemanly of habit, but his height and ugliness made him unsuitable for tragedy. He eventually returned to England where he was the beneficiary of a comfortable inheritance. John Sefton was born in Liverpool, January 15, 1805. Was a lawyer's clerk before becoming a provincial actor. He was hired by Cowell to play fops, old men, country boys, etc. Miss Wells came as a dancer. She married Sefton in 1831. After traveling the country with him, she returned to England, where she died. Miss Rachel Stannard was called "a fine, healthy dash-a-way actress, with prominent features of a rosy hue," suitable for sentimental ladies of comedy or facetious soubrettes. Louisa Lane was the future Mrs. John Drew, born in England, January 10, 1820. Her parents had hoped she would become a second Clara Fisher. She first appeared in New York as Little Pickle. Married at 16 to Henry Blaine Hunt; married George Mossop, 1848; married John Drew, 1850.

[3] Rolla and Cora were characters from Home's tragedy of *Douglas*. Grierson performed Rolla June 29, 1827.

[4] A Mr. Lee is mentioned as being at the Park Theatre,

*Theatrical Rambles of Mr. & Mrs. Greene*, Charles Durang

September 15, 1824, a recent recruit from London. Best in second tragedy roles and serious characters in genteel comedy, he seems to have disappeared after 1827.

[5]*The Golden Farmer* was a melodrama by Benjamin Webster.

[6]Wemyss brought Miss Emery over from the Surrey Theatre. She was best in scenes of intense passion, first appearing at the Chestnut Street Theatre November 11, 1827. Her career was cut short and she died in wretchedness and vice at the Five Points of New York City. Henry Southwell, who came from London, was called a dashing and spirited actor. He made his New York debut as Romeo at the Bowery Theatre, June 5, 1829. He died in 1841. Samuel Chapman, born in London, 1799, married Elizabeth Jefferson shortly after arriving in America. While managing the Walnut Street Theatre, 1830, he was thrown from a horse and soon died.

[7]*The Sleeping Beauty* was a romance play, author unknown. *Don Giovanni* was a burlesque by Thomas Dibdin.

[8]The Walnut Street Theatre closed July 25, 1827, to make the ring area into a spacious pit. Cowell resumed operations August 29, 1827, opening with *John Bull*, calling the building the Philadelphia Theatre.

[9]Mr. Wells was a clever ballet master and dancer of merit. He left the stage early to teach dancing in Pittsburgh and other western cities.

[10]Cowell ended his season November 3, 1827, with Cooper, Hamblin, and Mrs. Wood in *Venice Preserved*.

[11]Mrs. Austin was an accomplished singer with a range of nearly three octaves. She had a lovely personal appearance but no acting ability. Her last appearance in America was at the Bowery Theatre, May 8, 1835. Clara Fisher was a child prodigy who first appeared at Drury Lane in 1817. As an infant, her great successes were *Richard III*, *Douglas*, and Shylock. As an adult, she performed in musical comedy and farce. She continued to act until 1880. Died November 12, 1898.

*Theatrical Rambles of Mr. & Mrs. Greene*, Charles Durang

## XV.

NOVEL "CURE FOR THE HEART ACHE" — EXTAORDINARY CIRCUMSTANCE — TRIALS OF PROFESSIONALS — GREENE'S MANAGEMENT AT THE WALNUT STREET — THE WEST INDIAN DRAMATIC CORPS — JOSEPHINE CLIFTON — DAMAGED WARDROBES, ETC.

While in Baltimore, Mrs. Greene was cast for the part of Miss Vortex in the *Cure for the Heart Ache*.[1] As she had no book or part of the character, she called the Negro servant, Mary, and dispatched her to the theatrical book store for one, taking the precaution to write on a slip of paper the name of the book lest it should slip the darky's memory. Mary was a long time gone on her errand and Mrs. Greene's patience became exhausted.

Mary at length made her appearance in high glee, exclaiming "I'se got it, Missus."

Mrs. Greene asked her where she had been and what kept her so long; when the old woman, with an air of great satisfaction, handed her a square package labeled "magnesia," she said, "Why, Missus, I'se bin gittin' you de cure for de heart burn from de potterkerry, ob course! Don't tink I noes nuffin'. I'se read your 'scription, an' I'se got de physic."

An extraordinary circumstance occurred to Mrs. Greene while in Baltimore. The play was *Richard III* on the night in question. She felt very nervous all day and could not account for it. She knew her sister was ill, but did not think she was in any danger. She had to play the queen. As she was dressing she became wrapped in a state of clairvoyance of a

*Theatrical Rambles of Mr. & Mrs. Greene*, Charles Durang

mesmeric nature. She shook it off and concluded her toilet. Meantime, Mr. Greene received a message that Mrs. Bignall wished to see her sister. He kept the message from his lady, thinking it would be time enough to tell her when her part was done.

In the scene with Richard, where she encounters him on his warlike march, a vision came over the senses of Mrs. Greene just as she had finished her declamatory speech to the King. Her sister appeared before her in a dying state, as heaving her last breath in an attitude of prayer. She was seized with a fainting fit and was borne off the stage by those around her. That night she was conducted to the chamber of her sister, where she reposed in death.

The trying scenes of life that actresses go through, would, if related, smack more of the romantic than of real life occurrences. We have witnessed the pressure of life and its vicissitudes often surrounding the too despised actress, whose domestic virtues, truth, honor, and family devotions, should, or would if properly known by the religious or the pure philanthropists of society, cause a statue to arise in perpetuation of those hallowed attributes. They have a remarkable sense of the performance of duty in their profession. When their path of duty is crossed by the private tribulations of this life, ere the balm of consolation is poured into the bleeding wound, the professional task assumed, be it either in the role that her skill must elicit the laugh or that of the serious and pathetic to cause the tear to flow, the character to draw forth these passions must be honestly acted. Whether it be conscientious duty, ambition, or love of applause, it is ever performed to the letter. Then comes the private consolation, or the true indulgence of sorrows, sensible only to the afflicted. One signal instance out of many more striking facts was the foregoing.

Mr. Macready was playing *Macbeth* at Drury Lane Theatre. Lady Macbeth was personated by an actress of high talent and great private excellence, who has received the approval of the best critics. The model lady and actress was in the act of entering upon the stage when she received a letter by a messenger of the theatre. She glanced at the superscription. She knew the handwriting too well. Its contents

## Theatrical Rambles of Mr. & Mrs. Greene, Charles Durang

instinctively struck the chords of her heart. A pallor of earthly nature crossed her expressive features; but imperious duty assumed the stern composure of her character and with appropriate mien and gait she entered on the scene, thrusting the unbroken sealed letter into her bosom. When the curtain fell on the end of the third act, which she ends, she hastily sought a private corner, burst open the fatal missive, and with agonized intensity perused its contents. A shriek of agony convulsed her frame and features; but, soon resuming a rigidity of aspect as of marble, she folded the letter up, and with a tearless eye resumed a stern composure.

Her friends accosted her, but she could not command an answer, but hurried to her dressing room. The curtain rose on the fifth act. She entered with her wonted composure, braced up for the occasion, and concluded Lady Macbeth with excellence, apparently abstracted from her domestic woe. That note imparted the fatal intelligence of her husband's death! He died a lunatic in an asylum. Her life, her love had been devoted to the alleviation of his mental sufferings, yet such had been her sense of duty, that her grief remained passive in perfect abeyance to nature's call till she had finished her professional labors. Then did her sorrows burst forth in streams of agony too great for her noble heart, and it sank in the struggle. She expired with the letter pressed to her lips.

An offer was now received from the Lafayette Theatre at New York, corner of Leonard and Canal streets, erected by Gen. Sandford (subsequently destroyed by fire in 1829). But, as the managers were mere speculators, making money out of the actors' labor with no intention of ever paying them, the company left the concern *en masse*.[2] Mr. Greene obtained his salary through stratagem and left immediately for Philadelphia, arriving there in the nick of time, while Mr. W. B. Wood was organizing his company for the New Arch Street Theatre (this in 1828).[3]

This *corps* was numerically strong and talented, consisting of Mr. and Mrs. Wood, William Rufus Blake and wife, Mrs. Maywood, Miss Southwell, J. M. Scott (alias Big Scott), William Isherwood, Mr. and Mrs. Roberts, William

*Theatrical Rambles of Mr. & Mrs. Greene*, Charles Durang

Duffy, Samuel Chapman (stage manager), and other minors of utility reputation.[4] The late James W. Wallack, Sen., was the first star of the season, engaged at $200 per night, with other little oddities of that sort to keep step with the times that the Quaker City at that period could not pay for. The consequence was, in a few weeks, an end of Wood's enterprise and final managerial reign. At this period all the theatres in Philadelphia changed hands every season and no salaries paid.[5]

In May, 1829, the Walnut Street Theatre was to let, when John Greene and Samuel Chapman became its lessees, with Mr. Edmonds as the treasurer,[6] who was a *quasi* manager, indeed, a *bona fide* one. This managerial association in a short time blew up in a financial flare up, the charges and insinuations adverse to the treasury department ending in a legal arbitration which acquitted the Chancellor of the Exchequer—*viz.*, Mr. Edmonds—the finale being the dissolving of the partnership. During its existence they had a numerous stock *corps* and innumerable stars. Mr. and Mrs. Wood were here. Madame Ferron and Mrs. Pearlman sang without attracting. A most excellent ballet *corps* was introduced. The ballet master, Mons. Leon, a fine *artiste* but quite as droll in his manner as clever in his dancing, was eternally plying his nasal organ with snuff. One night while executing a *pirouette* of many revolvements, he plied his nostrils with huge quantities of snuff to the amusement of the auditors.[7]

Old Mr. Joseph Jefferson was here for a few nights with all the Chapman family. Mr. William Warren, ex-manager, now very feeble in every physical faculty, combined with mental decay, having lost a fortune by rash advisers and broken in spirits, was here as a stock actor but seldom appeared. Herr Cline, the rope dancer, was also here with kindred other novelties, but all to no purpose. After every imaginable novelty had been exhausted, the season suddenly closed on July 29, 1829.[8]

Alterations of the Walnut Street Theatre were now suggested. During this vacation John Greene & Co. rented the Wilmington, Delaware, Theatre. But poor Greene, through misplaced confidence and trusting his managerial business to other hands, got largely in debt and finally be-

## Theatrical Rambles of Mr. & Mrs. Greene, Charles Durang

came a bankrupt, resigning all thoughts of continuing in the Walnut Street management. He honestly withdrew from its control without resorting to the State laws for relief, and honorably compounded with his creditors.

  The theatre in Albany was now on the eve of opening under the auspices of William Duffy & Co. Mr. Edwin Forrest was engaged, when the sensational Indian drama of *Metamora*[9] was to be produced. Mr. Duffy offered Greene and his wife an engagement, which they accepted.[10] Selling all their furniture in Philadelphia, where they had indulged the hope of being permanently settled, they departed for the capital of New York, where they enjoyed a pleasant time till August. "Still waters run smooth." So did it with W. Duffy till a controversy arose between Greene and Duffy about business, when the Greenes seceded from Mr. Duffy's *corps* and went to New York, where they received an engagement from Mr. Thomas Hamblin for the Bowery Theatre.[11]

  At this time Mr. Somerville, a Scotsman, an actor, and a tenor singer of a roving, energetic spirit, was drumming up a *corps* of comedians for a professional tour of the West Indies. He succeeded in filling his company with choice talent, for actors are ever on the wing of immigration.[12] The Greenes joined him, as did Mr. and Mrs. Southwell, Mrs. Wheatley, Miss Josephine Clifton, Messrs. A. W. Jackson, Charles Lehr (the celebrated painter), and other known talent.[13]

  This company set sail from New York for their destined sphere of action in September, 1830, with propitious gales. In a few days out, while gently gliding over the billows of old ocean, a violent storm arose, in the course of which a tremendous sea carried away all the starboard bulwarks, literally swept the decks, and waterlogged the vessel. This occurred in the latitude of the Bahamas. A kind Providence saved the dramatic *corps*. The gale exhausted and modified to gentle, favorable winds, jury masts rigged and needful repairs made, their lucky star guided their shattered bark in safety to the Danish Island of St. Thomas, a very important depot for the contraband trade with the adjacent isles. The governor of the island was quite an original in humorous ec-

## *Theatrical Rambles of Mr. & Mrs. Greene*, Charles Durang

centricities and proved a patron to the theatrical tourists.

West Indian *corps dramatique* was of a diversified texture. It was composed of jeweled-minds of both sexes, indulging in groups on the deck in pleasant chit-chat on perils past, of the present, and the future in the promised sunny lands they were then approaching. Thus being scattered over the brig's decks, the observer beholds under the lea of the long boat, with an old tattered sail as a protective awning against Sol's rays, a sea boudoir for Monsieur Barbière and Madame Hurtan, fine opera dancers, in cozy *tête à tête*, talking over professional matters with French volubility and their great future. Although they performed their *pas de deux* most admirably on the stage, they did not always step or execute their *entrechats* in harmony.[14]

Mr. Barbière subsequently returned to the United States and became a cotton planter near Memphis, Tennessee, where, like another Caleb Quotem[15] he employed his various accomplishments in cultivating a little cotton, teaching French, the violin, with dancing. He continued to live respectably and independently, and we should be glad to learn that he still lives and prospers, for he was a very good fellow.

In this *corps*, too, was A. W. Jackson, late lessee of the Wintergarden Theatre at New York, with his dark, expressive looks—at this period seeking with youthful ambition the laurels of the tragic muse, even in the heat of tropical climes its bubble reputation. Always silent, but observant of passing events, philosophizing on theatrical speculations, he had his tribulations of life, but made a lucky hit in rebuilding the burnt-down Bowery Theatre at New York in 1845. Thus he soon acquired an independence which his well-directed thrift has increased. His study of dramatic philosophy has been sound. Mr. Jackson now resides in Brooklyn.

Miss Josephine Clifton, then but a Tyro in Tragedy's leading strings, looked like another Miranda, a child of Nature, "an Eve of an enchanted Paradise," during this voyage with her majestic figure usually reclined with book in hand, like another Cleopatra, in her cribbed and confined state room, on a large covered trunk converted into a sofa. She was then a novice in the profession, but ever dwelling in

## Theatrical Rambles of Mr. & Mrs. Greene, Charles Durang

ethereal thoughts. She was the paragon of good nature. During the tremendous gale of three days the vessel had passed through did she lie in a state of composure in her berth, silent but thoughtful, as if in prayer, giving no sign of excitement. Mrs. Greene said, in speaking on this subject (as she shared the state room with her during this voyage), that Miss Clifton, although apparently calm throughout the storm, inward agonies of their approaching dissolution marked vividly her then beautiful girlish face! For all then felt that the mountainous roaring ocean would soon be their eternal sepulcher.

After the storm had ceased, Mrs. Greene said to Miss Clifton, "Josie, I saw plainly that you were frightened."

"Oh, yes!" she replied, quoting a few lines from Byron's *Childe Harold*, on the ocean:

'Twas a pleasing fear,
For I was, as it were, a child of thee,
And trusted to thy billows far and near,
And laid my hand upon thy name, as I do here.

There was a kindred bright gem on board, an artist of rare abilities and peerless mind, but of strange and eccentric habits, a genius of mark, as his work proclaims. This man was Charles Lehr. He was attached to the *corps* as scenic artist. His paintings were ever the admiration of professors and all persons of taste in the arts. As a colorist in the Venetian style he is without a rival, and wherever his works have been seen, the critical plaudits of *artistes* have followed.

The waters had penetrated the hatchways and the frail chests, and drenched the entire wardrobes therein. The panic that followed the opening of the trunks, discovering their injured state, can better be pictured to the professional mind than described. "It was confusion worse confounded."

The leading tragedian, taking out of the trunk his Romeo and Hamlet dresses, said, "Look here, Mr. Manager, I am a ruined actor; these two dresses cost me over $200. I can never use them again!"

The leading lady, in the same category, exclaims, "I, too, am ruined! Behold my tragedy robes of gold and silver embroideries, completely destroyed!"

*Theatrical Rambles of Mr. & Mrs. Greene*, Charles Durang

The stage jewelry spoiled, the satins and velvets saturated with salt water inevitably gone and past restoration, the despair of the performers, as well as that of manager Somerville, was complete. The latter's stock wardrobe had just been new made for him at New York by the great *costumier*, Andrew Jackson Allen (of eccentric memory), composed of his famous gold and silver leather, a very perishable article which no ingenuity can restore.[16]

**NOTES**

[1] *A Cure for the Heart Ache*, a comedy by Thomas Morton, was first produced at Drury Lane, January 10, 1797.

[2] The Lafayette season began September 29, 1827, when Mrs. Greene made her first New York appearance as Elvira in *Pizarro*.

[3] The Greenes were back in Philadelphia for the opening of the Walnut Street Theatre season, May 1, 1828. The new Arch Street Theatre opened November 1.

[4] Mrs. Maywood, born in Bath, 1793, made her New York debut at the Park Theatre, September 30, 1817, (as Mrs. H. A. Williams) and was unimpressive, but attained some popularity outside the city. She attracted attention from her portrayals of male characters. Married Robert Maywood, 1828, and performed for several years on the Western stages. William Isherwood, brother to the more famous scene painter at the Chestnut Street Theatre, was never an outstanding actor. He died in 1841 while a member of the Park Theatre company. James Roberts was noted for his Scottish roles and comic songs. He performed as low comedian for the Bowery, Chatham, Lafayette, and (last appearance, 1832) Richmond Hill Theatres. He died in 1833. William Duffy, a native of Albany, New York (b. 1801), was considered one of the best general actors in the country—tall, well proportioned, energetic, indefatigable, and with a remarkable memory. He first appeared at the Pearl Street Theatre in his native city, 1822. He erected the first Buffalo theatre, 1835.

[5] The Lafayette Theatre reopened December 24, 1828, with the Greenes as a part of the company for a season that

*Theatrical Rambles of Mr. & Mrs. Greene*, Charles Durang

lasted until mid-March. Activity continued again April 6, 1829. On the 11$^{th}$ a fire in an adjoining building caused the total destruction of the theatre. The Greenes were back in Philadelphia in May of that year.

[6] The Walnut Street Theatre was rebuilt in 1829. The first lessees were Black and Inslee. The Greenes were added to the company in February. This management closed April 14. The following day, Aaron J. Phillips opened the Arch Street Theatre and engaged the Greenes for a term that lasted until May 20. The Greene-Chapman-Edmunds group, known as the Commonwealth Company, opened the Walnut Street Theatre on May 27.

[7] Madame Ferron, born in London, 1797, was a brilliant singer of the Italian school, coming to America with an established reputation in Europe. But she failed to equal her reputation here because this country was overrun with musical artists. Her powerful and melodious voice was diminished by a lack of expressive grace and charm. Mrs. Pearlman, who appeared at the Park Theatre for the first time, July 22, 1828, was judged to be an accomplished singer but rarely came before the public. Mons. Leon had been ballet master for the French *corps de ballet* before being brought over for the opening of the Lafayette Theatre.

[8] Seiltanzer Herr Cline first appeared in America, May 12, 1828, at the Bowery Theatre in his feats on the elastic cord and remained unrivaled until the arrival of the Ravels.

[9] *Metamora,* by John Augustus Stone, was a prize-winning entry in a competition sponsored by Edwin Forrest.

[10] Duffy and Forrest opened their Albany season June 9, 1829.

[11] Hackett and Hamblin became lessees of the Bowery Theatre for the season of 1830-31, opening August 2. Ireland lists the Greenes as members of the company from the outset. *Julius Caesar* was put up, August 11, with Cooper as Antony, Hamblin as Brutus, Mrs. Greene as Portia; *The Tales of Calas,* August 13, with Mrs. Green as Mme. Calas; etc. By October 30 they had departed, presumably for the West Indies.

[12] Somerville was looked upon as a useful general actor,

*Theatrical Rambles of Mr. & Mrs. Greene*, Charles Durang

especially effective in Scottish characters.

[13] Mrs. S. Wheatley (nee Mrs. Williams, not to be confused with Mrs. Frederick Wheatley) of the London and Dublin theatres was added to the Park company, May 17, 1815. She is said to have had an ease, gayety, and truthfulness about her personations that won the admiration of all. Miss Clifton, born in New York about 1813, first appeared at the Bowery at age 18 as Belvidera in *Venice Preserved*. Her wealthy mother had given her excellent training so she was an instant success. "Her surpassing beauty of face and person, her youth and attitude, her fine voice and impressive action, commanded a success almost unprecedented for a debutante, and she soon became an acknowledged star of the first attraction," so sayeth Ireland. She retired as the wife of Robert Place, a New Orleans manager, 1846, and died there the following year. Charles Lehr worked as a scenic artist for various theatres around the country. He was at the Franklin, NYC, 1835; Cincinnati for a production of *Aladdin*, 1844; etc.

[14] Madame Francisquy Hutin (also Hurtan or Houton) first appeared at the Bowery, February 7, 1827, introducing the modern French school of dancing to the American stage. It is said that she first appeared in light and scanty drapery which floated in air during her *pirouettes*, liberally displaying her symmetrical proportions, which forced the ladies in the lower tier of boxes to abandon the house.

[15] Caleb Quotem was a character in *The Review, or The Wags of Windsor*, a farce by Colman the younger.

[16] Andrew Jackson Allen, actor and costumer, was probably the first to work in theatrical gold and silver leather accessories equal to European manufacture. An advertisement in the New York *Mirror* states that Allen was a fancy dressmaker and manufacturer of "unapproachable gilt and silver leather," patented in 1817 for "theatrical and equestrian dresses and trappings, ladies' ball slippers, albums, portfolios, pocketbooks, hat leathers, coach trimmings, in short every variety of fancy and ornamental work."

*Theatrical Rambles of Mr. & Mrs. Greene*, Charles Durang

## XVI.

A MERRY GOVERNOR — FAMILY DISPUTES — HOW TO SETTLE THEM — MONEY PLENTY — *BLACK-EYED SUSAN* — MISS CLIFTON WITHDRAWS, ETC.

Arrived at St. Bartholomew, a Swedish colony, to repair our wrecked losses and to lay in fresh provisions, the inhabitants learning that they were dramatic missionaries, insisted that the company should remain for a few evenings and give them a taste of their quality. The public hall was fitted up for the occasion and was filled nightly with delighted audiences and the manager made money. The company then sailed for St. Thomas, their original destination, where they arrived on the 20$^{th}$ of October and immediately commenced an active campaign with success, under the auspices of its facetious Danish Governor, a character in his way, a truly original one.

During the season some unpleasantness arose in the manager's domestic affairs which militated against the company's private reputation, as such events necessarily do, especially in small communities as exist in the West Indies or its towns. Mr. Somerville became very jealous of his wife, who was a very handsome woman but not an actress of any merit. There was no obvious reason for this Othello feeling, so strongly felt by the manager as was indulged in by the misled noble Moor who, like Caesar, required his wife to be above suspicion. The company was daily subjected to listen to their conjugal altercations at the rehearsals and at all places. This proved such an annoyance to their business on the stage that they took a firm objection to its continuance. At length a separation was agreed upon by the parties.

*Theatrical Rambles of Mr. & Mrs. Greene*, Charles Durang

The facetious Swedish Governor was called upon to act as umpire in the matter, at least to give his sage advice; to which he did in this prompt candid style: "Send she back by de same ship dat she comed in. Dat is de vey I did sent my vife, by dam." This to Somerville seemed sound advice. So the lady, Mrs. Somerville, was sent to New York by the same vessel that brought the company out only two weeks before.

The business proved excellent, the houses overflowed on every night of performance, which were only twice a week. On the occasion of a national holiday, a grand effort was made by the manager and the governor to give it all due attention. The latter being an enthusiastic amateur of music, the said governor had a national Danish chorus prepared for the festival, to which many rehearsals with the full band were devoted. The governor in *propria personae* arbitrarily leading the orchestra with baton in hand, the most learned musician in the orchestra was not permitted to say one word in suggestion of any passages to correct an error or to explain any difficulty, nor even to open his mouth unless by the command of his Excellency. And by the same tyranny he ruled the audience, not allowing the auditors to applaud. If a few applauded with their hands or canes, he would instantly turn round to the house from his leader's seat and, addressing the persons whence applause came, shaking his fiddle bow at them, cry out, "Turn out them sticks!" "Kick out these sticks, officers!" scolding in the most violent manner. While playing furiously a running forte passage of double semiquavers, his head shaking as violently as his elbow, he would vociferate to Sandy Jameson[1] (the regular leader of Somerville's orchestra) or some of the other musicians in the band to play "piano, Mr. Horn" or "forte, Mr. Double Bass," "*fortissimo*, Mr. Trumpet," "*pianissimo*, Cornet," alternating his musical oral directions to the band with his crabbed rebukes to the auditory if they attempted in the least to applaud.

Henry Southwell made his debut in the West Indies as Romeo, as he did everywhere else, at London in 1826 and in Philadelphia at the Old Chestnut Street Theatre in 1827 with éclat. He was a great favorite throughout the West Indies' circuit. He was born in Ireland, possessed a fine figure, a face of the Apollo cast, and was a very good actor, but very

## *Theatrical Rambles of Mr. & Mrs. Greene*, Charles Durang

chimerical in mind.

Mrs. Southwell, his wife, was a fair specimen of a strong-minded woman, of stately figure, and expressive blonde features, a most worthy, industrious, and virtuous wife, possessing all the qualities that should adorn and command the sex to worldly respect. Southwell died in 1841 at Antigua, West Indies.

The once celebrated Mrs. S. Wheatley (nee Mrs. Williams) was a member of the *corps*. In 1816 she was a most attractive star at the Old Park Theatre, New York, and at the Chestnut Street Theatre, Philadelphia, at the same period. As a comic actress she stood in the first class at that day, indeed without a peer. Now, alas! time had altered her person into a stumpy fat figure, the freshness of youth vanished, a loss to an actress that no talent can supply to public satisfaction. In short, she was *passée*.

Somerville had engaged her for the Lady Teasle, the high and comic range of comedy heroines; but he came to the very natural conclusion, for the aforesaid reasons, that he had a more agreeable and suitable lady in the company, of youthful aspect and charms, that would prove a more able and popular representative of those characters, recommending to her the important role of elderly dames, then vacant in his *corps*. To this proposition she demurred as offensive to her feelings. However, on reflection, she very reluctantly assented.

The feelings that govern the sensibilities of theatrical talent are very natural, but very erroneous. The old performers never look back to what they were in the glow of youth, but vainly think that they must forever be bathing in the perpetual waters of youth, with the idealisms of a Pons de Leon. How often have we sympathized with the aged performer when time has stolen on them so gradually and softly as to be unheeded, transforming their youthful lines of beauty and vivacity into rigid colors of dingy tints, while yet in seeming feeling of physical powers they imagine themselves the same at seventeen, fifty-five, or sixty. The faded laurels that are still embalmed on their brows, to their dim visions are as verdant as ever. The plaudits of their palmy days, however, now

*Theatrical Rambles of Mr. & Mrs. Greene*, Charles Durang

faint in sound, still tingle in their ears. Few of the profession grow old gracefully; so flattering is its homage to genius and talent that few escape the intoxicating draft or ever again regain a sober sense from popular illusions. It is human nature.

Miss Josephine Clifton had not an elevated position in this company, being only in her novitiate state, seeking the honors of the profession through gradual advancement; not positively playing minor parts, yet promisingly ascending from secondary roles to the first. Appearing but seldom, Josephine had the more time to study the nature of the character. Her slow progress at this time was more to be attributed to delicacy of health than from any other obstacle, having just recovered from a serious illness incidental to the climate. Miss Clifton possessed a most engaging disposition. Kind and inoffensive, she gained the good opinion of all social grades, from the elegant and the accomplished to the more humble.

After a very delightful season, the Thespians departed for the charming little island of Barbados, parting in sorrow with their hospitable St. Thomas friends and their odorous groves. At Barbados the same professional success and social receptions from every quarter of its rich plantations attended them. The principal town, Bridgetown, contained about twenty thousand inhabitants and had a very neat theatre for effective dramatic performances, which was attended by intelligent and polished audiences. The company played only twice a week, giving great satisfaction.

The audiences that attended the theatre were intelligent and polished through European intercourse, attentive to the sentiments of the dramas, of the moral inculcated, exacting of the performers in their duties, liberal of applause when deserved, but never vociferous yet appreciative of that acting that was judiciously delineated. The planters and gentry were models of generous hospitality. Their domiciles were ever open to the actors for refreshments and their servants were at their call. At all times and places the courtesies of life were freely extended; and if sickness attacked any one of the company, the inhabitants of the isle were ready at the bed side to relieve the sick. No death, however, occurred, although several were attacked with the endemic of the climate.

*Theatrical Rambles of Mr. & Mrs. Greene*, Charles Durang

At this time a large British fleet had rendezvoused at this island. The flagship was the celebrated *Shannon* frigate that captured our *Chesapeake* in the War of 1812. The officers and seamen of the fleet, when on shore, liberally patronized the theatre. They had amateur performances among the ship's company on board their several vessels. The Admiral of the fleet requested the manager to produce the nautical drama of *Black-Eyed Susan*.[2] The request seemed queer, as at this time a court martial was being held on board the *Shannon* on a seaman for a misdemeanor of a similar nature for which William was to suffer death in the drama.

In order to give an accurate representation of it, permission was given to the manager, with any of his company, to visit the *Shannon* and to be present at the court martial held on board at their pleasure. Accordingly, Mr. Somerville, Mr. Southwell (who was to play William), Mr. J. Greene, and Mr. Charles Lehr (the artist who was to paint the nautical scenery) attended as the stage officials who were necessary to its effective production. As may well be imagined, this visit was not very agreeable to two of them, from the war reminiscence of 1812, the victory of the *Shannon* over the *Chesapeake*.

Both Greene and Lehr were natives of Philadelphia and staunch republicans. Southwell was a true Irishman, alive to his country's wrongs, consequently a worshiper of the ever hallowed Star-Spangled Banner. While Somerville's worldly neutral proclivities were "anything by turns and nothing long." They were all, however, received with courtesy and treated like gentlemen of an enlightened profession.

The court martial held its session in the great cabin, which looked very imposing. Mr. Lehr took a facsimile sketch of this naval assemblage, with others about the ship. In this way a most graphic representation of the nautical part of the scenery was given. The trial scene of William for mutiny could not have been more perfectly delineated on the stage. It almost gave a real picture of a court martial, for several of the warrant officers and forty of the crew, in their respective uniforms and naval insignia, were seated and otherwise grouped on this mimic trial. The effect was admirable

*Theatrical Rambles of Mr. & Mrs. Greene*, Charles Durang

and the applause most enthusiastic, especially from the Admiral and his brilliant suite, who filled four boxes with ladies of the island, the boxes being tastefully decorated with naval and national devices by Charles Lehr.

Mrs. Greene played Susan, it being her first appearance since her recovery from sickness. Her reception was most enthusiastic, and so continued throughout the performance. So warm was public favor, that on her adieu she was affected even to tears. After the run of *Black-Eyed Susan* she took a benefit, selecting *Theresa; or, The Orphan of Geneva* and *Nature and Philosophy*. The house was an overflow. Tickets for choice seats sold at a Joe, or eight dollars, the then current value of the *Joehannes*.[3]

The Barbados season approaching its end, Miss Clifton withdrew and embarked for New York.[4] The next island proposed to be visited was Trinidad, but Mr. Somerville had now become so unpopular with the company that a majority of the leading talent refused to accompany him thither. Besides, that island was deemed very unhealthy. The Greenes receiving an offer from a small select *corps dramatique* playing at Demerara, resolved to join that association, accompanied by Mr. and Mrs. Hutchings and Mr. Thomas Lennox, who seceded from Somerville's *corps*.[5] The manager offered them the most liberal terms to remain, but without avail. He had become obnoxious to them. So they organized and set sail for the colony of Demerara, a possession of Great Britain, which they reached in six days, regretting that they had to leave that "modern Eden," as they called Barbados.

The theatrical company was not very good and numerically small, yet the theatre was filled every night of performance, the audiences ever delighted with them. A house of a thousand dollars was a common occurrence. Mrs. Greene's benefit gave a receipt of sixteen hundred dollars. Tickets sold easily at two dollars each.

The population being small, and its patronage soon exhausted, it was deemed good policy to change their base of operations; so the itinerants set sail for the island of St. Vincent, one of the most elevated and rugged of the Caribbees. Kingston, the capital, had a population of all races known to

*Theatrical Rambles of Mr. & Mrs. Greene*, Charles Durang

ethnography, amounting to about eight thousand. Here they procured a large building wherein to erect a theatre, and with the assistance of some amateurs they were able to cast fully some popular plays. Thus strengthened, they performed for four months to full houses, tickets two dollars. The English population, with the Creoles of the place, evinced great spirit in their support. Col. Hardy, the commandant, allowed the band at the garrison to furnish the orchestra with the necessary music. The leader was a very capital musician, an excellent violinist, and could effectively arrange the parts for songs and concerted music. The band consisted of twenty-five, most of them solo players. They served to keep so isolated a place alive and the thoughtful mind from the sorry state of *ennui* or depression. Here the *corps* made money.

## NOTES

[1] Sandy Jameson may have been A. Jameson, leader of the concert orchestra at Vauxhall and musical director at the Chatham Theatre for the season of 1843-44. He was a violinist. In his memoirs, Leman remarked, "If he fiddles in another world, I am sure he will fiddle none but the liveliest tunes." He lived to the ripe old age of 90.

[2] *Black-Eyed Susan* was a melodrama by Douglas Jerrold.

[3] *Theresa* was a melodrama by John Howard Payne. *Nature and Philosophy* was written by "a Virginian" and published in 1830.

[4] Miss Clifton appeared at the Bowery Theatre on her return from the West Indies, September 21, 1831, as Belvidera to Hamblin's Jaffier in *Venice Preserved.*

[5] Hutchings, from the Philadelphia Theatre, had appeared at the Park, July 16, 1828, as Patrick in *The Poor Soldier.* Durang considered him a singer of little merit. He made no impression and shortly returned to England. Lennox was to follow this tour with appearances at the St. Charles and Mobile Theatres. Ludlow called him "a rather clever actor in Scottish characters."

*Theatrical Rambles of Mr. & Mrs. Greene*, Charles Durang

## XVII.

A VOYAGE TO OLD ENGLAND — AMERICAN ACTORS ON THE BRITISH STAGE — JOSEPHINE CLIFTON IN LONDON — A COUNTRY FAIR — STAGE COACH TRAVEL — AN ENGLISHMAN'S OPINION OF AMERICA.

The Greenes had for a long time decided to visit the fatherland, Old England. This wish was more professionally impressive from its being the land of Shakespeare and the numerous authors of the English drama, as well as the birth places of the most eminent of that drama's ablest illustrators from its fascinating mirror, the stage.

The motive of the native American actors, such as the Greenes, for visiting Europe was to see and judge for themselves. About that time America had begun to pay back with interest the obligations she owed to the mother country for the original stacking of her theatrical boards; for the old saw, "Whoever reads an American book?" was well answered by Wiley and Putnam, when their nationality was wounded through certain amputations on our literature by the publication of a catalogue of our native authors at London that proudly rebuked the ungenerous sneer. Their metaphysicians imbibed great and leading principles from our political justice and international axioms, and are largely indebted to the writings of Jonathan Edwards, the New England controversialist, and other eminent writers. Channing has furnished a laudable tone of charitable mildness in theology, and the moral freshness that gives zest to Emerson's essays is unequaled. In the words of an English author, "They smell of the pine forest; they have the verdure and freshness of their vast prairies; they make us feel that there is a peculiar tone of intellect for America as well as for the mother country."

*Theatrical Rambles of Mr. & Mrs. Greene*, Charles Durang

Judge Cooper has ably illustrated the pure principles of political economy with the warmest applause of British writers on similar subjects, while our novelists are Washington Irving, Cooper, Paulding, Bird, and others, not forgetting our brilliant females who form a galaxy of poetic and didactic writers and who have passed the critical reviews of the orthodox literary journals and magazines of Europe.

About 1831 and the ten following years, the London actors commenced their extraordinary transit to New York as stars, consequent upon the decline of the two national theatres of England. And this wild immigration culminated in the season of 1837 and 1838 in an insane struggle between the managements for extravagant expenditure for stars, operatic plays, pageantry, etc., attending to their ultimate ruin. After this nomadic star immigration of English stock actors, the tide began to turn and native American talent reciprocated the visits. This was deemed a bold attempt of untried histrionic talent, as all acting unweighed in the London balance of dramatic merit, either English or of any other country, was not current coin, but mere shinplasters.

William Pelby, manager of the Tremont Theatre, Boston, and Miss Josephine Clifton attempted the London boards despite prejudice and prophecies of failure. Pelby appeared at the Drury as Hamlet, and afterwards Brutus in Payne's play of that name for the benefit of the Philanthropic Society. Miss Clifton, on her return to New York from Barbados, appeared as Imogene in *Bertram* at the Bowery. She was the first American actress by birth who visited London as a star! She made her debut at Drury Lane as Belvidera in *Venice Preserved* in October, 1834, and afterwards played one of the spirits in *Manfred* with Macready. Neither of them were deemed prophets in their own land. Of Mr. Pelby, Mr. Cowell sarcastically remarked, "He is the first who lived exclusively on *amor patria* capital." He had a clumsy figure, rather a good face, and a very peculiar, husky voice. He could boast of originality of style, for he was unlike any one else or any thing the author intended.

Then followed in 1836, Edwin Forrest and Yankee Hill, both with success; Hackett, Mrs. Mowatt, and Mr. E. L.

*Theatrical Rambles of Mr. & Mrs. Greene*, Charles Durang

Davenport in 1846, also a success; Mr. J. Murdoch and Mrs. Bowers, followed by many others who now in 1863 go across the "herring pond" as often and with as much facility as they used to travel from state to state.

The removal of legal restraints in England on the acting drama has multiplied theatres of a minor character there *ad infinitum*. America and London are now on an equal footing, exchanging performers and novelties. So that mystery is solved and Yankee theatrical talent as well as all other talent stands co-ordinate with that of Europe; nay, getting a little ahead of our transatlantic cousins.

Mr. and Mrs. John Greene having acquired the means to take a tour to England, and being without any family to anchor their affections at home, they set sail on the first of August, 1831,[1] in the English ship *St. Vincent*, commanded by Captain Thomas, as jolly a mariner as ever stepped a vessel's deck. With a succession of fair gales they reached the Irish channel in fifty-five days (a tedious passage when compared with the present steam rapidity), where their reception was a bouncing gale of wind and rain. Under close reefed topsail the ship beat up the channel towards the Mersey, on which river is situated the city of Liverpool. The gale was frightful, with mountainous chopping seas making successive breaches over the rolling ship. They were fearful of the ship being cast about or going into stays if she should fail to claw off the land; and if so, her fate would prove inevitable and she must bilge on the rocky coast of Ireland or on the iron coast of Wales. At last they entered the chops of the channel, rescued from an ocean's burial, and after three days calm sailing arrived in Liverpool.

When our theatric tourists entered Liverpool, the theatre was a first attraction to their eager curiosity, at which temple a number of the London stars were then acting to very fine houses—Messrs. Vandenhoff, Blanchard, James S. Browne, Mackay, Miss Ellen Tree, Mrs. W. West, etc. Their performances, with their artistic details so well carried out, pleased them much. Veterans as they were, they could well appreciate the cleverness of their English professional brethren.

After a brief sojourn at Liverpool, they commenced

*Theatrical Rambles of Mr. & Mrs. Greene*, Charles Durang

their tour through the interior of England, gradually progressing towards the great metropolis. At one of the quaint old villages in Britain's Isle a fair was being, held with all the ancient customs. The Greenes, passing through it on the eve, were induced to stay for a day to enjoy those sports they had heard and read about. They put up at one of the old-fashioned inns, having the quaint sign of the "Hart and Trumpet." After a plain breakfast, not one of American profusion, Mr. and Mrs. Greene ushered forth to enjoy the passing fun and sports of the village fair, a novel scene to them and one which they had often assisted to represent on the stage in English dramas.

 The principal street ascended a hill. This was lined with stalls, displaying gaudy and gay articles of dry goods, such as handkerchiefs, ribbons, trimmed caps, and every variety of fantastic attire. Here the rustic maiden smiles and with innocent coquetry cajoles her beau into making her presents. Others were loaded with cheap toys. The penny trumpet and toy drums seemed favorite articles, nor did they let them be useless ones, for such a squeaking and drumming was seldom heard. Pork pies and gilt gingerbread were in abundance, while a portion of the ground was set aside for the cattle market, where were huddled cows that lowed continually, sheep that bleated, and pigs that squeaked. And shows of various kinds, from the fat lady to the Albinos, wild beasts, a canvas theatre, etc.

 On the wooden balcony fronting the green was a young lady with very black hair and very pink cheeks who danced with the clown incessantly. Gypsies were encamped near, and the never-failing sergeant with happy family paraded to the lively music, while they were followed up by a regiment of ragged little boys who in good time served to fill up his Majesty's army, William IV. It was a lively time.

 The next day our tourists departed in the coach for Birmingham, the center of England. The country folks were away by the dawn and the caravans, with their exhibitions, the show folk, etc., were on the road thither with the mail coach. This procession of the menageries, the pedestrians with packs on their backs, the showmen in their vans, the

## Theatrical Rambles of Mr. & Mrs. Greene, Charles Durang

dashing sergeant with his recruits in smock frocks, the gypsies bringing up the rear with their tawny faces and half Oriental dresses made a most droll but cheerful traveling train. Mrs. Greene had an inside seat in the coach from the window of which she gazed to the last upon heterogeneous procession; and had custom allowed it, she would have taken an outside seat with Mr. Greene, not only to have indulged in the personal sight, but to have viewed the country as they passed.

The approach to the stopping place, Birmingham, was pleasingly announced by the guard playing with much skill, "Home, Sweet Home" on the Kent bugle. Traveling in the English public coaches, for elegance and comfort, was probably the most agreeable mode that can be imagined, but it was very expensive. Railroads have superseded all this.

Their arrival at the hotel caused quite an excitement. The travelers were surrounded with a mob of curious persons with all the inquiring proclivities of the Yankee nation. They thought it really very anti-English. The next morning our tourists were beset with that very annoying English custom at hotels—after having paid your bill, the English eleemosynary hotel system of compensating servants, who beset you on every side as the traveler is about to depart with "Please remember the waiter," "The Chambermaid," "Boots," "Porter," "Cook," etc. This is an intolerable nuisance and should be abolished.

Recently, the host charged such exactions in the traveler's bill, but the practice is still to pay the servants, who receive no wages for their services, but give a premium for their places. Our tourists thought, "Being in Rome, we must do as Rome does," and laughingly handed over the donations of a shilling or so to the vehement beggars, stepped into the London coach, and away the travelers went merrily to the notes of the guard's bugle, when they arrived in a few hours in one of those dense fogs so frequent in the English climate, which destroyed the coveted view of the remarkable approaches to this mammoth metropolis. But dim as it was, they saw Hyde Park corner, and as the coach threaded its way through the narrow, crooked streets of this huge place, the vast concourse of promenaders, like the ebbing and flowing

*Theatrical Rambles of Mr. & Mrs. Greene*, Charles Durang

tide of a mighty river, attracted their wonder.

They put up for the night at the old "Bull and Mouth," often mentioned in Colman's comedies and established as a traveler's inn from the earliest days of London civilization. On the following day they sought and obtained comfortable lodgings in that well-known quarter of the city, Tottenham Court Road, where from time immemorial the respectable citizen of small means—the author, the poet, and artists—generally resided since the times even of its rural aspect. It is now past its suburban sphere and compactly forms the city, as Spring Garden does Philadelphia proper.

The taking of ready furnished lodgings and being furnished with meals, *ad libitum*, in the chambers is a very comfortable arrangement of living at London. Certainly the only mode of cheap living! The guardian of these domiciles is always a neatly clad landlady, the prototype of her prim clean household.

The ignorance of the lower classes of England on American subjects of social habits, the lineage or ace from whence they spring, are but imperfectly understood, even with the more educated it would seem. About thirty years ago many thought all Americans were Indians, or Negroes, or otherwise of an *outré* mixture of colors not approaching to any trace of their civilization. While journeying in one of their coaches, Mrs. Greene called the attention of her husband to a pleasing view, strongly resembling a spot in America. A woman passenger started at the remark, and keenly surveying both of them with curiosity and astonishment, exclaimed, "Be ee Mericans? for sartain?"

"Yes, ma'am," was the reply.

This somewhat puzzled her perceptions and, fearing she may have offended some superior persons, began in her Yorkshire dialect to apologize and asked them, "How come ee to speak English so soon?"

On Mrs. Greene informing her that all Americans spoke English, she stammered out fresh excuses and, raising her specs, examined the brownish cast of their faces; for their residence in the West Indies had given their skins a tawny tint, and the long sea voyage had imparted an additional

*Theatrical Rambles of Mr. & Mrs. Greene*, Charles Durang

bronze cast. Greene especially had very dark eyes, hair, and skin, which bothered the woman sorely.

"Well, I see ye is near white, and we larn't ee is all black as our coal, we wully air on e'er 'eds!" The woman's surprise was great.

## NOTES

[1]Durang is in error here. The Greenes must have left for England late in 1830.

*Theatrical Rambles of Mr. & Mrs. Greene*, Charles Durang

## XVIII.

A STRANGE VISITOR — THE GREAT BARE BACK RIDER — REUNITED WITH HERR CLINE — BEARDED INDIANS — VISITING THE THEATRES — T. P. COOKE — A REAL TRAGEDY, ETC.

About a week after the Greenes had been located in their London lodgings, the maid of the house announced to them that a man below desired to see them. They desired the servant to show the person up little stairs, when a shabbily-dressed individual, out at the elbows, patches on the knees, and slipshod, made his entree. A more forlorn and distressed piece of humanity could scarcely be found among civilized beings. His disheveled hair, neglected beard, dirty face and hands, and crownless hat, formed a wretched *tout ensemble.* This object the Greenes could not recognize at all.

After a pause he addressed Mrs. Greene, "You do not know me, madam? Yet you knew me once in another land, when Fortune showered gold over me and the applause of the American people echoed nightly in thunders on my novel acts of horsemanship! I was once the idol of the public. I am now an English vagrant. Do you now know me?"

The Greenes at once exclaimed, "Gracious Heavens! James Hunter, the once celebrated equestrian, who made his debut in Philadelphia at the Walnut Street Circus in the astounding feat of riding on the bare back of a steed without saddle or bridle!"

"The dame person," said Hunter with a sickly smile. "You did not know me, yet I am dressed in character now, for I am playing a different part."

*Theatrical Rambles of Mr. & Mrs. Greene*, Charles Durang

Poor Hunter further attempted an explanation of his degraded plight but it was quite obvious how it occurred. He flattered himself with a speedy restoration to health, to the exercise of his wonted powers and to riches; but all the symptoms of consumptive dissolution were marked on his face and body—the sunken eye, the hectic flush, the hollow cough, and the wasted flesh were only harbingers of Death's speedy dart. What a change from the time they first saw him! He was the first equestrian who rode on the bare back of a horse, which gave a wild, untamed look to the steed, as if he had just been caught on the prairies. It was a miraculous feat! Being the first who rode thus, as a consequence he made a fortune. Being a handsome and graceful little figure of a man, and youthful, the women adored him and the men lionized him. But through a weak mind and dissipated habits he lost all. Other riders were found in plenty to execute the same performances and he fell like Lucifer to rise no more.[1]

After some conversation on the past, the present and the future, Hunter took his leave. "Alas! poor gentleman. He looked not like the ruins of his youth, but like the ruin of those ruins." His exit left the Greenes lost in wonder, suggesting to each other what they could do to alleviate his tribulations, when the maid servant returned with a dirty card on which was written with a pencil, "Please lend me a shilling." Mr. Greene immediately enclosed a small sum of money in an envelope to him. They neither saw nor heard from him more, but they heard from others soon after that he was gone to another and a better world where his perturbed spirit we hope has found eternal rest.

Gradually their American friends discovered their whereabouts and established a most agreeable association, when they removed to a place opposite the Coburg Theatre, a very pleasant and lively location. Here were found as next door neighbors their old friend Herr Cline, the rope performer, with his father and mother, which rendered their subsequent sojourn in London very agreeable. The extension of their acquaintance among the profession caused them to pass many pleasant social hours.

All this time their West Indian guineas were oozing out by degrees in dear Londontown. Greenes was offered en-

*Theatrical Rambles of Mr. & Mrs. Greene*, Charles Durang

gagements, but he objected, fearful of a failure that might affect his native reputation; for he had gained it from the best critic of his native land, who acknowledged: "Many were the Dennis Bulgrudderys, both in Europe and America. He had seen them all, but none of them were fit to hold a candle to Greene." Johnstone (the father of the late Mrs. James Wallack) was the beau ideal of the Major O'Flahertys[2] and characters of that class. He looked and was the Irish gentleman of the Jonah Barrington school. And Power, for the valets, was the thing itself; the insolence and coxcombry of such parts he hit off delightfully on the stage, though the same style of manner made him exceedingly objectionable in a greenroom. There he was the very personification of hauteur. During his engagement in Baltimore he was invited to a party, the same evening having to play Murtoch Delaney in the *Irishman in London* and Dr. O'Toole in the *Irish Tutor*.[3] He got the prompter to ring up a quarter of an hour before the time. Not satisfied with that, he cut out all scenes in which he was not concerned, with the exception of those where the actors rebelled, and during them he stood at the side of the scenes telling them to hurry on. And during the scenes with himself he would tell them to talk faster, thus insulting both actors and audience. "But Greene excelled all; for the Teagues, the Murtochs, and the Looneys, the boys, the genuine, unsophisticated Paddy, with the natural genius for cutting canals and drinking whiskey, give me the native American-Irishman, John Greene."[4]

Madame Celeste at this time was playing her *ad captandum*, Melanga, of *The Wept of the Wish-ton-Wish*, quite a novelty to the Londoners, and drew astonishingly. *Victorine* was also played at the Adelphi, and was most powerfully cast, thus: Yates, Jack Reeves, O. Smith (the great demon actor), Mrs. Fitzwilliam and Mrs. Daley, all appearing in the piece.[5] Mr. and Mrs. Greene had the pleasure of visiting Covent Garden on the occasion of Miss Fanny Kemble's first impersonation of Mrs. Haller, in *The Stranger*—Mr. Charles Young as the Stranger, Mr. Warde as the Baron, Mr. Bently as Solomon, Mr. Meadows as Peter, Miss Goward (now Mrs. Keeley) as Charlotte, a cast of excellence.

*Theatrical Rambles of Mr. & Mrs. Greene*, Charles Durang

Miss Kemble's first engagement at Covent Garden enabled the proprietors to pay off a debt of £13,000. We cannot believe in any decline of the drama while her sister arts are actively progressive. In this faith we are unshaken. Whether the excellence of such actors as Garrick, Kemble, E. Kean, and the Melpomene of the British stage, Mrs. Siddons, etc., were buried with them, is of course a mooted point. The vista of time has given grandeur to their names and actions, but it is the nature of public admiration to look back upon all popular persons as unapproachable. It is first impressions that rule as a law of nature.

The vocal performances were very popular, as they were participated in by Mr. and Mrs. Wood, and W. Farren playing Justice Woodcock in *Love in a Village*, but the greatest attraction was T. P. Cooke as William, in *Black-Eyed Susan*. In that character he surpassed everything of the kind. As a melodramatic performer he was peerless; his fine muscular figure, combined with the graces of attitude, tended to qualify him eminently for those creatures of melodramatic imagination—the vampires, the Frankensteins, etc. The theatricals of England engaged the attention of the Greenes more than any other objects, as that subject took them to Albion's shores.

They were much amused with an Indian piece at one of the minor theatres called the *Long Rifle*. The characters were in the Indian costume, the savages wearing large whiskers and beards. Yet a very remarkable thing in this race is the absence or the scanty supply of beards or hair on their cheeks and chins. They heard the Indian names rather queerly pronounced, quite contrary to our aboriginal dictionary— Potomac as if writ Pot-o-mak; Powhatan, Pow-hat-an.

The salaries seemed very low in comparison with those given in America. A lady and gentleman of the profession, whose acquaintance they made, received only seven dollars a week as their combined salaries. Is it a wonder, then, that so many emigrate? Mrs. Hamblin was in England and had engaged several performers for her husband's theatre in the Bowery.

The Greenes were offered an engagement at Edinburgh, but as there had been an exciting event in amateur

## Theatrical Rambles of Mr. & Mrs. Greene, Charles Durang

theatricals that they were fearful might be prejudicial to the interests of public theatres, they declined. The facts were as follows:

A certain Lord, about 1835, married the young and beautiful daughter of a baronet. She was of a light, volatile disposition, vain and coquettish. A circumstance which pained her husband very much happened about a twelve month after their union. A young military officer, who had been once upon familiar terms with the lady, came to visit her at her house. His gay and thoughtless humor made him a great favorite. His attentions to her were observed, and displeased his Lordship. Major Blake would take no hint from any one, and it was thought that her Ladyship secretly encouraged his attentions from a desire to torment her jealous husband. His lordship, meanwhile, said nothing to either, but one evening, walking through the garden that fronted the mansion, he observed the Major standing on the terrace in front of the house, talking to his lady. He hurried to the spot, but ere he got there the Major had bade her *adieu*.

Some weeks elapsed, when the arrival of fresh visitors appeared to divert his Lordship from the terrible thoughts that played on his mind. To vary the diversions of the party, it was proposed that amateur performances of theatricals should be got up at the mansion. The Lord readily consented. A large hall in the mansion was fitted up in fine style. The play selected was *Othello*, which was rehearsed. The cast was curiously enough arranged. His Lordship was the Moor, her Ladyship was Desdemona, and the Major was cast as Cassio.

The piece went off with great *éclat* until the last scene, when Othello, overwhelmed with jealous rage, smothers his young wife as she lies in bed. This part the Lord, wrought to desperation by his fit of jealousy, performed so admirably and so naturally as to excite the wonder and admiration of all his guests. But imagine the horror and consternation when it was discovered that it was no piece of acting that his lordship had gone through, but a reality. The Lady had in fact been murdered! A coroner's inquest was held upon the body and a verdict of "accidental death" was ren-

*Theatrical Rambles of Mr. & Mrs. Greene*, Charles Durang

dered, which saved his Lordships life and reputation. From that time he became an altered man. The mansion was shut up and his Lordship went to the Continent to reside, where he died. His remains had just been brought home.

## NOTES

[1]Hunter became a reigning attraction at the Richmond Hill amphitheatre following his debut there on 1823, billed as the greatest bareback rider in the world. He left for England in 1829. His death came in 1839.

[2]Major O'Flaherty was a character in *The West Indian*, a comedy by Richard Cumberland.

[3]*The Irishman in London*, a farce by William Macready, first performed in America, June 5, 1793, at the John Street Theatre. *The Irish Tutor*, a farce by R. Butler, a piece popular with stage Irishmen, first performed in New York, Mar. 11, 1823, at the Park.

[4]Teague was a character in Thomas Knight's *Honest Thieves*; also in Robert Howard's farce, *The Committee*. Murtoch Delany from *The Irishman in London*; Looney M'Twolter from *The Review* by Colman the younger.

[5]*The Wept-Wish-Ton-Wish* was a burletta by W. B. Bernard, first brought out in America by Celeste at the Bowery, December 11, 1834. *Victorine; or, I'll Sleep on It*, a drama by J. B. Buckstone, was introduced to New York audiences, February 14, 1832, and became very popular.

*Theatrical Rambles of Mr. & Mrs. Greene*, Charles Durang

## XIX.

ARRIVAL HOME — NOSEY PHILLIPS — DRILLING THE SUPES — MISS WARING — STINGY GATES — ABOUT *THE HUNCHBACK* — A NICE LITTLE FIGHT — GREENE ARRESTED, ETC.

Homeward bound! Our travelers took their last meal in England at the house of Herr Cline, and on the same day embarked on board the good ship *Samuel Robertson* bound to New York. Whether actors are more unlucky at sea than other professional folks may be a mooted point, but their mishaps have been many and severe. The Charleston, S.C., company of comedians, after the burning of the Richmond Theatre in 1811, were cast away in a snow storm on False Cape on their passage from Norfolk to the South and only escaped with their lives. Many remember Powers' fate in the steamer *President*. Mr. Finn perished in a burning steamer on Long Island Sound in 1840, almost in sight of his "home, sweet home." The last time he ever acted was on January 8, in the same year, at the Chestnut Street Theatre for Madame Celeste's benefit. Theophilus Cibber was drowned in crossing the Irish Channel going from England to Dublin.

The Greenes left the Downs in January, 1831. The passage lasted a tedious and most boisterous forty-two days, five of which the ship hove to, they were without an observation, and there were snow storms prevailing nearly all the time. The gleams of a setting sun were eventually seen, however, in the dark west, and the welcome cry of "land ho!" was at length heard. Soon a New York pilot boat ran down upon the weather bow and they had a pilot in command of their quarter deck ere the night set in.

## *Theatrical Rambles of Mr. & Mrs. Greene*, Charles Durang

The ship anchored near the Battery and our travelers soon landed on their native soil, after an absence of two years, with the instinctive love that men of every clime feel for their country. They exclaimed, "Welcome, my own, native land!" As they landed the weather suddenly changed to an eastern hail storm. They cast a farewell look on their old ship, weather-beaten as she was, minus her bowsprit and fore-top-mast. Still they felt an interest in her from old associations. They reached a Bowery omnibus sleigh near Bowling Green and in it wended their way to their old lodgings near the Bowery Theatre.

When the Greenes arrived from their English trip the Chatham Theatre was open under the management of Moses Phillips, better known in dramatic circles as Nosey Phillips, a cognomen given by his fellow actors from his large aquiline nose and a propensity he had of nosing out other people's business. Greene and wife received an engagement at this theatre.[1] Among the performers was Mr. Daniel Marble, then unknown to that fame which afterwards crowned him with laurels, and had not death interfered he would have amassed a large fortune by his Yankee impersonations. In the Chatham Theatre he was filling the role of tragic heroes. He was an excellent comic actor and a good, generous-hearted man.[2] Mr. and Mrs. Charles Thorne were also members, and their merits and talents were then rising into notice.

The theatres in New York were poorly heated. One very bitter, cold night a tragedy was being played wherein supernumeraries as soldiers were busily employed. Greene, not having anything especially to do, was politely requested to arrange the supernumeraries for the court scene. At the time of this request Greene was standing before a fire, twisting a sword in his hand, and this made the blade red hot with the fire. Some of the performers asked him what he was doing that for.

"Oh, only to keep my hands warm on the stage, where I have to be in the next act," was the reply.

"Ha! ha! ha! a very good joke," said one of the inquirers.

Greene arranged the supers on the stage and up went the curtain on the scene. While the principal characters were

*Theatrical Rambles of Mr. & Mrs. Greene*, Charles Durang

acting in the front of the stage, a ludicrous confusion took place amongst the supers at the back and sides. Greene, in directing them to take certain positions in the scene, played a prank by passing their rear lines and touching each super on the leg with his hot sword, as if ordering them severally to take some particular position. The men became restless and danced like bears on a hot griddle. Greene, as if ignorant of the cause, doubled his zeal in arranging them. Some ran off the stage. Others lifted up their feet alternately, like chickens going to roost, standing on one leg at a time, while others swore vengeance on the captain of the supers *pro tem*. The best of the joke was the gallery boys, who made game of the supers always on seeing their confusion, without knowing the cause hissed and hooted the awkward squad. The scene was consequently destroyed and that favor was never requested of Greene afterwards.

The houses were well filled every night, yet without any assignable cause the theatre suddenly closed. At this juncture Greene received an invitation from Messrs. Duffy, Jones, and W. Forrest, then the lessees of the Arch Street Theatre in Philadelphia, to play a round of Irish characters with them. This offer he accepted, while Mrs. Greene received one from Mr. T. Hamblin, to act in the Bowery.[3] When Greene's benefit came off at the Arch Street Theatre, Mrs. Greene, by the permission of Mr. Hamblin, went on to Philadelphia to perform for her husband's benefit. The piece selected was the popular drama of *Presumptive Evidence*.[4] Greene made a great hit in the part of Price Kinchel. Indeed it was a most masterly piece of acting.

Mrs. Greene returned the next day to her situation at the Bowery. She had been cast for Portia in the *Merchant of Venice* but being absent two days, and that by the permission of the manager, the part was transferred to Miss Waring, then a very promising young actress, who arose to very high honors subsequently in the profession. She is the present Mrs. James Wallack. No doubt the occasion was seized upon to place the young lady in Mrs. Greene's place. This only serves to show that an actress should never leave off her slippers till she is dome with them or some person will make them fit.

*Theatrical Rambles of Mr. & Mrs. Greene*, Charles Durang

The great Fanny Kelly (for there were three great Misses Kelly) received a very flattering offer to visit America. She declined to do so, for, said she, "If I leave my slippers in the London green room, some one will soon slip into them."

Mr. Hamblin now got up the popular drama of the *Rent Day*, playing Martin Heywood himself; Toby, George Jones; Bullfrog, W. Gates.

Gates was one of the greatest favorites that ever trod the old Bowery boards. He had made a great hit as Jem Bags. Who can ever forget his appointment for "down by the pump." The b'hoys of the Bowery thought him beyond immortality. After he threw off this mortal coil, his noisy patrons would hardly credit the fact till they saw him quietly inurned. His obsequies were a public demonstration. By his fellows he was nicknamed "Stingy Gates." He was a very quiet actor, yet it is doubtful whether he was entitled to that great merit claimed for him. The truth is that full one-half of those actors called good or superlative were made so by being placed in good parts. Fine parts play themselves, bad ones have to be made by the ingenuity of the performer.

Mrs. Hamblin, an excellent actress in those days, was the Rachel, and Miss Waring was Polly. During the summer of this season the Greenes seceded and went with John Barnes, who had withdrawn from the Old Park in the summer of 1832 and established himself at the Richmond Hill Theatre.[5] The corps was a strong one. Jacob Woodhull became the stage manager, having left the Park where he had long been a laborer. There were also Mr. and Mrs. Hilson, John Henry Clarke, J. M. Field (or Straws), Dan Marble, Mr. Phillips, Mr. and Mrs. Greene, Mr. Charles Young (the dashing widower), and Mrs. Duff, the talented pretty widow.

During this season the handsome Young, whose locks were now grown gray, contrived to make Mrs. Duff, the great tragedienne, accept his hand in marriage. And after some negotiation the nuptial ceremonies were duly solemnized, first by an Episcopalian clergyman, then at the lady's request by a Catholic priest, she being always a strict communicant of this church. But she never lived with Young one minute after the marriage. It was truly a most strange freak in her, and can

*Theatrical Rambles of Mr. & Mrs. Greene*, Charles Durang

only be explained by supposing that she was given to moments of hallucination.

This company, composed of all the New York favorites, first-class performers in every line, made a most signal failure. The reasons were many and potent for this result. The theatre, built by Richard Russell, was out beyond Varick Street, then a poor suburb of the city. The times were commercially out of joint. And to end all, the cholera broke out frightfully and put all to flight. Mr. Jacob Woodhull died by the disease, being about 40 years of age.

The *Hunchback* was brought out here with a good cast; Hilson as Master Walker; Modus, Mr. Clarke; Field played Stephen; Mrs. Barnes was the Julia and played it well; Mrs. Hilson as Helen was also excellent. The beautiful play was first produced in America at the Arch Street Theatre in Philadelphia for Duffy's benefit. It was brought out in a hurry, studied from Saturday to Monday and only one fair rehearsal was had for it. Of course the words were committed to memory but the characters of the drama were not digested. Therefore it was imperfectly understood, yet it pleased the few persons that witnessed it.

A similar fate attended it at the Richmond Hill Theatre in 1832. There being but one copy of the play, the actors engaged in it copied out their respective parts. It was only cast on Saturday and was played on the Monday following. It gave infinite satisfaction. The Press was unanimous in its praise, eulogizing that which should have met their condemnation. The performers performed a feat of great study but, after the words are memorized, the main labor of an actor is to study the nature of the character, and if he has not seen it acted before it becomes an effort of mind wherein genius directs the player in its true delineation. The piece was not truly understood until the Kembles developed its beauties in the following season. And although admired by people of taste and literature, it failed to draw houses until the Kembles acted in it.

A fatality seemed to attend all of Sheridan Knowles' excellent plays when first produced here. W. B. Wood, in his personal recollections of the stage, often speaks very sensibly

*Theatrical Rambles of Mr. & Mrs. Greene*, Charles Durang

on this subject. At the Chestnut Street Theatre, Knowles' favorite play of *Love* was first produced on a benefit night. According to the custom of those days it had been partially read in the Green Room and once regularly rehearsed. As an inevitable consequence, it failed and was for some time utterly neglected by the public.

Mr. and Mrs. Greene entered into an engagement with Messrs. Duffy, Forrest, and Jones, managers at the Arch Street Theatre. The managers had long been their personal friends. But ere Greene departed for the Quaker City, he determined to make an effort to get the back salary due him from the Chatham manager, Nosey Phillips, who, with his usual consistency of character, would persevere in being on the debtor side of the ledger, *per contra*, showing no credit. He at once insolently refused any settlement of any kind. He ingloriously repudiated all managerial obligations.

Mrs. Greene was sitting in a lower room of the house where the interview took place between her husband and Nosey Phillips. It was at first a calm one, very piano, but all of a sudden it became stormy. Over her head Greene at intervals fired a demurrer at the head of the delinquent in the shape of a pitcher of cold water, a large piece of ice hitting the manager's pate. Then a few words, and presto, a missile in the shape of a chair, then other portable articles that were lying about the room went wham, bang. The confusion worse confounded increased to a whirlwind of rage and turbulence. Barnes, with his usual placidity, endeavored to allay the storm, to smooth the belligerent creditor.

At length Greene descended to Mrs. Greene, took her by the arm, and went homeward. But after thus passing two or three blocks they found that they were pursued by a hue and cry of police officers, with the exclamation, "There he is! there he is! arrest him!" So the pugnacious John Greene was surrounded by these myrmidons of the law, and was captured as if he had been a thief or a cunning pickpocket. After a stout tussle Greene was prevailed upon to go with the officers quietly, and soon they had him safely in the locked up at the station house.

By this time some of the company had heard of this disgraceful case. J. H. Clarke came at once to the rescue. He

*Theatrical Rambles of Mr. & Mrs. Greene*, Charles Durang

detested Phillips and first saw Mrs. Greene safe to her boarding-house, it being after night when this fracas occurred. He desired her to be comforted, saying that nothing probably could be effected for Greene towards his release that night, but that it should have his earliest attention.

Clarke, like a good and sincere friend, returned to the watch-house ready with the necessary bail early in the morning to at least release his friend Greene from "durance vile." Nosey Phillips, who had been the cause of this *émeute*, sat up in the watch-house all night to be ready with his charges against the prisoner before the sitting magistrate in the early morn. J. H. Clarke sat on the theatre steps opposite all night, too; and the moment the judicial officer entered and took his seat, the case was heard *pro et con* and most summarily dismissed. It never came to trial, Nosey being content to set off his battered pate versus the salaries due to the actors. Greene and his friend Clarke returned home to breakfast after a repentant fast.

## NOTES

[1] Phillips opened at the Chatham on March 11, 1831. His management ended in April.

[2] This was Marble's first year in the profession. He was soon to gain a reputation as a portrayer of Yankee characters, particularly through a play especially written for him by E. H. Thompson, *Sam Patch*. Marble's first appearance at the Chatham occurred April 11, 1831, for the benefit of the prompter, Mr. Nelson. He paid $20 for the privilege of performing.

[3] Ireland lists Mrs. Greene at the Bowery in the role of Druda in Buckstone's *Ice Witch*, April 2, 1831.

[4] *Presumptive Evidence*, sometimes called *Bohemian Mother*, a domestic drama by J. B. Buckstone.

[5] Barnes actually opened the Richmond Hill Theatre on May 23, 1832.

*Theatrical Rambles of Mr. & Mrs. Greene*, Charles Durang

## XX.

ARCH STREET THEATRE — SOMETHING WRONG ABOUT THE MONKEY — A BAD BREAK — FIRE — UNFORTUNATE REMARK — AT NIAGARA FALLS — STAGE COACH ADVENTURE, ETC.

Mr. William Duffy, whilom manager of the Arch Street Theatre, was at this time lessee of the Pearl Street Theatre, Albany, and appointed John Greene stage manager at a yearly salary, receiving the same whether playing or not, the Greenes having no interest in their benefits when thus announced, which were put up at Duffy's discretion.[1] They emigrated to the ancient burg or city of Albany and took up their quarters at the Washington Hall, a large and airy hotel adjoining the theatre. The latter was a neat, compact building, quite large enough for the city's patronage then, as all thought when they saw Master Burke play to empty benches. He was now in a state of adolescence, in a transit of fiddling over acting. His acting powers not attracting, he abandoned them afterwards and devoted his attention to music.

Mr. Greene remained as William Duffy's prime minister for several years. During this time among the actors and actresses composing the company were Mr. and Mrs. Logan, and all the little Logans; the late Clara Woodhull, daughter of Jacob Woodhull (she afterwards married Mr. Pickering and died of cholera in New Orleans); Miss Almira Dunham, Mr. David Johnson, etc. The stars were as follows: Mr. and Miss Priscilla Cooper, Edwin Forrest, the beautiful Miss Phillips, Mr. and Mrs. Blake, Mr. H. Finn, Mr. Oxley, Mr. A. A. Addams, Miss Hughes, Madame Ferron (the vocalist), Mr. and Mrs. Barnes, the Kentucky Giant, Porter, with Major Stevens, the celebrated Dwarf.[2]

During Greene's management at Albany, Charles

## *Theatrical Rambles of Mr. & Mrs. Greene*, Charles Durang

Parsloe, of pantomime notoriety, was playing one night the part of the monkey.[3] He did not seem to be very nimble; he sprang lamely from fence to tree. He had lost his usual quick, queer gesticulations of the animal and would every now and then run to the wings out of sight of the spectators and quickly return as if relieved of something. Greene saw something was afoot and determined to find out what was the matter. He saw little Harry Knight[4] running from one entrance to another to meet Parsloe whenever he came off. There seemed to be a sympathy between the Monkey and Knight; both seemed under some animal influence, or some other spiritual effect of the day seemed to move them physically and together, perhaps some cordial spirit corked in a small bottle to allay the thirst brought on by undue exertion.

The Monkey's agility was at fault. It was a lame job. At last Greene discovered that the Monkey's dyed stockinet dress, made of elastic web so as to fit the body like the natural skin to resemble the Monkey, and which dress had been dyed brown, was old and worn out, bursting in its seams and texture; and at every leap it was giving way. Harry Knight had a pot of brown ochre and a brush out of the paint room, so that whenever a rent occurred in this decayed monkey costume, Parsloe would jump to one of the side wings and Knight would paint the introductory white skin over. So it went on very lamely till the finale of the piece.

John Greene himself was once playing Smart in the farce of the *Rendezvous*.[5] This smart lackey makes his entrance through a center window in the back part of the scene. Not being very remarkable for agility, in jumping into the room from the window he made a rent in his pants, which for the moment was irreparable. He danced about the stage like Gabriel Ravel in his Brazilian Ape. Mrs. Anderson was playing Rose, and Smart should have run to her as her lover; but instead of doing so he jumped around the center table, keeping his back to the audience, playing many antics n the background to hide the rent in his unmentionables. But Rose, with all her efforts, could not get him down to the footlights to go on with the dialogue, which was necessary to give the plot of the piece. She began to think he had lost his senses. At length

*Theatrical Rambles of Mr. & Mrs. Greene*, Charles Durang

he communicated to her by stratagem his sad predicament. They vamped some dialogue that was not from the author, during which time they thus whispered side speeches, "Then go off and repair damages as best you can. Take that table cover with you and I will sing here."

Greene seized the hint, wrapped the table cover around him as a cloak, and made his exit triumphantly, while she whispered to the prompter to ring in the orchestra. The song was not to have been sung till later in the piece. The leader and band ran into the orchestra, wondering why they were summoned before the time, and were taken at a *non plus*. But Mrs. Anderson, with great presence of mind, winked at the leader and giving as a cue, "As there is some confusion in the house, I think I will sing the 'Dashing White Sergeant.'" He took the hint and struck up the symphony and she sang it to a double encore. By that time Greene had donned a new pair of white pants, entered at the end of her song, and they finished the scene with great *éclat*.

One night Greene was busy at the theatre preparing the bills for the next night's performance when a sudden alarm of fire rang through the theatre. He was tormented by the interruption and went on writing, saying that it was not his property that was on fire. Shortly after, one of the carpenters came running into his room, exclaiming, "The hotel next door to the theatre is all in flames, Mr. Greene!"

Mr. Greene threw down his pen and rushed in to save his wardrobe, an actor's first thoughts when those tools whereby he works are in danger of destruction. Many of the actors boarded there, and a scene of the greatest confusion followed. Some of the performers escaped from the hotel and ran out with their dresses, carrying them into the theatre contiguous for safety. The hotel was soon wrapped in flames and the theatre closely adjoining caught fire under the eaves and the roof was beginning to burn rapidly. Through the exertions of the firemen and citizens they succeeded in saving the theatre, although greatly injured by the fire and water, while the performers were compelled to remain in the theatre all night. There was no performance that night nor the next. The landlord of the Washington Hotel soon procured another house in the neighborhood, when his boarders removed from

*Theatrical Rambles of Mr. & Mrs. Greene*, Charles Durang

their temporary lodgings to the new quarters. After the repairs of the theatre, the Thespian banner was again hoisted on the gable of the house.

In 1835 Mr. W. Duffy conceived the idea of erecting a new theatre in Buffalo, now a vastly growing place. He visited that city, soon had the theatre under contract, and in a short time built for opening.[6] There was a great deal of go-ahead energy about Duffy. Although of seeming listlessness, a *jejune* way, yet, like a Turk when aroused, of great activity. *Ad interim* an opposition arose to rival his efforts in the Eagle Theatre, but Duffy forestalled this rivalry and opened his campaign first with flying colors, Mrs. Fanny Jarman playing on the opening night Mariana in the excellent play of *The Wife*. Mrs. John Greene delivered the opening address. Mr. Cooper and daughter and Emma Wheatley added to the attractions, as well as Mr. and Mrs. Charles Green—a useful pair.[7]

There is a proverb which says, "Think twice before you speak once," which was most aptly illustrated in a pleasure trip of our histrions to Niagara Falls during the summer. Mr. William Wheatley, with the Greenes and some other notables of the sock and buskin, arranged a visit to this sublime phenomenon of nature's water works! It is a very pleasant little drive along the banks of the picturesque Niagara River.

Everything being harmoniously fixed, the parties departed on a lovely balmy morning in different vehicles. To this party was added the new members of the company, Mr. and Mrs. Charles Green, with whom most of the party were unacquainted except by repute. The lady had acquired some fame through the partiality of the Pittsburgh audiences, where she had a large circle of friends who gave her a large and flattering benefit as a testimonial to her abilities and private worth.

To this couple Mr. Wheatley was personally unknown. It so happened that a halt of the party occurred at the half way house for the purpose of taking some refreshments and while there they assembled in the parlor of the inn, when Mrs. Charles Green's complimentary benefit at Mr. Wemyss' Pittsburgh Theatre became the topic of conversation. At that

## Theatrical Rambles of Mr. & Mrs. Greene, Charles Durang

moment Mr. Wheatley entered the room, unaware of the presence of the beneficiary, and joining in the chit-chat remarked quite unreflectingly that he deemed "it strange that that little humbug should have received any testimony of the kind, as it could not have been from any talent she possessed." John Greene, who was doing the amiable, and was about to introduce the gentle couple to Wheatley, felt hurt for his friend's brusqueness and hastened to repair this breach of courtesy to strangers, lest further unpleasantness might follow.

This *contretemps* of Wheatley's thoughtless expression preyed upon his spirits during the balance of the tour; his gaiety, friendly and gentlemanly intercourse and courteous deportment in social relations are ever marked as his shining characteristics. He feathered the arrow that wounded his own feelings. He was so mortified that he never offered any explanation or apology, but remained moody throughout the trip.

The cataract where it first falls into its eternal depths of boiling cauldrons arouses curious emotions. The first look at this stupendous spectacle of nature is a terrific shock of mind and body. When amazement subsides into its hollowed sublimities, a divinity would seem to shape your thoughts to love and adoration for a beneficent Providence!

Players are cruelly subjected to insults of a mortifying nature, both publicly and privately, and that too often without any mode of redress from the mean and cowardly source from which it may proceed. But this detracts not from their honor or professional vocation. How often are they attacked in ambush by the press, debarred of all remedy of reply. An incident occurred in their travels in sober New England, the land of morals and steady habits, where the dude assailant, in this case, lived and claimed to be a model representative of those virtues and doctrines that give them their high position in society.

The Greenes were then performing in the state of Vermont. After going through a performance they took the stage coach for another town at half past twelve in order to reach the place early in the day for the play on that night. The stage was full and the night very dark, so that they could not

## Theatrical Rambles of Mr. & Mrs. Greene, Charles Durang

recognize each other's faces. A gentleman, one of the passengers, commenced descanting upon the performances of the evening before. Of course the Thespians were on the *qui vive* to hear some flattering things upon their abilities and personnel. Alas! the grapes were sour to the taste of the performers. The leading lady (Mrs. Greene) he was very much pleased with, "she was a tolerably fair actress, a tall, fine figure, majestic deportment," and to use his phrase, "well up in her part; but her companion (meaning Mr. Greene), who of course was not her husband, but she merely took his name, was one of the most cutthroat looking scoundrels he had ever seen, a hanging look, strongly marked."

Mr. Greene was much piqued, yet controlled his temper and replied, "I think, sir, your judgment correct and very liberal."

This loquacious gentleman, delighted to have his judgment confirmed, continued, "Why, sir, that fellow's looks would condemn him before any intelligent jury in the Union! Such palpable and marked villainy I never saw so forcibly imprinted by Providence on man's face to warn the unwary, and the lack of forecast of those unacquainted with Lavater's science of physiognomy. That man's proclivities may be sworn to by an utter stranger."

Greene facetiously acceded to what he said, "I agree with you, sir, with one exception. We should draw more charitable conclusions in relation to the lady's connection with the cut-throat gentleman, who I understood is truly married to her, having the truth of that from a gentleman who was present at the ceremony."

"Oh! my dear sir, all that may be, but women are whimsical, contrary personages, that anything they do can never be a surprise." Thus he ran on with the theme, criticizing after is own peculiar views the company and the acting of the performers, still lamenting that so fine a woman should associate thus with such a hang-dog looking fellow.

The stage stopping to change horses just before daylight, John Greene, in a lark, invited the critical gentleman to take a glass with him. This was accepted. The bar had a flaming light behind it. The glasses were served. Greene took off

*Theatrical Rambles of Mr. & Mrs. Greene*, Charles Durang

his hat and the "villainous, cut-throat countenance," so artistically abused, appeared to the critical traveler who had so unsparingly traduced him. He was at once struck dumb. He could not believe his senses. He could not drink to the salutation of John's proposal to drink to his health! He drew back, pulling his hat over his eyes, ashamed of his brutal behavior.

Greene coolly observed, "Good manners, truthful words, and charity are blessings to society. Without them all is anarchy."

John Greene was naturally of a most quiet disposition, of inoffensive manners; but if offended, of very pugnacious temperament. And although a very short man, he was a very muscular one, with bull-dog courage. Yet on this occasion, as on others, he repaid his reviler with sarcastic jokes. John Greene pitied the man's dismay, for he had inquired for some other mode of conveyance, too ashamed to return to the stage with those he had so thoughtlessly slandered. None was to be had. However, he reluctantly resumed his seat and when daylight fairly developed all the faces of the passengers, the long, silent look of each other's expressive face after the war of words may be better imagined than described.

Greene very emphatically introduced to the confounded critic, "My wife, sir."

The gentleman nodded, stammered some inaudible apology, and repentantly hung his head. Moral: Never slander in the dark, for the light of day will expose your crime. Speak truth or be silent.

## NOTES

[1]Phelps has the Greenes appearing at the Pearl Street Theatre as early as 1830, Mrs. Greene making her debut as Calanthe in *Damon and Pythias*, and Greene as Murtoch in *The Irishman in London*. Their returns to Duffy's management at Albany continued until Duffy's death in 1836.

[2]Cornelius A. Logan first appeared at Tivoli Garden, Philadelphia. He became manager of several theatres and a popular comedian in the West. His daughters were actresses Eliza, Olive, and Celia. Miss Clara Woodhull was Jacob's youngest daughter. Although young and pretty, Ireland found

*Theatrical Rambles of Mr. & Mrs. Greene*, Charles Durang

her "not remarkable for any eminent ability." She married the tragedian Alexander Pickering, but fell victim to yellow fever in New Orleans, dying at the age of 19. Miss Elmira Dunham was engaged by Ludlow, along with her sister, Emeline, 1826, for the Mobile theatre when the Greenes were a part of the company. She made her first New York appearance at the Bowery, September 24, 1833, as Nonna in *The Sleeping Draught*. David C. Johnson made his first stage appearance, March 15, 1820, as Henry in *Speed the Plough*. Eventually, he was a successful caricaturist. Miss Pricilla Cooper was the daughter of Thomas A. Cooper. She was introduced to the stage at Cooper's benefit as Virginia in *Virginius*, February 17, 1834. In 1839 she married Robert Tyler, son of President John Tyler, and served as presiding lady in the White House for the three years of Tyler's presidency. Miss Lydia Phillips was a favorite at Drury Lane before coming to America. Her appearance was that of high breeding—tall and dignified, graceful in action, with a restrained acting style. Henry J. Finn, born at Cape Breton about 1790, first appeared at the Park, January 16, 1818, as Shylock. He had a classical education from Princeton College and later studied law. He was of exemplary character, an accomplished painter, and a skillful writer of plays and other literary efforts. He died on the steamer *Lexington*, which burned in Long Island Sound in January, 1840. John H. Oxley, a native Philadelphian, first appeared in New York at the Park in *Hamlet*, August 16, 1836. Tall, well figured, slender but muscular, he was a traveling star throughout the United States and the West Indies. He was also involved in management. Augustus A. Addams was acting in his native Boston as early as 1823. He married Mary Duff, but his ill treatment toward her bought on a divorce. He was an actor of great promise, which fell short because of carelessness and dissipation. Miss Elizabeth Hughes from Covent Garden made her American debut at the Park, 1831, where she was a popular musical actress. She eventually returned to England to become Mrs. Fenwick. Major Stevens, the dwarf, first appeared on the stage in *Tom Thumb* at the Park, November 12, 1824.

*Theatrical Rambles of Mr. & Mrs. Greene*, Charles Durang

[3]Parsloe's forte was performing the monkey in the pantomime *La Peyrouse*. Portrayal of monkeys was a popular feature around this time. The melodrama *The Dumb Savayard and His Monkey* was at the Park, August 29, 1831, with Master Wieland, who, in the words of Ireland, "scratched and jabbered after the most approved fashion of stage monkeys." Mons. Gouffe (The Monkey Man) came over from London in 1832 to exhibit his dwarfish physique and muscular agility. Parsloe was pleasing New York audiences with *The Cabin Boy and His Monkey* in 1833. Master William Blanchard was the ape in *The Planter and His Dogs* at the Bowery in 1835. And by 1840 the Bowery was billing the spectacular "Gnome Fly," Signor Hervio Nano (Harvey Leech), who alternately imitated a baboon and a fly, displaying feats of extraordinary strength.

[4]Henry Knight, son of a famous London comedian, made his American debut at the Park, October 9, 1827. Had his leg cut off on the railroad between Baltimore and Philadelphia and died from the effects.

[5]*The Rendezvous; or, All in the Dark*, a farce by Ayton.

[6]The cornerstone was laid for Duffy's Buffalo Theatre on January 4, but the company performed in Buffalo off and on prior to 1835.

[7]Fanny Jarman, born in Hull, England, 1805, was a leading actress in Dublin before appearing at Drury Lane as Juliet, 1827. Her American debut was in the same role at the Chestnut Street Theatre, 1834. *The Wife* was a tragedy by James Sheridan Knowles. Emma Wheatley performed at the Park for her mother's benefit, June 25, 1834 (she was not yet 13), an imitation of Fanny Kemble's Julia in *The Hunchback*," to great applause. Mr. and Mrs. Charles Green joined Duffy's company in February, 1832.

*Theatrical Rambles of Mr. & Mrs. Greene*, Charles Durang

## XXI.

A TRAGEDY INDEED — MURDER OF MR. DUFFY — A SUIT AT LAW AND ITS RESULTS — FANNY JARMAN COMPARED WITH ELLEN TREE.

The new Eagle Theatre at Buffalo progressed to rapid completion, and was far superior to the first edifice; therefore the tide of public patronage set in for the Eagle Temple to the detriment of the others.[1] Mr. Duffy deemed it expedient to beat a retreat to his headquarters at Albany, where he intended opening with the neat comedy *Two Friends* with some other light pieces.[2]

On this opening night a very melancholy incident occurred that shed a solemn gloom over the company for a long time and eventually dissolved its organization under the Duffy dynasty. The part of Valentine in the *Two Friends* was to be performed by Mr. John Hamilton, but about the time the curtain should have risen it was found that no Mr. Hamilton was present to appear in the part. An inquiry was made as to his whereabouts but to no purpose. He was *non est*. Mr. Greene, the stage manager, and Mr. Duffy consulted about the matter; and Hamilton not appearing at the last moment, they prepared a substitute to read the part. At this point of the dilemma the delinquent made his appearance.

Mr. Duffy in an excited tone said to him, "Sir, you are late. What is the meaning of this?"

To which Hamilton replied with perfect nonchalance, "I don't mean to play tonight."

"Your reasons, sir?" asked Mr. Duffy.

John Hamilton in a very insolent way said, "I have not been paid up."

"How much is coming to you?"

*Theatrical Rambles of Mr. & Mrs. Greene*, Charles Durang

"Eight dollars," replied Hamilton.

"Why, is that worth making a difficulty about?" said Duffy. "Why not go to the office and get your money?"

At that Hamilton became quite abusive. The manager became quite enraged. And finally it ended in a desperate quarrel in the green room, the result of which was the substitution of another play.

This recusant performer went into the front of the house, and wickedly attempted to interrupt the performances. The police were called to put him out and he was at last ejected. The warfare waged warmer from day to day, the parties becoming more exasperated, until one night *Ellen Wareham* and *A Husband at Sight* were announced.³ Mr. Duffy acted in both pieces, Cresford in the former and Frederic in the latter.

While he was reading his part over in the green room he was standing near a large mirror. Mrs. Greene stood opposite to him reading hers. When Hamilton entered she saw his figure in the mirror and was struck with the fiendish expression of his face, which caused her to dread some fatal issue between them. The manager was called on the stage and Hamilton followed him closely. Her alarm was now redoubled. She saw that foul intentions were purposed by this little fiend incarnate towards Duffy and followed him closely on the track. In her trepidation she rushed to Miss Dunham's dressing room, told her fears, and both of them proceeded behind the scenes with the vague hope that by their presence to disarm Hamilton in his awful intention of feloniously assaulting Duffy. The latter, however, was on the stage and the former, evidently foiled in his dread intent, passed through the side stage door to the auditorium. The two ladies congratulated themselves as the probable interments of having averted for that time at least the fatal blow that might then and there have been consummated—a murder most clearly intended. Things were safe so far. The performances went on, were finished without interruption, and all departed in peace to their homes, little dreaming of the bloody drama that this fatal altercation was to end in.

The next morning the company assembled in the green room only to learn the sequel of this bloody quarrel.

### *Theatrical Rambles of Mr. & Mrs. Greene*, Charles Durang

Having met as usual for the rehearsal business, the first call of the call boy that should summon them to the stage was the announcement to the congregated *corps* that John Hamilton had killed William Duffy and afterwards cut his own throat, which report was not true but thus amplified as all such things are. Duffy had been seriously stabbed by Hamilton, who was in prison then. The facts elicited were as follows: Hamilton, under strong excitement, had been drinking all the evening before; and after his conduct and ejection from the theatre, his vengeance knew no bounds. But with the effects of liquor his feelings arose to desperation and bloody views. "Blood Iago! blood Iago!" seems to have imbued his mind. Mr. Duffy had rooms in the theatre but took his meals at the American.

Dropping in at the Washington Hall adjoining the theatre, which had been rebuilt, he saw Hamilton standing with others in the barroom and remarked, "I thought you were in jail by this time."

This provoked an angry response and more heated words followed, till Hamilton precipitated himself on Duffy in a most hostile manner, knife in hand. Duffy in self-defense raised a chair but it was too late. The assailant evaded the barrier and inflicted a serious wound in the abdomen of Duffy, who fell to the floor. Dr. Stadts was immediately called in and the wounded man was removed on a litter to his rooms, where the wound was sewed up and every attention paid to his case, with hopes that a speedy recovery would result. For some two or three weeks daily bulletins were issued, giving varied statements of his condition. One day the most flattering hopes were put forth and the next the reverse, all hopes being gone of recovery.[4]

The theatre of course was closed *sine die*. This was also a catastrophe to the purse of the actors, who seldom or never had a bonus or reserved fund to draw upon. In this event Mr. Greene proposed to the company that an effort should be made to start a scheme. It met general approbation and Greene obtained a hall in Troy and a loan of scenery and wardrobe. Thither the company went in combination.

*Theatrical Rambles of Mr. & Mrs. Greene*, Charles Durang

While they were thus playing one night to a full house the play of *Pizarro*, Charles Webb as Rolla, about the third act, the company received the news of Mr. Duffy's death. The intelligence was received with a shock to their feelings, as they were impressed with the belief that their manager's recovery was quite certain. They felt it the more as they honored and loved the man for his friendly and parental care of their interests and welfare. He had some hauteur about him at times but his heart was benevolent.

Mr. Greene announced the melancholy event to the audience, with oppressed feelings, at the end of the act, saying in a faltering voice, that, "The memory of their manager was dear to them, by all revered, and when only assured but yesterday by his medical attendants of his safety, the sudden news of his death overwhelmed his brother performers with regret and sorrow. To alleviate our oppressed feelings, and out of respect to his memory, the company through me, as their manager, would desire to close the performances of the evening with the act just finished. The audience can have their money restored to them by calling at the box office of the theatre. In according thus to the sympathies of the company, it will be deemed a liberality of generous feeling ever to be engraved on their hearts."

The audience was a motley assemblage of hard working mechanics, under whose rough manly forms the hearts of true Christianity beat purely; and deeply sympathizing with the players in the bereavement of their manager, quietly withdrew from the house, not one demanding the price of their ticket to be returned. The enemies to theatrical institutions cannot refuse their approbation to moral and pious deeds like these, as evinced by the performers and so beautifully responded to by the industrious, hard-working mechanics who have the good taste to seek their few hours of relaxation from laborious duties in witnessing instructive amusements.

The entire troupe started immediately for Albany to attend William Duffy's obsequies. The cortege was large and imposing, the concourse of citizens and his friends were numerous. The deceased was a native of Albany and the respect

## *Theatrical Rambles of Mr. & Mrs. Greene*, Charles Durang

paid to his memory was universal, and spoke trumpet-tongued as to his townsmen's estimation!

The performers returned to besiege Troy again with fresh alacrity, which did not last as long as the Trojans' siege. One was ten years, the Thespians' not ten weeks. On the night they were to play *Venice Preserved* the hall was crammed with all the Trojan artisans to see "the plot discovered," as they have it behind the scenes. Charles Webb was to act Pierre but was missing at toll call when the curtain should rise. This, with him, was not a novelty. It was a pity, as he was a very good actor. Well, it was found necessary to change the pieces, the only resort in such cases. This it was feared would arouse the ire of the audience, but it failed to do so. They were determined to be pleased and seemed quite as well satisfied with the make-shift change as though they had made the selection themselves, applauding the actors in all their short comings to the very echo.

But things were brought to a conclusion at Troy by the executors of the Duffy estate. They called in the scenery and wardrobe that was belonging to the estate. In settling Greene's account with the executors, it was found to owe Greene $1,600, they having been engaged at a yearly salary. This, in Greene's estimation, would have been nothing but for Duffy's death. His ability to manage the theatres under his control would soon have liquidated so large a debt due to a performer. Besides, he could well rely upon Duffy's honor for a just settlement at any time. But like all theatrical property thrown suddenly into the market, it never brings one-fourth of its value; therefore Duffy's assets were not available after his death.

As it was, Mr. Greene became involved in an annoying lawsuit with the executors, attended with heavy expenses and loss of time and temper, and gained nothing, but spent what money he had on hand. Such are the result of lawsuits, which devastate more property than earthquakes or tornadoes and are more tormenting than the plagues of Egypt.

Thus thrown suddenly out of situations and a just debt hardly earned by the death of Mr. Duffy, they were again cast upon the world's ocean without a chart, compass,

## *Theatrical Rambles of Mr. & Mrs. Greene*, Charles Durang

or rudder, adrift with an actor's capital, which sometimes amounts to nothing. But the professionals, however they may be encircled by tribulation, are ever fertile in expedients. Another traveling scheme was devised, and by some means they gathered with their professional rake a scanty set of scenery—a street, a wood, a chamber, on its back a palace, a kitchen, a prison, with a green baize curtain, and a meager wardrobe. They formed a *corps dramatique* of five gentlemen and two ladies, of whom Mrs. Greene was one. They ventured once more to shell the Trojans, who were good and true folks. From thence they wended their way to Plattsburgh, of glorious memory, with its beautiful historical views on the lake shores of Champlain. But that did not crown them with success. Their purses grew lighter as they moved from place to place.

At length Mr. and Mrs. Tiernan (Miss Jarman that was) and Mr. Thomas Ward, passing on their way to Montréal through one of this company's stopping places, came in contact with them. Mr. Ward was desirous of forming a legitimate company for the Canadas, as he purposed to connect Montréal with Québec, where excellent theatres and enlightened audiences made proposals for Greene to engage with him. They offered him the stage management and it was accepted, with the proviso that the whole of his troupe should also be employed. This was also agreed to and they all started together as a great combination.[5]

On their arrival at the City of Montréal, that *corps* was divided. To John Greene's portion was assigned Mr. and Mrs. Henry Knight, Mr. and Mrs. Lewyllen, Hughes, Adincourt, and Whitney. Mr. Abbott, Mr. Tiernan, and Mrs. Tiernan were sent to Québec.[6]

Mrs. Tiernan still kept the name of Jarman, her maiden name, being identified more popularly with the name of Fanny Jarman of Covent Garden, London, an actress of great merit and private worth. And we think (we know with odds against that opinion) that in every attribute of her art and lovely personal qualifications she was superior to Miss Ellen Tree. Circumstances shelved her at Covent Garden, where in the season of 1828 and 1829 she led the juvenile business. Mr. Fawcett, the stage manager, sent her the part of Oriana to play in the *Inconstant*.[7] Mrs. Jarman sent it back with the message that if her daughter played in the piece at all it must be bizarre. It is said that Fawcett remonstrated in a friendly manner but without avail. At the end of the season in May, Miss Jarman was discharged. Miss Fanny Kemble made her debut at Covent Garden in the next season of 1830 as Juliet with a success unprecedented; Romeo, Abbott, Mercutio, Charles Kemble.

While in Canada the drama of the *Heart of Midlothian*[8] was produced for the purpose of gratifying public solicitation of seeing Mrs. Jarman's beautiful and impressive impersonation in the affecting Jennie Dean-'s. When she first played it at the Chestnut Street Theatre, Philadelphia, her acting of the plain, virtuous Scotch girl (spoken in rather a polished lowland dialect) melted a crowded audience to tears. She was the very embodiment of gentleness and truth. Her forte was in the sweetness and light shadows of domestic pathos. Her simple appeals to royalty and power were a perfect personification of eloquence. What force and beauty she would have given to the trial scene in this drama had it been properly dramatized! Why that most important and effective scene should have been omitted by the dramatizers of the three first dramas we cannot divine. The difficulty was, of course, that the trial scene precedes all the action of the piece.

Mrs. Greene was cast for Madge Wildfire, wherein she achieved a great success. And she acknowledged that to Mrs. Tiernan's excellent instructions in this wild creation of Walter Scott's she owed much of her pantomime business, which was most effective. Thus aided by her own conceptions, she gave to the audience a truly great character. She was highly complimented by acute critics who had witnessed Mrs. Egerton's Madge Wildfire, the original in London in 1819. They gave Mrs. Greene the merit of masterly delineation. A great artist is capable of being a great teacher.

Notwithstanding they had a good company and commanding star talent, the season proved a comparative failure to the managers, who very honorably and promptly paid as agreed upon.

*Theatrical Rambles of Mr. & Mrs. Greene*, Charles Durang

## NOTES

[1] The erection of the Eagle Theatre was completed in 1834 and was opened by Dean and McKinney. Duffy had been performing in Buffalo from June to September of that year. Phelps claimed he had been making money.

[2] *Two Friends*, a comedy by M. R. Lacy.

[3] *Ellen Wareham*, a domestic drama by Buckstone; *A Husband at Sight*, a farce by the same.

[4] Ireland calls the man James Hamilton. The altercation occurred in 1835; Duffy died on March 12, 1836. Hamilton was tried for Duffy's murdered on April 29 and 30.

[5] Ward and Dinneford had leased the Québec and Montréal theatres early in 1836 to be used for a summer season.

[6] The Lewyllens had only recently come to America from England and had been members of Ward's Pittsburgh theatre. Adincourt and Whitney are significant only for their obscurity. William Abbott, who would become a partner with Ward in theatre management, made his American debut at the Park as Beverly in *The Gamesters*, September 28, 1835. He died an actor's death, being seized with a stroke while on stage, 1843. Tiernan, born in 1804, was from the Dublin theatre. He first appeared at the Park as Romeo.

[7] *The Inconstant*, a comedy by George Farquhar.

[8] *The Heart of Midlothian*, a melodrama by Thomas Dibdin.

*Theatrical Rambles of Mr. & Mrs. Greene*, Charles Durang

## XXII.

WITH RUFUS WELCH — ACQUITTED OF DUFFY — SECTACLES AT THE WALNUT STREET THEATRE — VACHE, HIS ECCENTRICITIES — MISS ELLEN TREE — PITTSBURGH THEATRE, ETC.

The company made their *exeunt* out of the Canadas into the "States," as they are called there. The season over, the Greenes then beat their course to Albany, where they then fell in with General Rufus Welch, who, giving Greene a hearty shake of the hand, exclaimed, "You are the man I have been looking after. I want your wife and self forthwith for the Lion Theatre at Boston. Name your terms."

Greene named his terms, which were large, and asked the General if he would give them. "Yes, all right; come with me at once to the land of pumpkins and notions. You are the cheapest on my salary list."

Over the hills to Boston town did Greene and wife coach it. They found Welch's stage *corps* to consist of David Ingersoll, Collingbourne, Mr. and Mrs. Kent,[1] and Irish Fields, as he was called, all assembled at the building they were to occupy as an amphitheatre. The members composing the ring performers were capital and numerous. Grand melodramatic spectacles were brought out, such as *Blue Beard* with the music, "*Rienzi, El Hyder*, etc.[2] The general spared no expense in the accessories to the pieces. The result proved the houses were meager and the losses very heavy, so severe that it was announced the house must close forthwith.[3]

The General assembled the entire company, explained matters, and offered them means of removal to another place. Mr. and Mrs. Greene did not, very fortunately, require his assistance. The weather was very cold and snowy when they started in the stage for Philadelphia, by the way of

## *Theatrical Rambles of Mr. & Mrs. Greene*, Charles Durang

Connecticut. Before the Canadian tour, the trial of Hamilton, the comedian, for the murder of William Duffy, the lessee of the theatre at Albany, took place. Mrs. Greene was subpoenaed on this trial as a witness to testify as the state of Hamilton's mind towards the deceased, as she had witnessed much of the attending circumstances that transpired between them ere the fatal deed was committed. This was a most distressing situation to her who had never been near a court before, to be summoned upon so solemn a case. To accuse, or palliate friend or foe before a tribunal of justice was dreadful! The position was one of the most trying, regretting, as she had to do, the death of a friend like Duffy was to her; yet oppressed in heart and pride of profession in beholding a former associate standing at the bar of a criminal court, with whom she had oft conversed and performed; imbued with all the merciful feelings of a female heart, always charitable even towards the most guilty. Feeling for a young man whom the heat of passions superinduced through the demon intemperance had brought to this awful state, she felt that her truthful evidence must weigh heavily against him. Yet she hoped for his acquittal from an ignominious death or from the degradation of a former honorable life to that of a felon's doom.

Her testimony went greatly against Hamilton. In vain did his able council, through strict cross examinations and searching questions of a confounding and embarrassing nature, endeavor to invalidate her conscientious statements that had been given with all the simple purity of truth. When she was released from the tortures of a witness box, she swooned and was taken home in a state of insensibility.

After a laborious investigation and a most elaborate defense by his advocates, the jury retired, and after a long consultation returned with a verdict of "not guilty." His escape was a miracle. Hamilton showed Mr. Greene after his liberation a large lump of opium he had concealed in the lining of his coat. This in the event of his conviction he would have swallowed sooner than to have been consigned to the State Prison.

Hamilton was originally a printer, a native of Albany, and had some talent as a low comedian. With a few good qualities of the man, he was very passionate and, when

*Theatrical Rambles of Mr. & Mrs. Greene*, Charles Durang

aroused upon some trifling, imagined wrong of a demoniac nature. He was at the Arch Street Theatre in Jones, Duffy, and Forrest's reign in 1831. This dynasty was rather favorable to his advancement. He wandered to the West, a most unhappy, broken-hearted man, and, as we learn, died there.

The citizens of Albany, after this trial, appreciating Mrs. Greene's merits and the interest which her appearance at the criminal tribunal as a witness had created, excited them to offer her a complimentary benefit on the eve of her departure for Philadelphia. Mr. Blake, then lessee of the Paul Street Theatre, had kindly offered the use of his building. The house was well filled and the proceeds were a very seasonable relief to their exhausted finances. Their movements were now as whimsical as the winds of the heavens. They had been and were driven north, south, east, and west with the changes of the weather cock. About January, 1837, they reached Philadelphia, where they soon received an engagement from F. C. Wemyss, lessee, manager, and actor of the Walnut Street Theatre; Mr. A. W. Jackson stage manager.[4]

Here everything seemed to run smoothly, a happy and contented company, business good, and a liberal audience. They had some hope of a permanent situation. After all their wandering, this was a consummation devoutly to be wished.

The *Wrecker's Daughter* was represented for the first time, with Edmund Conner as Black Norris, Joseph Proctor as Edward, and Mrs. Greene as Marianne. It pleased much. The spectacular drama of *Thalaba* was got up by William Barrymore. It produced in six nights $3,285, the greatest average receipts of any piece ever produced by Mr. Wemyss at that theatre. The *Bronze Horse*, revived, was played with it; the latter piece had an immense run on the previous season, although got up without much expenditure.[5] It is a curious thing in theatricals that those got up pieces, as they are termed, on whose attractive qualities most reliance is placed, generally produce disappointments, and those on which lesser means are bestowed give unexpected successful results. Public dramatic attractions are a puzzle, as difficult to solve as that of the riddle of the Sphinx.

N. B. Clarke[6] figured in these pieces prominently. As

*Theatrical Rambles of Mr. & Mrs. Greene*, Charles Durang

a melodramatic actor he was very popular. He went west, where, as stage manager and actor, he was well known. He became a great favorite at Chicago, as the stage manager for Mr. J. B. Rice, and is at present stage manager at the New Bowery.

Mr. J. B. Rice formerly belonged to the Walnut Street Theatre, when he married Miss Mary Anne Warren, a daughter of the late William Warren of the late Chestnut Street Theatre. Mr. Rice established the regular drama in 1852 in Illinois, erecting theatres at Chicago and Milwaukee and realized a large fortune in theatrical and land speculations.[7]

In Milwaukee he commenced in a hall which was filled to overflowing every night. He was beloved as a man and a manager. The company was small but composed of great ability. Mrs. Rice was an excellent actress and one of the best soubrettes to be found on the stage. In fact, the talent of the Warren family is hereditary.

Mr. Wemyss closed the Walnut Street season on the 11th of April with Mr. Conner's benefit. He was then becoming a fast-rising actor. As Glaucus in the *Last Days of Pompeii* he made a hit, while the piece itself, with all its magnificent scenery and machinery, made a failure, paradoxical as it may seem.[8] Mr. and Mrs. Greene were then transplanted by Mr. Wemyss to Pittsburgh, where he opened the theatre on the 2nd of May with a newly organized company.

The season was a brilliant succession of triumphs. The stock actors were nearly the same, except the addition of Mr. Vache, a native of Philadelphia, who had been an amateur of one of the private Thespian companies, *viz.*, "The Boothenian Association." This gentleman was quite a genius in the arts, an artist on the stage and an artist on canvas. As a portrait painter he would have excelled if he had made it a profession. His portraits of the members of the Walnut Street Company in 1837, done on the walls of a large dressing room in that theatre, executed with willow charcoal, were *facsimiles* in spirit and likeness of the persons so traced. He had capital scenic ideas in machinery and, as a correct costumer and make-up of characters, was without a rival on the stage. He played first as an amateur at a small theatre in North Third Street above the old Northern Liberty Town Hall, in

*Theatrical Rambles of Mr. & Mrs. Greene*, Charles Durang

a large hall in the Exchange Hotel, in 1834. It was kept by Mr. Vesey, and was afterwards converted into a neat theatre by the late Joseph Jefferson, Jr. He made his first appearance as a regular at the Walnut Street house, Philadelphia, as Pierre in *Venice Preserved* in 1835. He had a manly figure and a good face, with that almost indispensable adjunct to all actors—a musical voice. But tragedy was not his forte. He finally emigrated to the Bowery Theatre under Mr. Hamblin, where he became truly eminent in old men and eccentrics. In make-up of character parts of strong humor, his dress, face, wiggery, and all those art attributes that mark a true artist, his breadth of coloring struck the eye and ear at once, while his delicate shading, mellowing and blending of its various tints, gave a rich Rubens picture of dramatic delineation. Poor Vache, while thus endowed, was of an eccentric turn. Like most actors after the labor of the night, especially if accompanied by the heartfelt approbation of the audience, he was wont to enjoy an hour or twain as a *solatium* of the performer after a tiresome performance. He then enjoyed the Lenten feast and the sparkling glass of ale, or some inspiring beverage of the sort. As they are generally men of taste, they try to secure that article of approved taste that may bear eulogy in quaffing.

In the vicinity of most theatres there is generally a *sans souci* libation snuggery, where the histrions may enjoy in private "the feast of reason and the flow of soul." One of these temples was kept by a blind retired actor by the name of Daniel Sinclair, whose real name was Gauger. The house stood opposite to the Bowery Theatre with the insignia over the humble portal, "The Little Pewter Mug." At this draught exchange, where the actors most did congregate, Dan Sinclair was the host, and here did Vache take his "night caps" Like Macbeth.

Dan Sinclair, after he became afflicted with blindness, left the stage per force, but went about as a blind star, in the various towns where he had been in his day as a performer, getting eleemosynary benefits, playing the blind father in the *Bohemian Mother*, without the least pathos or effect, a proof that the real things are not effective on the stage.

## Theatrical Rambles of Mr. & Mrs. Greene, Charles Durang

Poor fellow, in his case and Vache's, it was proved that "evil communication corrupteth good manners," for Sinclair fell a victim to the liquids of his trade. He dropped down suddenly in his own barroom just as he was lifting a glass of spirits to his lips, was carried to his bed, whence he never arose again but in his spirit! He should have remembered the old playhouse motto as he held the glass in his hand—*Veluti in Speculum*—mentally, at least, if even his vision was gone.

Vache was eccentric but genial in his disposition. Everybody liked him on and off the stage. But sometimes he would unwittingly become oblivious with his fellow roisterers and would miss the door of his domicile, which was in a like row of houses back of the theatre in Elizabeth Street. In going home *solus* late in the morning, his vision dancing in circles *à la valse*, he was bothered to find his own door and generally rang at four or five doors, terribly alarming the inmates, before he chanced to get to his own bell pull. The denunciations of poor Vache in annoying them from their rosy dreams may well be imagined.

One night he rang vigorously at his door and the many sleeping boarders were gradually awakened. But they indignantly swore they would not get up to let him in; so with a grunt they severally composed themselves again to sleep. Again the bell pealed forth its sharp rattling tones, and no longer able to endure the noise, one of them went down, intending to inflict chastisement on the offender; but found Vache, to his surprise, had left his own door and was ringing a Triple Bob Major at the bell of the next house.

"What are you doing there?" cries a voice from the third story window.

"Police! Police! where are you? Take this fellow up," Vache's fellow boarder called out. "What are you doing there?"

"Gentlemen," cries Vache, in his most affable style, "excuse me, pardon me, for thus disturbing your slumber but the truth is I live in one of these houses, but which is my dwelling I can't for the soul of me find out. So I tried them all as I went along." His fellow lodger led him into his own hall. But after all, he contrived to get into a wrong chamber and a wrong bed. The rightful owner of the bed came in soon

*Theatrical Rambles of Mr. & Mrs. Greene*, Charles Durang

after and finding his bed was tenanted requested Vache "to go to his own room."

"Certainly," replied Vache. And not having undressed himself, he got up and walked out of the room.

The boarder who let him in was an early riser, and on going down in the morning found what seemed to be a dead body at the foot of the stairs. It was Vache, who was sleeping with all the calmness of a good conscience and plentiful draughts of whiskey.

Mr. Wemyss' Company received at Pittsburgh a new star. Miss Ellen Tree was on her way to the North from New Orleans, where her success at the St. Charles Street Theatre had been unprecedented. This lady and highly polished actress of the drawing-room school, made her appearance at the Iron City in the *Lady of Lyons*. Her performances were received with all that enthusiastic admiration that her fine talents merited. The Pittsburgh audiences have fancies of their own; some of them very singular; however they are right in being independent and not swayed by the opinions of others. Thus many preferred the Pauline of Mrs. George Barrett to that of Miss Tree's. Mrs. Barrett was an attractive actress in person, grace, and manners. Miss Tree could scarcely be equaled. She is very intellectual in her acting and clearly in the possession of a pathos not surpassed by any of her contemporaries.

During the engagement Miss Tree played Viola in Shakespeare's *Twelfth Night* and Mrs. Greene was cast to the lady Olivia, the counterpart to Viola. The language of this comedy is quaintly difficult, but poetical and beautiful. It is seemingly crabbed, as it was the style of composition of the time of Shakespeare and his contemporaries.

Mrs. Greene feared undertaking so responsible a character as that of Lady Olivia to Miss Tree's Viola. She had conceived so great a veneration for the magnificent actress that she was seized with a sudden depreciation of her own ability, and was so much afraid of marring the beauty of it by any awkwardness that it threw her into agony and she experienced such a paroxysm of stage fright that she never forgot the awful sensation. Though conscious of being letter

## Theatrical Rambles of Mr. & Mrs. Greene, Charles Durang

perfect, she felt at the moment as if she could not recollect a single word. All her part blended into misty indistinctness and a sensation of giddiness and faintness came upon her. In fact, her nerves were tightly strained by anxiety and were reacting. There was no real cause for the distress. The spasmodic affection passed, excitement lent her energy, and she acquitted herself to the admiration of audience, critics, and, more than all, the lady who shared the task with her and who transmitted, as it were, like electric sparks, her light and her judgment.

Mr. and Mrs. Hodges now shed their light on the Pittsburgh boards for some nights.[9] Their handsome persons and pleasing performances made them very attractive. Their success served to lengthen the season greatly to the delight of the company and the benefit of the treasury. The theatre kept open till the latter end of April.

Mr. Hodges was a well educated tenor, but like most vocalists was generally in a state of semi-hallucination, always in the abstract status about business. A good story is told of Dumas. Dumas appointed Mr. Hodges his stage manager, an office for which nature, habit, and experience rendered him totally unfit. No man in America could be found so incapable. Mrs. Hodges may be remembered as the beautiful, sensational, melodramatic Miss Nelson, and subsequently as Mrs. John Brougham, who appeared at the Covent Garden Theatre, London, during Mr. Fawcett's stage management with success.

After the close of the Pittsburgh Theatre the company dissolved, some returning to the Walnut Street Theatre, others going down the La Belle River to the towns on the Ohio and Mississippi. Thus did the Greenes float their way down those romantic rivers till they reached New Orleans, stopping on their way at various towns to collect gold and silver bouquets from their green banks. Mr. and Mrs. Greene made an engagement at the Camp Street Theatre, boarding at the same house with Mr. and Mrs. Cowell and their youthful daughter, Sidney Cowell, afterwards Mrs. Bateman, the mother of the now celebrated Miss Bateman.

*Theatrical Rambles of Mr. & Mrs. Greene*, Charles Durang

## NOTES

[1] David Ingersoll, a native of Philadelphia, where he made his debut in 1830 as William Tell. He first appeared in New York at the Bowery, December 27, 1833, in the same role. Ireland said of him, "His personal appearance was fine, and his natural abilities were in every way of a superior order; and had discretion guided his career, he might have lived to become the first of American actors." He died in St. Louis, 1837, at age 25. W. Collingbourne, from the minor English theatres, was an accomplished dancer, clown, and a fair singer. His name was eventually shortened to Colinborn and his colleagues, going one step further, shortened it to Colly. He was a favorite with the Boston audiences. Mr. Kent, formerly from Drury Lane, made his American debut, November 1, 1821, as sir Anthony Absolute. He played bluff and hearty men with distinction, as well as being useful in operatic pieces. Mrs. Kent, formerly Miss E. Eberle, was an attractive soubrette and vocalist.

[2] *Blue Beard*, a melodrama by George Colman the younger; *Rienzi*, a dramatization of Bulwer's novel (also versions by Louisa H. Medina, J. B. Phillips, and Miss Mitford); *El Hyer*, a melodramatic spectacle by William Barrymore.

[3] Welch opened the Lion Theatre in early November, 1836; the place closed in April, 1837.

[4] Francis Courtney Wemyss first performed in America at the Chestnut Street Theatre, December 11, 1822. He was a light comedian of worth, but more importantly a manager of theatres in Pittsburgh, Philadelphia, and Baltimore.

[5] *The Wrecker's Daughter*, a tragedy by James Sheridan Knowles; *Thalaba* was probably adapted from Southey's epic poem (1801) *Thalaba the Destroyer*; *The Bronze Horse; or, the Spell of the Cloud King* was an operatic romance. E. S. Conner, born in Philadelphia, 1809, left off tailoring for small roles at the Arch and Walnut Street Theatres. Although he became effective in both comedy and tragedy, melodrama was his forte. He later went into management. William Barrymore was also a fine melodramatic actor and a stager of the genre. Durang described him as tall, handsome, gentlemanly

*Theatrical Rambles of Mr. & Mrs. Greene*, Charles Durang

and intelligent but "very eccentric and irritable in his disposition."

[6]N. B. Clarke (real name Belden), born in Cincinnati, 1810, made his stage debut at the Chatham Garden Theatre, 1830.

[7]Rice retired from the theatre, 1856, and became mayor of Chicago. Mary Anne Warren, a Philadelphia native, made her debut at the Walnut Street Theatre, 1837. She retired from the profession along with her husband.

[8]*The Last Days of Pompeii*, a melodrama by Miss Medina, was called by Ireland one of the most popular of its genre ever produced. It was first put up at the Bowery, February 9, 1835, and ran for a month straight. There was another version by Charlotte Barnes. The piece was often revived.

*Theatrical Rambles of Mr. & Mrs. Greene*, Charles Durang

## XXIII.

THE BATEMANS — CHARACTERISTICS OF A NEW ORLEANS AUDIENCE — MRS. GREENE'S BENEFIT — MELANCIIOLY FINALE TO A SUCCESSFUL DEBUT — THE STAGE AND PUIPIT — COURAGE OF AN ACTRESS.

Mrs. Cowell played at the St. Charles, the father and daughter (Sidney) at the old Camp Street Theatre. Mrs. Cowell was in very delicate health at that period and was often confined to her room. She died the following February. Mr. Cowell in his memoirs thus refers to his bereavement: "The nature of my task prevents me from giving even a sketch of the beautiful Crescent City as she is now, but to me she must ever be most dear as the depository of one unlettered tomb on which I never shall have length of days enough to rain upon remembrance with many eyes" The little Sidney became a finished actress and had lived to see her daughters, once infant prodigies, ripened into beautiful womanhood— one withdrawn from a profession that the other has so successfully pursued that she has passed the ordeal of London criticism.

Mrs. Bateman possesses literary abilities, natural and acquired, of a high caliber. Well read in *belles-lettres*, she has assisted the acting drama with much novelty of an enlightened nature in original and adapted pieces. She adjusted the beauties of Longfellow's admirable poem of "Evangeline" into a dramatic form for her youthful daughter's debut. In that lovable heroine she elicited infinite precocious talent. Geraldine is another effective character in her repertoire. Thoroughly schooled in stage business, with a

*Theatrical Rambles of Mr. & Mrs. Greene*, Charles Durang

good figure, a well modulated voice, graceful action, and a good education, there is nothing to prevent the young lady from rising to the top of her profession, unless, indeed, the dangerous excess of adulation should suppress that youthful ambition by checking further study, which is the only salutary guard to attain that excellence so coveted, and without which the desired goal is never reached.

Mr. John Sefton joined the Company soon after this. These nights were the most trying and laborious times that she ever went through during her professional probation; no slave experienced harder work than Mrs. Greene. She performed seven nights a week for five months without one day's intermission, for be it remembered that the theatres in New Orleans were open on Sunday night. Often will the overtasked actors and actresses exclaim in sorrow with Rosina in the old operatic farce, *How Sweet Is Rest on Sunday*. Yet in the New Orleans and Mobile theatres it was denied to them. It is a vicious French custom, "more honored in the breach than the observance."

The patronage of the New Orleans audience toward its favorite performer is proverbially liberal. On benefit nights the receipts, however large at the doors, are mostly accompanied by the presentation of a purse seldom less than six or eight hundred dollars, and sometimes a thousand to the beneficiary. This may be considered as an exaggeration, but it is so. Mrs. Greene, at this season, received a highly honorable testimonial of this kind as a just tribute to her public talent and private virtues. The communication was headed by George W. Randall, Esq. of the *Picayune* newspaper, and ran thus:

> To Mrs. Greene—Madame: Feeling desirous that you should hereafter entertain a better opinion of the citizens of New Orleans than you now can, after haying had such a benefit on Friday last, we would now most respectfully request of you to engage the Camp Street Theatre for one night more, for a benefit, that we may say to you emphatically, and prove it by deeds that we can appreciate genuine dramatic talent. There are those among us for whom you have beguiled many an hour

*Theatrical Rambles of Mr. & Mrs. Greene*, Charles Durang

that would otherwise have passed wearily away in Albany and other cities of the Union, and we regret that circumstances forbade your having a crowded house on the late occasion. Should you be pleased, Madame, to honor us with another opportunity of showing our good will. Address your reply to Mr. G. Wilkins Bendall, Editor of the *Picayune*, stating what evening will be convenient for you. In such case, we feel assured that the house will be made a bumper by MANY FRIENDS.

New Orleans, April 9, 1839

The tender was accepted. The comedy of the *School of Reform*[1] was the play selected Mrs. George Barrett as Mrs. Ferment. The house was very full, the receipts large with private donations. It was, in every sense, a substantial benefit to those it was intended to serve and honor. This night closed the season, the actors and actresses leaving as usual for healthier climes during the hot months. Mrs. John Greene, however, engaged the building for one night more nearly all the performers volunteering. When after paying charges, they cleared six hundred dollars. Thus strengthened in pecuniary resources, they left their generous patrons of New Orleans in "good health and spirits," as Diggory says.[2]

Doctor Lardner about these times occupied the theatres with his astronomical lectures with much profit to himself. His illustrating machinery was a great hit, and being novel was largely upon public approbation. Mr. George Holland,[5] the comedian, came out with magnificent illusions on the same evenings at New Orleans and Mobile, and the learned Dr. lighted up his planetarium oratory.

At one time, while the Greenes were sojourning at New Orleans, a magical progressive city of harlequin phases, they were domiciled, or had apartments, in a very convenient building for a wayfarer called "The Arcade," wherein were congregated James H. Caldwell, George Barrett, and Mr. Barton, the latter one of the old school actor, and for several years acting manager for Mr. Caldwell at the Crescent City, a calm, moral, dignified gentleman in manners, but of eccen-

*Theatrical Rambles of Mr. & Mrs. Greene*, Charles Durang

tric ways, not offensive however, but rather of garrulous vein. He was more of a reader than an actor, and was the person who advised Charlotte Cushman to make an effort to essay tragedy after she had lost her admirable voice by some freak of nature during her voyage to New Orleans, a misfortune sufficient to have crushed a spirit less buoyant than her own.[2] He became her elocutionary teacher and brought her out as Lady Macbeth for his benefit. The rest is known. Charlotte still lives and reigns! But poor Barton is no more. This amiable man and melancholy genial spirit of truth, of honor, and mental enrichments was much afflicted with asthmatic affections. He retired to his native England, where he taught elocution as a means of living.

When the Greenes left New Orleans for Cincinnati, the boat on its way there stopped in Louisville, Kentucky. John M. Scott, learning that the Greenes were on board, waited upon them at the boat. He was then playing an engagement at Mrs. Drake's theatre. Scott, on his return from the boat, told Mrs. Drake of the circumstance and she immediately dispatched a messenger to Mr. Greene with a wish to engage them; but ere the messenger got to the wharf, the steamer had departed for the Queen City. Before their arrival there, however, the mail had forestalled their coming with a letter with terms from Mrs. Drake. They returned in the next boat.

Here they found a congregation of stars—E. Forrest, J. R. Scott, Webb, and Mrs. George Barrett. Sheridan Knowles' play of *Virginius* was acted, with Forrest as Virginius, Webb as Appius, John Greene as Dentatus, Mrs. Barrett as Virginia, and Mrs. Greene as Servia. The stars were as numerous, as those of the firmament. Miss Davenport succeeded, playing such parts as Young Norval, Dumb Boy of Manchester, while Celeste followed with her clap-trap *French Spy, Devil's Daughter*, and other *omnium gatheram* dramas![4]

It was during the performance of one of these pieces that a very distressing accident befell one of the performers in the *Spy*. James Rowe, a young aspirant for stage honors, expressed a desire to play the part of Toney, a part to which Mr. Watson had been cast but which he very cheerfully resigned to the ambitious Rowe. The character he sustained with great éclat, having made quite a hit on the night in question. While thus elated with his success, he was joking and gymnasting behind the scenes. While striking attitudes with his drawn bayonet in his hand, his foot caught some projection on the scenery and, in trying to extricate himself, he fell on the naked bayonet which pierced his body some six inches. This was at first unperceived by those who saw him fall, as they thought it only a sham; but on his not stirring at all for some moments, they were led to examine him, when to their horror he was a corpse. He was instantly conveyed to the green room and laid on a sofa. Physicians were in attendance, but in vain. All surgical aid was fruitless.

Mrs. Drake allowed the performances to go on, being overruled by others. She regretted it much on the following day. The denunciations from every quarter were loud and severe. The press was strong in censure. The young man was much respected in Louisville. He possessed worth and talent. His funeral obsequies were largely attended by citizens and all the performers.

Many have heard of Mr. Charles Parsons, tragedian and minister of the Gospel, the stage and the pulpit, and the pulpit and the stage. Mr. Parsons was studying for the church, and a very prominent actress was also in a similar state of grace. We believe their purposes were true and founded in sincerity and good faith. We cannot see how the profession of a player, if pursued with propriety and moral conduct, can be incompatible with pure religion. Many persons deem it inconsistent and impossible. Such impressions are uncharitable towards a class of human beings endowed with a taste for the arts and clearly of cultivated intellects as the followers of a literary profession.

Mrs. Siddons, whose life, talent, genius, and virtues are history, and as such adorns England's annals in the arts and the drama, affords to our thoughts a striking illustration. On being saved from a fearful death, burning on the stage, she silently returned thanks to God for her preservation; and in describing her own mood of mind, exclaimed, "Never did I feel more devout nor have a firmer faith in an everlasting

## Theatrical Rambles of Mr. & Mrs. Greene, Charles Durang

providence." Much ignorant fustian is preached against the profession as to its personal modes and its evil disseminating influences. Allow us to close this prosy moral subject with an anecdote that occurred in the late Mr. W. B. Wood's family, a private circle even without fear, without reproach.

About the year 1816, the tragedy of *Bertram* (then new) proved highly successful in Philadelphia. It was strongly criticized on account of its alleged immoral plot and drawn characters. It would seem wonderful that, if these objections were well founded, it should have been written by a clergyman and authorized for public performance by the Lord Chamberlain, with the addition of a thorough revival by the licenser, a person at that period in London remarkable for his rigid adherence to morals in dramatic plot and language, as well as required absence of all political, anti-monarchical references. With us, as elsewhere, the tragedy was severely scathed by the press. Mr. Wood, in his *Recollections*, related the unpleasant event in the following judicious way: "These severe strictures were not confined to occasional essays or notices, but, in our case, at least, proceeded from the pulpit, no doubt from the error of referring only to the original printed edition, unaware of the fact that every doubtful line of illusion had been carefully struck out by the licenser, whose authorized copy alone we followed. On one occasion the speaker became so much hurried away by a mistaken impression, as boldly to appeal to his audience and ask what estimate could any one make of the feelings or the principles of that woman—of her perceptions of right or wrong—who could be found capable of representing the heroine of this shameful production. I know not whether the gentleman was aware that the unfortunate person who the week before in discharge of her professional engagements had been representing this character was at the very time a regular member of his own congregation and was seated on that Sunday as she usually was in her accustomed place at church, which was in close proximity to the speaker and in full view of every person present." This lady was Mrs. Wood, the manager's wife. We observe that she was always very strict in her religious observances. How often have we heard the strange ejaculation, "Who do you think I saw at church? Why Mr.

*Theatrical Rambles of Mr. & Mrs. Greene*, Charles Durang

and Mrs. — of the theatre! Who would have thought of seeing them there!" As if really they thought the actors were not human beings, or beings of another organization. If players are not equals in the sight of God with their brethren, they are bound by the same human laws in all things here.

    Mr. Hodges now opened the Nashville theatre, in Tennessee. Learning that the Louisville theatre was to close, he offered the Greenes an engagement. It was accepted and thither they went and were most kindly received, professionally and privately before which audience they continued to appear with yearly creasing appreciation of their merits.

    Their first stopping place was at the City Hotel at Nashville. The manager, however, had furnished apartments in the theatre, which were very comfortable and had the appearance of a home, to which he politely invited the Greenes, a most convenient arrangement.

    The theatre opened with the *Stranger*, Mrs. Greene playing Mrs. Haller, which was attended with a most painful accident at the end of the fourth act, where the introduction of the Stranger to Mrs. Haller takes place. The well-known tableau forms a striking incident in the play. The Stranger, making an exclamation at the sudden appearance of his repudiated wife, starts and makes an exit while the wife falls fainting into the arms of her protectors, the drop-curtain falling as quickly as possible on the picture. This curtain had attached to its barrel a heavy iron bar to give rapidity to its descent. The group not being far enough back from its line, in its descent it struck Mrs. Greene just above the ankle of the left leg, confusing it seriously. In this awful state of suffering, her ankle bound up, she contrived to finish the part and to go through the arduous fifth act with the Stranger. Many of the audience, out of sympathy for her sufferings, desired the act to be dispensed with.

    The next night she, thus invalidated, appeared as Bianca in *Fazio*,[6] as no substitute could be readily procured in so brief a time; and on the following night limped through the Widow Melnotte on the occasion of Mr. Hodges performing Claude Melnotte, sooner than have the piece postponed. At the close of this performance she was conveyed to

*Theatrical Rambles of Mr. & Mrs. Greene*, Charles Durang

her chamber, where she remained painfully confined to her couch for above six weeks.

During this time the spectacle dramas of the *Mountain Sylph* and the *Deep, Deep Sea* were successfully produced as novelties *par excellence*.[7] Mrs. Greene was greatly missed in all those pieces. Her next appearance was when only partially recovered, so that she could limp along like the lady with the cork leg. She appeared as the Widow Greene in the *Love Chase*.[8] This effort laid her up again.

## NOTES

[1] *The School of Reform*, a comedy by Thomas Morton.

[2] Cushman's *Macbeth* was first brought out at the Charles Street Theatre, New Orleans, April 23, 1836.

[3] Probably the character in Goldsmith's *She Stoops to Conquer*; although other Diggorys appeared in Jackson's *All the World's a Stage* and Lunn's *Family Jars*.

[4] *The French Spy*, a melodrama by J. T. Haines; *The Devil's Daughter*, a melodrama by George Almar.

[5] George Holland came to America under an engagement at the Bowery Theatre. A highly entertaining comedian and comic singer, with a bit of ventriloquism and barnyard imitations, he was a loyal employee of Caldwell for several years and a favorite in New Orleans. At this time he was traveling as Dr. Lardner's agent and manager. Lardner gave astronomical lectures using a planetarium that occupied an entire pit, valued at $13,000. Its motion was powered by a small steam engine.

[6] *Fazio*, a tragedy by H. M. Milman.

[7] *The Mountain Sylph*, an opera by Barnett and Thackery; *The Deep, Deep Sea; or, The American Sea Serpent*, a burletta by Charles Dance.

[8] *The Love Chase*, a comedy by James Sheridan Knowles.

*Theatrical Rambles of Mr. & Mrs. Greene*, Charles Durang

## XXIV.

WEIGHTY ACTORS — METAMORA AND THE INDIANS — A LUDICROUS SCENE — GENERAL JACKSON AND THE ACTORS — A TRAVELING SCHEME, ETC.

Charles Parsons, the mammoth actor of native hue and Methodist preacher, suddenly abandoned the clerical robes and donned again the sock and buskin. It seems a curious coincidence that he made his debut from the pulpit to the stage in the part of Dr. Cantwell in the *Hypocrite*.[1] The actors enjoyed the joke if the audience did not. Parsons now played a star engagement, which all actors will do when they can. In choosing this character he insulted common sense by his attempting to throw odium on the professors of religion; but to the credit of the supporters of the drama be it said, he played to empty benches.

The return of Mr. Parsons to the stage certainly added weight to it for at this time the western stage could boast of three immensely weighty actors of about the *avoirdupois* of 290 to 320 per man. Who was the largest we cannot decide, but they were giants. These were named Big Scott (J. M. Scott), Parsons, and Raymond. The best-named of this big trio very foolishly committed suicide by drowning himself because someone said that Parsons was a better actor than he was. Soon after, Parsons assumed the character of the preacher, which left the great western dramatic field open to Scott to tear the passion to pieces. That Raymond should have drowned himself for that or any other cause was a very foolish act. However, Parsons' restless disposition was continually see-sawing between the two professions. He again threw off the parson's habit and became a stage star again. Probably the profits of his clerical position did not equal the

*Theatrical Rambles of Mr. & Mrs. Greene*, Charles Durang

actor's, or the groaning responses of his congregation were not so agreeable as the clacquers of the pit and boxes of the theatres. He returned to expiate his sins there.

Wemyss gives a very amusing account of Parsons when he was his stage manager at Pittsburgh in 1838. At that time he was studying theology with a view of ordination in the ministry. We give one of his official reports to his employer:

MY DEAR WEMYSS—

Mrs. Shawls engagement, no go. First night, $165; second night, *Lady of Lyons*, $126; third night, *Ion*, $80. What do you think of that? This place of Pittsburgh is not worth the attention of any manager. I am disgusted with it, and never again, in my professional character, will I visit it. A monkey-show, at a fip a head, is equal to their deserts, and fully adapted to their intellectuality. More is beyond their conception. Blast them! I am almost sick of the ways of management, if such is to be my success, and I think you will agree with me too. Therefore, if I was not already engaged to you at Baltimore, I should, I think, decline the whole matter; but. as it is I will do all I can to make things go right.

Yours truly, C. B. Parsons.

Mr. Parsons excelled in Indian heroes, and one of these characters he chose for his benefit. On this occasion Mrs. Greene performed a squaw of some interest in the piece. At the close of the performance he took off his wampum belt and presented it to her as a testimonial of the pleasure her impersonation of the part gave him. She wore it ever after in the character of Nahmeoke in *Metamora* when she played it with Forrest.

A funny scene occurred on one of the nights he was playing *Metamora* in the west. Nahmeoke is assailed by a squad of Indian traitors. Metamora springs from a covert and, presenting his rifle over the shoulder of his squaw, exclaims, "Which of you have lived too long?"

## *Theatrical Rambles of Mr. & Mrs. Greene*, Charles Durang

The two, who were instructed to advance from the group, were a very tall and a very short one. Both had been libating with whiskey and were greatly afraid of Forrest's rigorous treatment of supers. Well, forward came this long and short of it. The short one came officiously first toward Forrest. Forrest sternly fixed his wild and piercing eye on his two victims. The short Indian, becoming nervous and alarmed, fell rolling on the stage. The big 'un—the six foot two inch one—followed suit, and fell on the little 'un. Both grappled each other as they lay on the floor and commenced a roly-poly game across the stage, while Forrest stood with his rifle over the shoulder of his squaw, who was convulsed with laughter. But to add to the fun of the scene neither of them would get up; but each blaming the other, pummeled one another well, till at last they rolled off near the wing, and then rising, fled incontinently from the wrath of the red Indian.

It is seldom that Forrest's risibles can be excited. His nature is at times quite irascible when he is crossed in stage business that has been well digested by rehearsals. But to laughter, however ridiculous the passing event may be, before the public he does not lose the identity of the character he is invested with, which is of course of the serious phase.

However, no rule without an exception. John Greene once won a bet from Forrest. The wager was that in playing a certain stolid, idiotic, stupid character in one of his pieces, he would force him for once to a smile or a giggle, when most deeply absorbed in the passion of the scene. This bet occurred during a rehearsal wherein Greene had this nondescript part to play and in which Forrest was giving instructions how to play it.

"If I follow your directions strictly, I shall surely cause you to laugh in spite of yourself," said Greene.

"Don't trouble yourself about that. I am not very impressible, and feel the responsibility of my own character too much to care for the ludicrous. I'll take the responsibility."

"Very well," replied Greene, "the blame be on your own head."

Greene and his comrade were to enter when Forrest

*Theatrical Rambles of Mr. & Mrs. Greene*, Charles Durang

was in one of his most impassioned speeches, in a whirlwind of passion. They entered at the cue; and to the questions put to him, Greene turned with a face so ludicrously stupid that it seemed a wooden mask from which no ray of intelligence could emanate. Forrest looked at him a minute and turned his head to recover his gravity. Then with an extra amount of sternness to conceal his hysterical desire to laugh he again endeavored to face the dense blank, idiotic countenance, on which no smile had dawned, which awaited his pleasure. One look was sufficient. The irrepressible fit of laughter burst forth; which proved contagious to the audience and a general laugh responded from all parts; all except Greene, who was as inflexible as a marble statue. John won his bet and it was paid.

John Greene was always a great admirer of General Jackson, and the question may be asked, without fear of contradiction, "who is not?" For "e'en his faults did lean to virtue's side." "Ingratitude, more strong than traitor's arms" can never veil his noble patriotism and deeds from that soil where floats the banner of Union Stars, illuminating freedom's soil! A star of glory himself!

Mr. Greene and a party of friends being on an excursion of pleasure near the famed Hermitage in Tennessee, and long wishing to visit this second Mecca of American patriotism, seized upon the present opportunity of gratifying this ardent wish. The Honorable Felix Grundy had favored Mr. Greene with a letter of introduction to the old Spartan sometime before. No opportunity offering for its presentation until now, the desired visit was at once resolved upon and thither the Greene party went, and was all most cordially and hospitably received by the old hero.

Mr. Greene said that at the first interview with the General the party seemed embarrassed in his presence, but such was his easy, friendly manner, so simply courteous, that all were at once placed at ease, as if in a friend's house in familiar intercourse, conversing freely on the topics of the day, but never broaching any political subject involving diversity of opinions of the past or present himself, but awaited questions of that sort from his guests. Mr. Greene ventured to touch upon some of his Indian campaigns and his hair

## Theatrical Rambles of Mr. & Mrs. Greene, Charles Durang

breadth escapes, which he most pleasantly and modestly recounted, relating many interesting anecdotes not known or referred to by historians and seemingly avoiding anything that might be construed into political personal references, never self opinionated, but quite affable in all things, indeed, in his social moments the reverse of all those idiosyncratic attributes so often charged to his stern character.

Gen. Jackson was very remarkable in personal appearance—tall and sinewy of frame, but then very attenuated, his features strongly marked with self will and determination, the gray eye still clear and flashing fire, the hair iron gray, stiff and wiry, with a high and expanded forehead. So did stern native majesty sit paramount on that care worn brow.

The General invited the party to dinner and introduced them to his family. There were three or four children at the table, all orderly and well behaved. To them his attentions were often turned. The table and family assimilated to the pilgrim style, in simple neatness, remarkably clean in every article, the meats plentiful and well cooked, but no luxurious attempt. The Generals conversational powers were easy and pleasant. At times he would appear feeble and evidently exhausted. A pause would then intervene and anon he would rally his physical powers. The mind again sparkling, he would commence anew his electrifying remarks, imbued with much humor and shrewd points. He did the honors of the host with grace and dignity, imposing no restraint upon his guests; at least his native good breeding imposed no such feeling, the marks of a true gentleman.

He showed the party through his drawing and ante-rooms wherein were many curious relics. One room was hung with the portraits of his officers, whom he called his children. When the party left the mansion, the General accompanied them to their coach, shaking all of them cordially by the hand. He stood at his entrance gate as they drove down the road until they lost sight of each other. It was the last time they ever saw old Dentatus.

A traveling scheme was now formed to go to Jackson, Missouri. The company was made up of stars, young, mad actors, some decayed of the *passé* type, a heterogeneous

*Theatrical Rambles of Mr. & Mrs. Greene*, Charles Durang

cast who could fill a stage or "pit, as well as better men," as Falstaff avers. One performer, especially, who played Pizarro, was of the sawdust school, a spouting blower in a horse drama, ever ready in horsemanship attitude to throw a fore-spring or a back summersault from an over desire to be felt as well as heard and seen by the spectators. Such actors ever looked like the Jack of Clubs, inevitably the same. It was a company of much individuality, always striving at making original points and out-heroding Herod.

Mr. Charles B. Parsons, a native of Connecticut and a weighty actor of some 225 pounds, now came forward with a new project. It was to become the lessee of the Cincinnati Theatre and also of the Louisville house; or in lieu of that plan, to build a new one altogether. He had engaged a young architect to draw plans for the same. In this new enterprise of building or leasing, Parsons invited John Greene to participate in as a joint partner. In this operation Greene desired time to consider a proposition then fraught with so great a responsibility.

The season here finished satisfactorily, when they started on the usual river circuit. In a few months subsequently, the Greenes and *corps* departed for the upper sections of that country towards Nashville, Tennessee. After a long detour through the States of Mississippi and Tennessee, the itinerants arrived at Louisville, where they met with Charles B. Parsons.

Mr. Greene, having agreed to his proposition of erecting a new theatre, had brought with him the plans accurately drawn, with the estimates and building specifications, etc.; and giving some new views thereon, to which Parsons very calmly replied that, "he should not want them now, that after his benefit, which would take place that week, he should withdraw from the profession and return to the church he had thoughtlessly abandoned."

To which Greene dryly made answer, "With Domine Samson, I can only say, 'good gracious.'"[2]

223

*Theatrical Rambles of Mr. & Mrs. Greene*, Charles Durang

## NOTES

¹*The Hypocrite*, a comedy by Isaac Bickerstaff.
²A character in *Guy Mannering*.

*Theatrical Rambles of Mr. & Mrs. Greene*, Charles Durang

## XXV.

DOWN THE RIVER — THE JEFFERSON FAMILY — SILVFR CUP VERSUS TIN CUP — FREE AND EASY HOTEL ACCOMMODATIONS, ETC.

The Greenes once more descended the Ohio and reached St. Louis. Here they met their old theatrical friend and manager, Mr. Ludlow, who had his theatre open at this place, wherein Edmund S. Conner was casting his stellar rays over its boards in the sock and buskin line.[1] Ludlow engaged the Greenes to play a few nights in conjunction with Conner. Mrs. Greene opened in *Mrs. Haller*. The second night as Catherine in *Love*,[2] and also played the Widow Melnotte, and many leading parts with Conner as the hero. At this time the late Joseph Jefferson (the father of the present popular comedian,) had his company, consisting mostly of his own family, playing at Alton, Illinois. The names ran thus: Mr. Adams, Charles Burke (his step son), Mr. Germon, Mrs. Jefferson, Mrs. Germon, little Joe and Cornelia Jefferson (brother and sister), and other auxiliaries.

Jefferson had a very pretty set of moveable scenery with which he could erect or cause an impromptu theatre to arise in any hall with two hours labor. He was an excellent scene painter and machinist, as well as a fair comedian.[3] So far as comedy and farce went, his family *corps* was quite *au fait* and truly a model traveling association of theatricals. Thus was the Jeffersonian fraternity perambulating through the Far West when the Greenes fell in with them.

It was Jefferson's purpose to form a circuit of the various towns on the upper Mississippi, and with that intention made a proposition to Mr. and Mrs. Greene to join him in the speculation. It was agreed to by the parties, the place of meeting together being at Quincy. Jefferson, having great

*Theatrical Rambles of Mr. & Mrs. Greene*, Charles Durang

experience in the above localities, was sanguine of success; and for this purpose rented a large hall to erect his theatre in. But, alas! the Quincy grapes proved sour.

Unfortunately for the drama, there had been a religious revival at that place. The liberal minded, merry, moderate citizens, and the *bon vivants* of whiskey toddies, the licentious card players, the vulgar jig dancers, etc., had become suddenly pious. They were forbidden by their religious exhorters to attend profane stage plays, filled with Satan's examples; so that all the converted absented themselves from their old amusements, lest they should be marked as backsliders and sinners. But hypocrisy was quite apparent in their latent practicing of evil of all kinds.

The business failing to pay the current expenses here, the *corps* moved to the town of Hannibal, where the receipts were larger and so partially repaired financial damages. From thence they went to Dubuque, Iowa, a then growing town, and which now contains a land office, three churches, a lyceum, a bank, four hotels, a printing office, and a number of large stores. Vast improvements since the Jefferson *corps* was there in 1840.

Joseph Jefferson and family subsequently emigrated to the city of Mobile at the invitation, *on dit*, of Mr. Charles Fisher,[4] a brother of the celebrated Clara Fisher, who was not an actor but a gentleman of refinement, intelligence, and of great literary acquirements. He was secretary to the Gas Company of Mobile. The President of that company was a Mr. DeVandal, who had leased the theatre from Mr. Caldwell, who was its owner. Hence he had commissioned Mr. C. Fisher to engage a company for the season of 1843.

Mrs. Richardson (nee Miss Elizabeth Jefferson, Mrs. Samuel Chapman, and now Mrs. Richardson) had been a season or so before at the Mobile theatre where, through her very versatile talent, she had become a powerful favorite. In the course of human events, her husband, Mr. Richardson, was accidentally killed at Baltimore, where he carried on business of a mercantile nature. In due course of time, Mrs. Richardson became the happy wife of Mr. Charles Fisher of the Gas Company and, in a few years after, a widow for the

*Theatrical Rambles of Mr. & Mrs. Greene*, Charles Durang

third time. The usual uncertainties attending all theatrical speculations overtook the Mobile theatre about this time, which, we believe, was under the management of an eccentric Frenchman by the name of Jules Dumas, who had been an *attaché* of the Ravel *corps* as a traveling agent and an interpreter in their first essays in America. As a proprietor of a theatre he seemed *au fait* in all the tricks of the trade. He kept adjacent to the theatre a well appointed restaurant. Knowing the social qualities of the profession generally and as an accomplished *restaurateur* and wily manager, he took "time by the forelock," as an expert financier, and paid one half of his salaries, or sometimes the whole, in choice libations.

    Mrs. Richardson had, through solicitation, become the manageress of the theatre, her popularity and cleverness as an actress suggesting such a policy by the lessee. So the new season commenced under her auspices and Charles Fisher's, whose influence was co-extensive with the upper crust of Alabama society. The brilliant status of Mrs. Richardson attracted Joseph and his brethren and sisters to her theatrical throne, a most imposing nucleus around whom this Jeffersonian family concreted with infinite felicity; *viz.*, Mr. and Mrs. Wright, Mr. and Mrs. MacKenzie, Mr. and Mrs. Germon, Mr. Joseph Jefferson and his two little prodigies, Joseph and Cornelia. The other parts of the company consisted of Mr. and Mrs. Hodges, Mrs. Stewart, Mr. Cowell, and Mr. Morton.[5]

    Poor Joseph Jefferson died at Mobile of yellow fever, November 24, 1842, aged 38. The grandsire of this Jefferson dynasty was one of our first glorious comedians that adorned our first theatre of 1794 at Boston, New York, and Philadelphia. He died at Harrisburg, Pa., in 1832.

    E. S. Conner was starring at Mobile this season, when it was announced that "a splendid silver cup would be presented to the tragedian by a committee of gentlemen who had long admired his public talent and private virtue. As there was a struggle for bumper benefits in a failing season, Cowell, who had a benefit coming off, hit upon a similar expedient of drawing a house. As the stars had monopolized nearly the entire season with their benefits, the stock actors had hard

*Theatrical Rambles of Mr. & Mrs. Greene*, Charles Durang

work to squeeze in their beneficial appeals, always few and far between. As a piece of savory satire upon star humbuggery of the day, we beg to give his bill of fare on that occasiont:[6]

MOBILE THEATRE
under the management of Mrs. Richardson.
FAREWELL BENEFIT
of
MR. JOE COWELL,
Prior to his departure for some place, but where,
he don't know, nor will any body care.

At the close of the performance, of course, Mr. Cowell will be called out—but if not, he will go out—and have a splendid wreath thrown to him from a corner of the 2d tier, and be addressed from the stage-box or by one of a committee of gentlemen who have long admired his private worth and public services, and be presented with an elegant tin cup; to which he will make an extemporaneous reply prepared for the occasion after the manner of other distinguished artists. Among the many luxuries that could be named for both mind and body, such as old wine, old books, and old boots, might be mentioned old plays; but Old Joe Cowell, being desirous to please everybody, has made a selection of one about his own age; two, born within his recollection, and another that never saw "the light of other days" till now, called <u>Joe Short</u>.

Now Joe Cowell having the <u>Assurance</u>—not London—but of many friends, that they intend to <u>Meddle</u> in his favor on this occasion, begs in a <u>Courtley</u> manner not to <u>Dazzle</u>, but, inform the public that his benefit will take place on Friday evening, August 7th, when he hopes it will not be considered <u>Pert</u> his recommending the patrons of the drama to keep cool and <u>Harkaway</u> to the theatre, and have the <u>Grace</u> to give him a <u>Spanker</u>.

The performance will commence with the first and

*Theatrical Rambles of Mr. & Mrs. Greene*, Charles Durang

second acts of

LONDON ASSURANCE.

Sir Hartcourt Courtley, Mr. Bridges; Dazzle, Mr. Ludlow; Meddle, Mr. Cowell; Max Harkaway, Mr. Germon; Charles Courtley, Mr. Morton; Grace Harkaway, Mrs. MacKenzie; Pert, Mrs. Germon, after which, not a star, but a real comet from some-where so far down east that his childhood was passed in breaking day with brickbats, will appear and sing the Pizen Sarpient.

By particular desire of Age Tomorrow. In which Mr. Ludlow will personate seven characters. Marie, with a favorite song, Mrs. Richardson. To be followed by a new farce called

JOE SHORT.

Principal characters by Mr. Cowell, Mr. Anderson, Mr. Wright, Mrs. MacKenzie, Mrs. Wright, and Mrs. Germon..

To conclude with the "Widow's Victim.." Jeremiah Clip (with his inimitable imitations), Mr. Cowell; Jenny, Mrs. Richardson; Widow, Mrs. Mackenzie.

THE TIN CUP

will be exhibited on the day of performance, and a deposit at George Cullum's made at the bar by the committee, for Cowell's friends to drink to his success in a bumper!

The company continued their whimsical adventures through an entire circuit of the new towns of Illinois, all springing up in the midst of the beautiful prairies, as beautiful as those we have read of in the amusing Arabian Knights entertainments. Now those flowery plains are becoming dotted with picturesque villas and villages, thriving manufacturing towns, and stately cities.

Their mode of traveling was of the most primitive

## *Theatrical Rambles of Mr. & Mrs. Greene*, Charles Durang

style of the early emigrants—in a large covered wagon with a team of six horses, nothing less, each horse decorated with a string of bells. Thus they jogged on as merry a set of undone fortune seeking Christians, as any in Christendom, with jest, story, and song to Galena, a prosperous town in the lead district.

All the new towns in Illinois, *viz.*, Springfield, Jacksonville, and others, in the midst of those paradise gardens, are growing places. And they presented to the eye of our perambulating Thespians original and heavenly sights of primitive nature in scenic grandeur as just discovered by man but touched by his magic wand and suddenly becoming dressed in all the beauties of art.

On their journeys they often met with large groups of Indians seeking like themselves new places, or a local habitation without a name. On the arrival of the company at a hotel with a lofty sounding name, but of a most woebegone aspect and dilapidated state—probably one of those old granite one story rough houses first constructed by the French fur traders in this district, to which the American emigrants had added wooden tenements of a very fragile style—Mr. Greene asked for a private room for self and wife, and was shown into one on the ground floor with neither lock nor latch of any kind on the door, and which proved to be none other than the general receiving room of the tavern, where the guests of all orders were passing through, lounging about, or throwing themselves down to repose on its benches. In such an apartment Mrs. Greene could not change her clothes, wash herself, or arrange her dresses for the night's performances. However a screen of matting was constructed in one corner for a sleeping apartment, *pro tem*, and thus with a pine knot lighted did she make her toilet and read over her part for the play. Nothing more primitive could be looked for even in the days of the patriarchs. After they had retired for the night to their rough couch, the boarders of every caste would enter, and very coolly seat themselves and discuss the affairs of the country, the market prices, etc. It was the model of a free and easy society upon the most approved original plan.

The theatre was filled every night with a generous

*Theatrical Rambles of Mr. & Mrs. Greene*, Charles Durang

paying audience. They made another detour to the several places on their return towards Galena. At length they reached a place called Lancaster. They put up at a log house dignified by the name of a tavern, wherein the post-office was located. Another incident occurred here. The first morning after their arrival Mrs. Greene was awakened by a slight noise, and starting up suddenly found a man standing with one foot on the trundle-bed occupied by herself and husband, reaching over their heads. Alarmed, she called out with vigor for the reason of this intrusion upon her privacy, when the man very coolly replied, "he was going to sort the mail and was fishing the letters out left in the interstices of the logs." Being satisfied with his answer, she drew the patched coverlet over her head, while this postmaster industriously pursued his official duties.

They arrived safely at Burlington, the capital of Iowa, not so large a place as Dubuque. This then Territory, now State, was crowded with Indians, who were then holding a large council fire at this place. Our gentlemen became quite intimate with their great war chief, Kisacush. This Indian brave spoke English very plainly and seemed remarkably well bred. He dined with them frequently during the company's stay, and Greene has told us that he was quite *au fait* in table etiquette and equally a critic in dramatic entertainments.

*Theatrical Rambles of Mr. & Mrs. Greene*, Charles Durang

## NOTES

[1] Ludlow was featuring Conner in his St. Louis theatre late in November, 1839.

[2] *Love*, a drama by J. S. Knowles.

[3] This would be Joseph Jefferson II, father of the famous American comedian.

[4] Charles James Berry Fisher, the youngest brother of the popular Clara Fisher. He seldom performed, but was connected with various literary and theatrical enterprises. He took over the management of the sporting and theatrical paper, *Spirit of the Times*, in 1833, but relinquished control two years later. He died in Mobile, January 20, 1859, at the age of fifty-five.

[5] Wright's wife was Mary Ann Jefferson, sister to Mrs. Richardson. Alexander Mackenzie was married to Hetty Jefferson. The Germons were also a part of the Jefferson clan.

[6] This item is nearly verbatim from Cowell's *Thirty Years Passed Among the Players*. Cowell wrote, "I had a right to a benefit during the twenty weeks, but the season had been so monopolized by sometimes two and three stars at a time, that I had to continue a week longer for a vacant night."

*Theatrical Rambles of Mr. & Mrs. Greene*, Charles Durang

## XXVI.

THE CITY OF THE DEAD — A RETURN TO NEW ORLEANS — A MOST AWFUL SCENE — THE TWO FANNIES — THE COMEDIENNE AND THE *DANSEUSE* — GEORGE HOLLAND AS MINE HOST.

The company's next halting place was at Palmyra. Here they found the races in full operation, the Greenes and their companions visiting the course every day as did all the fashionable families of the place and its vicinity.

The company now visited the thriving settlements of Prairie du Chien, Caseville, and Madison. The former is about five miles above the Wisconsin River; situated on a beautiful prairie, long settled by French traders. Their descendants are half-breeds. This country abounds in mineral wealth, lying between the Mississippi and Lake Michigan. Traveling to Madison by stage, where they expected to take the steamboat, they had to wait two days at what they called a hotel. But it was nothing more than a shanty, at the rear of which three warehouses stood in a melancholy state, empty, as a sign of non-commercial trade.

The city proper, the capital of Wisconsin, originated in speculation. It was laid out magnificently on paper. Some public buildings were raised—two hotels, forty or fifty dwellings—but it looked like a city of the dead. The long deserted black wharf first struck the players with despair. The city looked as if it had been suddenly deserted by its inhabitants, as if followed by the plague. Kitchen utensils strewed all around, pieces of bed coverings left behind, window frames smashed, broken pieces of furniture lying in every direction. Doors left open only proved that a fatal contagious disease had been a busy assailant there, that death ruled.

## *Theatrical Rambles of Mr. & Mrs. Greene*, Charles Durang

Naught but a starved cat with a skeleton of a rat before it was seen. It was the only thing alive. And we believe to this day that the place, like Herculaneum and Pompeii, lies buried in the ashes of oblivion. If it has been excavated by the hands of industry and commerce, we have never heard of it.

It was surrounded by miasma exhalings as fatal as the Pontine Marshes around Rome. The company of players might have offered ghost exhibitions here, for they would only have had an audience of ghosts to have flitted before them. So they joined in the exodus, ran down to the steamboat landing, where fortunately the boat had just touched for passengers. They hurried on board with all their baggage, overjoyed to escape from a scene so truly wretched and desolate. Away they steamed on the Mississippi, and only reached Prairie du Chien to behold that sickness had forestalled their arrival. For at the boarding house where they stopped they found every room littered with empty medicine boxes, pill boxes, and vials.

The cholera tremens came on them again! They fumigated the house, built large log fires at every chimney, threw chloride around, and seemingly conquered king cholera and gained renewed spirits; for Jefferson came in with the news that he had obtained a great stone building to perform in, that he met a happy response from the citizens of the place, and that all was alive to see a play.

The town was salubrious and money plenty, and Jefferson gave a singing quotation from the farce of the *Agreeable Surprise*:

> A toast's not worth a fig
> Without a lusty jorum,
> Hey popularum jig,
> Hey jingo popularum, jig popularum?"

"The bills for a play are out for to-night," says Joe Jefferson—*ecce signum*.

The house was crowded in every part. The inhabitants were pleased to ecstasies, and were hospitable and generous to those who entertained them.

## *Theatrical Rambles of Mr. & Mrs. Greene*, Charles Durang

There was a proposition made for the company to proceed to St. Paul, but the Greenes were forced by a previous engagement to return to New Orleans, where they had signed a contract with Mr. Ludlow, the manager of the New American Theatre. So they proceeded by way of Quincy and Stephenson on Rock River to their place of destination, sailing down the Mississippi. They left Mr. Joseph Jefferson's company with heartfelt regret, for they were in it truly as members of the family. A more pleasant professional association they never enjoyed in a life of forty years on the stage. The management was patriarchal, the feeling was that of brothers and sisters. Isolated though they were from all other refined society, or the domestic comforts of home, sweet home, they partook in every sense of savage life, nor did their morals suffer thereby.

Mrs. Richardson continued for same time on the Mobile stage (as late as 1852), as Mrs. C. Fisher. After Mr. Fisher's death, she finally retired from the profession and successfully established herself at New Orleans as a teacher of music and singing, and is now preparing two promising daughters for the stage.

Our readers must pardon this Mobile digression from our Greene travelers. To them we beg to return. At Dubuque a singular but painful sight attracted the attention of Mr. Greene and wife. On their arrival at the hotel where they were to put up, they were met in an official way by a very large, good natured looking Negro man. He obsequiously stood watching their entrance into the hall and seemed quite desirous to give his services to their wants. His sable countenance was vivid with smiles and good humor, his large white pupils of vision rolling in their orbits like sparkling foams of seas with delight at their returning thanks to his attentions. He turned out to be the cook of the hotel and, during the sojourn of the Greenes there, he was always most assiduous in his attentions to them.

One fine elastic morning Greene and wife took a promenade around the place to view its novelties and beauties, when their attention was aroused by a loud tumult of an approaching mob, accompanied by hideous yells and oaths, mingled with the piercing groans of agony of a human being.

## Theatrical Rambles of Mr. & Mrs. Greene, Charles Durang

It was the demoniac populace lynching a Negro man, a punishment inflicted for stealing clothing, as alleged. At length, getting a view of the poor wretch thus being unmercifully flagellated, they saw, with affliction, that it was the laughing hotel cook lashed to a cart-tail and flogged through the streets as it was drawn along. His screams were appalling. His wife ran from her labors to implore mercy from those fiends in human shape who were thus scourging him, on her knees supplicating the God above for a mitigation of his sufferings. The human monsters heard her not, but casting her savagely aside, she fell on the corpse of her husband, who thus expired.

The Jeffersons having made up their minds to return to Mobile, the company traveled down the river together. In two week's time the Greenes found themselves once more in dear, wicked New Orleans, as they expressed themselves.

The leading lady at the American house was Mrs. Farren, one of the greatest favorites of the Orleanites, as they called her "their own." Mr. Conner was the leading gentleman and the stock company were all of equal talent and great merit.[1] The theatre was very handsome, well lighted, and, what was much better, was well patronized. The magnificent St. Charles loomed aloft under the government of Mr. James Caldwell. Of course that theatre was in a flourishing condition.

A fiasco occurred with Caldwell's negotiation with the celebrated actress Mrs. Fanny Fitzwilliam and her mentor, Mr. Buckstone.[2] Mr. Caldwell felt certain that he had secured their services for his theatre. But from some untoward circumstance they refused to appear at the St. Charles and appeared first at the American with tremendous success. She opened with her versatile *Widow Wiggins*,[3] where her unique Italian and French imitations of song, dance and dialect acting took the natives by storm, while her racy Irish widow capped the climax of the most inimitable comic performances ever beheld on their boards.

On the first night the house was but a shy *domus*, to use the actors' phrase. It was not half full. But such was the powerful impression she made on that night that seats for the

*Theatrical Rambles of Mr. & Mrs. Greene*, Charles Durang

ensuing ones were difficult to be got. The town rang with the name of the brilliant, joyous, fascinating Fanny Fitzwilliam, who gave her auditors on the night before fits of side-splitting laughter, wonder and delight. Her music dwelt on their ears, her dance dazzled their eyes.

As a comic singing actress she had no peer, her character delineations were so true to nature. The houses were crowded from parquet to dome throughout the season, for which long period the manager found it necessary to engage her—a star engagement without a precedent. The same persons attended the performances nightly, such were her enchanting qualities. In truth, her acting, her melody of voice, her arch hoyden looks and manner only increased her popularity on each succeeding night till the end of the season. She was truly a dramatic and operatic nonpareil.

But what made the actress' attraction so much more extraordinary was that the Divine Fanny Ellsler,[4] the glorious *danseuse*, "the Venus of the light fantastic toe," who turned the heads of all the young ladies and ravished the hearts of all the young cavaliers, now danced on the same nights at Caldwell's temple, filling it with maniac crowds to surfeit. Fanny Ellsler's tickets sold at three dollars each. Half the people who wanted to see her terpsichorean feats could not get in at all. Every foot of standing room was occupied. Yet did these rival stars thus continue *pari passu* to draw crowds to the end of this season.

At the end of the season at the American, Ludlow sent his company to Mobile, where the only building the manager could procure to produce his performances in was a cotton press warehouse in the suburbs of the city and which could only be reached by a rugged crooked avenue; while manager Caldwell's new theatre was in a central and fashionable location, elegantly constructed, and in every respect affording in itself a charming resort for a tasteful, liberal public such as constituted the auditory of Mobile, the depot for the state of Alabama.

This effort of Ludlow's was to present Fanny Fitzwilliam to the Alabama public, who had heard of her colossal fame and were rampant to behold the joyous, sparkling Fanny. But this proved a fiasco. The theatre was too remote,

## Theatrical Rambles of Mr. & Mrs. Greene, Charles Durang

the road too bad and difficult to either ride or walk there, the accommodations too uncomfortable when there. The houses were thin and Fanny's salary too large to be paid out of the Lenten receipts.

J. H. Caldwell, with *his* Fanny, out-tripped Ludlow's Fanny. So, as "discretion is the better part of valor," after a brief show of colors, Ludlow decamped with his star and *corps* back to New Orleans to drop the curtain of the season in the Delta City, where Fanny Fitzwilliam threw off her merry comic robes, donning her traveling ones, and went North, or up the Mississippi.

The *corps* disbanded and the Greenes left for Philadelphia to visit their many friends and relatives in the Quaker City. While there they played an engagement at the Arch Street Theatre.[5] In the fall they took up their line of march again for New Orleans. Arriving at Cincinnati on their way thither, they tarried at the latter place in consequence of the yellow fever raging at Orleans. There they awaited its exit from that city, which the winter weather soon expelled.

Mr. and Mrs. Greene were here offered an engagement, but this summer recess they had allotted for holiday and physical recreations. The weather being yet pleasant, they were resolved to prolong its enjoyments, as their labors had been long and arduous; and meeting with many old friends and professional collaborators, especially ancient George Holland, a man of many parts of sterling worth, they told George that they wished to remain and wanted board. He replied that he was in want, too, only he wanted boarders. This was cheerful news to Greene, and the Greenes forthwith took board at Holland's domicile, where they found to their general joy the Cowell family, Slomans, and the charming Miss Mary Rock, all in family union.[5] Here was a home improvised at once.

To descant upon George Holland's humor, his love of jest, or *raconteur* of merry companionable qualities to make happy the domestic circle would be superfluous information to the profession. As a caterer of the creature comforts of life on the most liberal scale, he could not be surpassed. They had an extra dinner, one to which they had invited some of

*Theatrical Rambles of Mr. & Mrs. Greene*, Charles Durang

the choice *beaux esprits* of the city. Holland determined that it should be a piquant dinner, a novelty worthy of Epicurus, a Roman feast. He provided rare and choice collections of pickles and spices to sharpen the appetite, to strengthen and stimulate the stomach. The courses were numerous and various, from turtle soup to vermicelli soup, pies of a curious shape spiraling up like gothic towers, a chicken its pastry formed to look like a fine hen sitting over her young brood, a boiled turkey floating in oyster sauce, a Yorkshire pudding, beef *à la mode*, etc.

The dining hall opened into a large yard. The doors were opened, the guests ushered in and seated, when Holland, at the head of the table, assumed the character of grand carver. He commenced operations on the gothic towers, when out flew numerous birds, some cooked, others in their native singing state. The turkey then became the object of attack, when suddenly the host disappeared in a summerset and was next seen in the yard. He declared he had been upset by his attempt to carve that old native bird, whose age might have taught him better manners. He walked back to his place with the greatest coolness, enjoying the astonishment of his guests, assuring them he had thought the turkey was always a bird of tenderness, but the ancient that intruded into their presence had broken his carving knife. Here was a catastrophe! However, the dessert with Madeira and Champagne would drown all disappointments. It was feast of reason and the flow of soul. He was one of the kindest hearted, fun loving, mirth provoking landlords that ever brightened the performer's pathway.

## NOTES

[1] The American Theatre season of 1840-41 began on November 10.

[2] Ireland called Fanny Fitzwilliam (nee Fanny Copeland) "one of the most delightful comic actresses of the age. She made two successful visits to America, her last being in 1842. She began an engagement at the American Theatre, New Orleans, in February, 1841. J. B. Buckstone was considered a very clever farceur, a contributor of more than 150

*Theatrical Rambles of Mr. & Mrs. Greene*, Charles Durang

plays and pieces which were popular in America. He made his acting debut in this country on August 17, 1840, at the Park Theatre in his own comedy, *Single Life*.

[3] *Widow Wiggins*, a piece requiring rapid changes of character, was expressly written for Fitzwilliam by Buckstone.

[4] Fanny Ellsler first appeared at the Park Theatre on May 14, 1840. She came to this country with a European reputation that created immense local excitement. Her American engagements were a series of triumphs, but her business agent, Henry Wickoff, extracted severe terms for every one of them, never less than $500 per night and a clear benefit, or half of the night's gross and a clear benefit.

[5] The Greenes were at the Arch Street Theatre for a very limited engagement. During the summer they gave dramatic performances in Albany.

[6] Mr. and Mrs. John Sloman first appeared in New York at the Bowery Theatre on February 4, 1827. Mr. Sloman, a Christianized Jew, was a passable farceur, but excelled in comic songs. Mrs. Sloman was considered "too coldly classical to suit the multitude." Mary Rock (Mrs. Murray), from Dublin, first appeared in New York, November 19, 1827. A lady of considerable ability, pleasant features, and a sweet voice was diminished by the popularity of Clara Fisher. She spent most of her career on the Boston stage. She was best in genteel comedy, but was also a harpist.

*Theatrical Rambles of Mr. & Mrs. Greene*, Charles Durang

## XXVII.

*LONDON ASSURANCE* — STAGE DRESSES AND DRESSING — ENGLISH OPERA COMPANY — JOE COWELL AS A BONIFACE — A SERENADE AND ITS RESULTS — A CONFLAGRATION — A MAN OVERBOARD — THE LITTLE MAGICIAN — THE BONNET OF 76 — DUVERNA AT THE CHATHAM — ANDERSON, THE STAGE MANAGER — BACK TO NEW ORLEANS.

At this season the popular comedy of *London Assurance*[1] was brought out with the following excellent cast: Sir Harcourt Courtley, Mr. George Barrett; Dazzle, Mr. James S. Browne; Max Harkaway, Mr. John Greene; Meddle, Mr. J. Cowell; Dolly Spanker, Mr. Sloman; Charles Courtley, Mr. Pearson; Cool, Mr. Reader; Lady Gay Spanker, Mrs. Greene; Grace, Mrs. Sergeant. The scenery and furniture were truly splendid, equaling any theatre on the continent. The press was loud in praise of its admirable production, and Mrs. Greene, one great objective in these sketches, received the highest mead of adulation for her truthful impersonation of the dashing equestrienne! This cast is worthy of a record here. Mr. Manvers, the tenor, followed with English Opera soprano, Madame Brichta.[2]

The success of *London Assurance* was so great that they organized the cast as a body, played it at New Orleans, and the company was sent to Mobile to bring it out there. As it required some time to produce it properly, the company in the meantime were to play three pieces, among them was the *Stranger*, Mrs. Greene as Mrs. Haller. She wore the usual costume on the occasion, the traditional one of this German drama, *viz.*, a silver gray silk with white lace coiffeur. One of the newspapers tartly criticized this dress as incorrect, but

*Theatrical Rambles of Mr. & Mrs. Greene*, Charles Durang

was pleased with the rendition of the character. Why he so found fault with it, he did not please to say.

How often do we see ladies representing characters in the 13$^{th}$, the 14$^{th}$, or in the 15$^{th}$ centuries, in the *bon ton* of the present day, while the males in the same play will be dressed in shapes, tunics, etc., sometimes in Roman and Grecian tragedies. Some of the ladies of the present day dress Ophelia in *Hamlet* in crinoline. Even those stars to whom we might look for a correct judgment and appropriate costume are often the opposite to the character represented. *Par* example, Mrs. Austin, the celebrated vocalist and actress, when she first appeared in Philadelphia and Baltimore in 1827 wore in Rosina as a reaper, a rich silk velvet bodice, trimmed with gold lace, and white satin petticoat. Truly, a most inappropriate costume for a poor reaping rustic girl. Such a violation of costume must have struck the most common observer, yet it passed unnoticed by the sage critics. Forsooth, a star had canonized an error!

In playing a beggar, the costume should be rags and patches, clean to be sure, but not fine. If acting a domestic, a plain, suitable apparel. If a historical character, consult the authorities of history, the best pictures, or well-informed artists thereon. In the purchase of materials, buy the best velvets, silks, satins, etc., as being the cheapest in the end, as more durable and more effective than imitations, though many imitative things show best on the stage at night. For instance, stage jewelry, as it is called, of Birmingham manufacture, shows more brilliantly at night than the real Simon pure; and a set of those may be purchased, say for $300, that will look more costly than thousands of dollars worth of real jewelry. Silks and velvets show their real value at night and never become shabby.

Mr. Joe Cowell had made quite a sensation through the Southwest as Meddle. Indeed, he played it with much natural racy humor. He made it tell, a difficult task where there are so many good parts in the comedy to divide the applause with. Cowell was now waiting in New Orleans until required to appear in *London Assurance*, and when he did appear as Mark Meddle, he made a popular mark. We do not

*Theatrical Rambles of Mr. & Mrs. Greene*, Charles Durang

purpose in our desultory sketches to follow events chronologically, but as they involuntarily arise upon our memory as we sketch with pen and ink.

On the arrival of the so-called English Opera Troupe at New Orleans, a funny incident occurred in *rencontre* between the tenor or baritone (we now forget which of the troupe's members it was) and the stage manager of the St. Charles, the then veritable Joe Cowell. All who knew Cowell's genial proclivities for social conventions, especially after the laborious duties of the night's performances were truly discharged, know that to him indulgence was the Elysium of pleasure, when composed of congenial friends and brethren of mark and humor. Cowell was a man of infinite complacency of mien and manner, but a Talleyrand in shrewd perception, who, in jocular sarcastic sneers when eulogizing persons or "damning in faint praise" some notable personage, surpassed all compeers. His face and smile were blandness personified. When in genial converse he would draw forth his large silver snuff box and liberally inhale the pulverized tobacco. The manner, the jeer, and expressive sneer so good-humoredly expressed can never be forgotten by those who were pleasingly entertained with his quiet conversational remarks. He was at all times undisturbed, even when in a sea of troubles.

His autobiography of *Thirty Years Among the Players* abounds in sneering pleasantries of the kind. His significant fling at Mr. and Mrs. A. Wood at their idiosyncratic acting, to say the least, was unkind and in bad taste, a qualified praise better left alone. In speaking of their performance in the *Stranger*, he says, "They frequently played together such characters as Mrs. Haller and the Stranger. They threw so much reality into the scene that they literally appropriated all the sorrow to themselves; positive sobs and tears by turns, at each others plaints and penitence, would so interfere with and divert the sympathies of the audience as to draw all recollection of the imaginary character in pity for the sufferings of Billy Wood and his wife. And so on with others. We think that the highly respectable characters of those late performers deserved more appropriate record. Talent exists in all times however rare genius may be on the stage; but high-toned

## Theatrical Rambles of Mr. & Mrs. Greene, Charles Durang

honor and respectability are not so perpetual to all its professors or any other portion of the human family. The wearing of their private mantle might adorn many of the high magnates of the present stage.

This manager and actor often sat up with his *convives* till the cock gave the hint for the night cap; and so departed, all exhausted with good humor, to seek restoration from that great nurse of nature—sleep. But Cowell made it a *sine qua non* with the host of the hotel that when he retired to his dormitory nothing in creation should disturb his slumbers till he, himself, awoke and rang for servants; no, not even if the edifice was on fire. The arrival of strangers or stars after his sleeping hours would often break his privacy on the score of business. Cowell had taken time by the forelock and prepared himself with the *lex talionis* in case he should be thus disturbed, and ordered that there should be a large bucket of water left in his room every night.

The expected opera troupe arrived late at night at the hotel and the first inquiry was for the manager, to learn if a rehearsal could be called in the morning with a full band. No time was to be wasted. Mr. Manvers did not know of Cowell's prohibition of being called upon at unseasonable hours; but some wags, looking out for a joke, pointed out his room to the singers and away they went in full chorus, headed by Mr. Manvers, who first knocked gently at the door.

No answer, another knock, then a vigorous call, "Cowell! Cowell!"

Being all in a merry humor, they began to sing the glee from *Cymbeline*:

> Hark! Hark! The lark of Heaven's gate sings,
> And Phoebus 'gins arise,
> His steed to water at those springs
> On chaliced flowers that lies;
> With every thing that pretty is,
> My manager sweet arise,
> Arise, arise, slumbering Cowell!"

At the end of the strain, the door opened and the con-

## *Theatrical Rambles of Mr. & Mrs. Greene*, Charles Durang

tents of the bucket fell in a deluge over the manager and his troupe.

"Hallo! stop! stop!" cried Manvers. "We did not come to rehearse the oratorio of the *Deluge*. What is the meaning of this!"

Confusion, worse confounded, was raised by the drenched vocalists; and when Cowell's vision of sleep disappearing, he recognized the voice of Manvers. He immediately donned his *robe de chambre*, descended to the drawing room, making a graceful *amende honorable*, and "the mistakes of the night were crowned with a merry morning," as the tag to the comedy has it.

They brought out *London Assurance* after many delays at Mobile, and it ran wonderfully for ten consecutive nights. Then the company returned to New Orleans to the St. Charles, which had been occupied by the Italian Opera, which went to Mobile. Thus the dramatic and opera companies alternately occupied those cities.

The Italian Opera met with the most enthusiastic success. The houses in the spacious St. Charles were nightly overflowed with the elite of fashionable society. Seats were engaged for the entire season. Indeed, a perfect furor prevailed. The *artistes* were perfect in all respects. As lyric actor nothing could equal Sig. Salvi.[3] He had a pure cultivated tenor of extensive register. In vivid expression and sympathetic power, he reminded all of the elder Kean. Signora Rossi was a most beautiful woman, equally effective in all qualities with the *artiste* Salvi. Her voice was of the organ tone. She had an excellent school, well balanced division of her register and rich in quality. Her eyes were magnificently inspiring, with a fine person. She was a lyric actress of powerful expression. The operas with the grand accessories of the St. Charles Theatre could not have been surpassed in Europe, certainly not in America.

One Sunday afternoon, while the opera furor was at its apex, the dramatic *corps* were sitting at their lodgings in cheerful conversation when the alarm of fire was given. The cries were loud. They all rushed to the door, when they beheld the St. Charles Theatre in flames.[4] On that night an opera was to have been sung. The excitement to listen to it had

## Theatrical Rambles of Mr. & Mrs. Greene, Charles Durang

been tremendous. The house would have been crowded with at least three thousand persons. Had the fire broken out when the house was thus filled the loss of life would have been awful.

This beautiful temple, as it was called, had no parallel then in this country and hardly since. In many respects it equaled the Philadelphia Academy of Music and in some decorations surpassed it. The fire originated in an adjoining yard and, reaching an open window in the theatre, it soon communicated to the flammable material of canvas and all those flimsy articles which the mimic world is composed of. The whole interior was soon in flames. As if a train of powder had been laid, it suddenly exploded. Naught could be saved such was the rapidity of ignition to all parts. Messrs. Cowell, Pierson, and J. S. Browne, keeping their wardrobe in the theatre, lost all of it. All the dramatic wardrobe of the theatre, most valuable properties, scenery, music, etc., was a total loss. What the Italians lost we do not know. Everything was lost except a portion of Robert Macaire's dress, which all know consists of rags. In this conflagration the great entrepreneur James H. Caldwell lost a fortune and the performers their season's employment.

The Nashville theatre, at this crisis of the Greene's fate, was to let. The lease or its ownership was in Mr. Caldwell's hands. Mr. Greene was advised to take it. The suggestion was adopted and in conjunction with Mr. Joe Cowell he became the lessee. They organized a good *corps*, consisting of Messrs. Barrett, Cowell, Greene, Anderson, Germon, Sergeant, R. Russell, Mesdames Mueller, Germon, Sergeant, and Greene. A respectable *corps*.[5]

This theatre then stood on the sight of the present Odd Fellows Hall. The company took passage on a swift steamer bound up the Mississippi for Nashville. Barrett, who remained behind for some reasons best known to himself, was to follow in two weeks. They started with a strong head of steam, not a "fair wind," as used to be said in olden times. When about two miles from land, a cry was heard of a "man overboard!" All hands rushed to the gunwales to see who it was. None could recognize him. He was rapidly receding

## *Theatrical Rambles of Mr. & Mrs. Greene*, Charles Durang

from sight. The headway of the boat was stopped, but ere the steamer's boat could be lowered and manned, the floating man seemed to rapidly disappear. Yet, from what could be seen of him, he did not struggle but floated on his back like an expert swimmer. The rowers bent manfully to their work, soon overhauled the man, and pulled him into the boat. The lost one proved to be a Mr. Cripps, one of the musicians. When thus restored to the deck he appeared perfectly calm and easy though thus rescued from the jaws of death. It appeared that he slipped off the steps into the water in descending from the upper to the lower deck. When requested to describe his sensations, he very coolly said that he knew every exertion would be made to rescue him in time for rehearsal.

The company reached Nashville in about fourteen days, when the theatre was found in a most dilapidated condition, requiring many repairs before it could be opened. Mr. George Barrett soon joined the *corps*, and by his professional ability and polished suavity became a profitable card. He opened in Ambrose in the neat petite comedy of the *Two Friends*,[6] a character he made his own.

The charming Fanny Fitzwilliam and that excellent dramatist, little Buckstone now arrived on their way to New York and entered into an engagement with Greene, who flattered himself with the prospect of crowded houses. And so it would have proved but that this joyous daughter of Thalia was suddenly taken ill on the stage and was taken off in a swooning state. She was very ill indeed. This sad event marred her engagement and nullified poor Greene's golden prospects. "Trifles light as air" oft ruin the most brilliant theatrical events.[7]

The Hon. Martin Van Buren, being on a visit to Nashville, was invited to the theatre and very graciously accepted the invitation. The excitement to see the Little Magician politician, and certainly polished gentleman, gave a receipt of $500. Greene vauntingly proclaimed him the best star of the season, he producing the largest receipts and at no cost.

The season being now far advanced and the paying business on the wane, the performers began their exodus north and east. So Greene shut shop and joined them in

## Theatrical Rambles of Mr. & Mrs. Greene, Charles Durang

travel, reaching New York in "pretty good health and spirits," as Gregory says in the farce of *Turn Out or Turn In*.[8]

Being tendered an engagement at the Tremont Theatre, Boston, they accepted, and Mr. Greene opened in Dennis Brulgruddery, making a most successful impression, the press being unanimous in eulogy upon the naturalness and legitimate raciness of this Irish gem of lower life.[9] But to Mrs. Greene they were almost uncivil; nay, cavalierly ungallant to the sex, in speaking of her Lady Caroline Braymore. When critics lightly use their pens they know not how they lacerate feelings. They should temper justice with charity and gently scan the softer sex. The bright particular stars that now, 1841, emblazoned the theatrical horizon were Edwin Forrest, Josephine Clifton, Daddy Rice—the great original Jim Crow, Thomas Barry, Mr. and Mrs. John Brougham, Miss Clarendon, George Vandenhoff, etc. In the stock company, and great favorites with the Bostonians, were Mr. and Mrs. John Gilbert and others of good calibre.[10] The season did not answer at the Tremont Theatre and it closed in February for a month; and then, as if in derogation of the drama, opened with a circus and stage pieces, or a half and half mixture.

The circus scheme did not succeed. The coalition of the performers of the drama and quadrupeds failed. The horses were trotted away and the bipeds resumed their original positions. But all in vain. "The times were out of joint," the salaries were not forthcoming, and the Greenes seceded, accepting an offer of an engagement from Mr. J. Adams for the Albany Amphitheatre, wherein, much to their distaste, were circus performances. But here the business was equally dull, "stale, flat and unprofitable," so the objectives of these sketches transferred themselves to New York where they entered into an engagement with Messrs. Jackson and Duverna, lessees of the Chatham Theatre.[11]

Gen. Welch had engaged the Park Theatre and was playing such horse pieces as *Mad Anthony Wayne*, *Putnam*, etc. He offered the Greenes situations; and being sure of their money with the noble General, they readily accepted. There they remained six weeks, when the General removed his

*Theatrical Rambles of Mr. & Mrs. Greene*, Charles Durang

large *corps* to Philadelphia where they most successfully performed to tremendous houses at the National till summer.

John Greene's fame was now culminating to the star point. The manager of the Boston Museum offered him an engagement of two weeks on star light principles. This was his first and last appearance in the stellar role. It was an eminence he never coveted, although at this time many good stock actors, as well as inferior talent, were thus aspiring, and, as such, have been sanctioned by public sentiment. His ambition was to be a plain stock actor of the Jefferson, the Wood, the Warren, Blissett, etc., school, where he had received his professional initiatory lessons.

Mrs. Greene accompanied her husband on his tour to Boston. It being for two week, he did not go with any intention of playing there. That, fickle jade fortune played on this occasion a fantastic trick.

One morning, taking one of her old fashioned walks, she observed a crowd looking anxiously at a large playbill poster. She stopped and became a star gazer also; where, lo! to her wonderment she saw, in flaming large letters, a half a foot in length, the name of Mrs. Greene, announced as her first appearance in her "Memorable Bonnet of 76." Prodigious!

"Here I was a star! not owing to my intellect or to the brains that should make a star," said the lady, "but to my *outré* old fashioned head gear."

She had worn the antique bonnet when she was in Boston before in the *Cobbler's Wife*.[12] Its appearance then was always the signal for peals of fun and laughter. The house was crowded. Mr. Greene was quite successful in this starring tour, realizing a handsome sum of money.

They returned to New York. Then they concluded an engagement with Mr. Burton for the Arch and Chestnut Street theatres, Philadelphia, where they remained till Mr. and Mrs. Charles Kean arrived, they appearing at the Chestnut street, under Burton's management. The company was sent alternately from one house the other, as circumstances required. The Keans were very successful. The season closed at the Arch Street house in July, 1846.

At the end of the season of the Arch Street Theatre,

*Theatrical Rambles of Mr. & Mrs. Greene*, Charles Durang

the Greenes took an engagement under Mr. William Duverna of the Chatham Theatre, New York. Their salary was barely sufficient to pay board, no benefits to be given by agreement, and to play on Christmas day, New Years, and 4$^{th}$ of July, afternoons, or evenings, and no extra payment for this service. Greene was bound to play all the hearty old men, melodramatic heroes, low comedy, old men in farces, etc.; Mrs. Greene, the heavy business of tragedy and seriocomic dramas, old women, and chamber maids. Quite enough for one person with all the crudities of that category of various lines.

Mr. Duverna sailed during the season of 1845 to England in quest of novelties and returned with Miss Anna Cruise, who opened in Rosalind in *As You Like It* and soon became a favorite. She was considered best in singing parts and chambermaids. She remained in the company over a year. Mrs. Flynn, Mrs. Juda, Mrs. Nichols, Mrs. LaForrest, Miss Reynolds, Miss Philips, John Winans, Mr. Bellamy, S. Johnston, Stafford, etc., were members of the company. The houses were generally well filled, but the prices were very low, the audiences coarse and ill-bred.

Mr. James Anderson, once the prompter of the Park Theatre and the first Chatham, was engaged as Duverna's stage manager. He was an Irishman and a most strict disciplinarian. If he took a dislike to any performer he would do everything to annoy the poor wight. If his whims of friendship alighted on him, then his situation was a paradise. He was very capable but very tyrannical, very ill natured if etherized, and very different when breathing the purity of oxygen, He had, however, very good points in his character; but they were so intermingled that to separate the tares from his virtues would prove a Herculean task. He retired to a farm he purchased in a romantic nook, a kind of Irish cabin, isolated from the bustle of the world, yet surrounded by the beauties of nature and in the highest state of cultivation.

The Greenes did not long remain at this minor theatre, which had the news boys for its chief *habitués*. They soon removed to the Bowery upon increased salaries.

Robert Place, the lessee of the American Theatre, New Orleans, made them a large offer for his establishment,

*Theatrical Rambles of Mr. & Mrs. Greene*, Charles Durang

most eligible both as to position and profit, which they accepted. Bait a managerial hook with good business and a large salary and you'll find the bait and hook readily swallowed without much patient angling. So in September, 1847, Mr. and Mrs. Greene again took wing for New Orleans by the land route of Albany, Pittsburgh, Ohio River, to the Crescent City of the Mississippi, playing one week at Albany and about six weeks at Cincinnati under Rockwell's management. At the request of Mr. Logan they played for his benefit at Bate's Theatre, the play being *Douglas* with Miss Eliza Logan in the role of Young Norval; Old Norval, John Greene; Lady Randolph, Mrs. Greene.

During this time, a very sad event occurred there, resulting in the death of a very promising young actor named Morris. He rehearsed his part in the morning with his usual health and spirits and died before night while in his own room in conversation with a friend. He was engaged to be married at the time to Miss Rowe, whose brother was the young man killed by falling on his bayonet behind the scenes while playing Tonio in the *French Spy*. A strange fatality attended this family.

## NOTES

[1] *London Assurance*, a comedy by Dion Boucicault, first performed in this country on October 11, 1841, "with an attention to scenery, furniture, and appointments hitherto unattempted on our stage." The most popular play of the season, it received nearly fifty performances. The run at the St. Charles was from December 20, 1841 through March 7, 1842.

[2] The English Opera Co. made its first American appearance at the Park Theatre, September 9, 1839, with Beethoven's opera *Fidelio*. During his career in this country Manders' voice suffered from our climate and over-exertion, allowing him to appear only at intervals. His farewell benefit occurred at the Astor Place Opera House, November 22, 1849. Madame Brichta first appeared in New York at the Bowery, March 20, 1829.

[3] Sig. Salvi first appeared in New York at Niblo's Garden,

*Theatrical Rambles of Mr. & Mrs. Greene*, Charles Durang

March 22, 1849, in *LaFavorita*.
　[4]The St. Charles burned on March 13, 1842.
　[5]The Greene-Cowell management in Nashville was for only a few weeks in July, 1842. Cowell has written the business was bad.
　[6]*The Two Friends*, a comedy by M. R. Lacy.
　[7]Fanny Fitzwilliam drew badly. Cowell wrote that the best house brought $211 and the smallest $38.
　[8]*Turn Out or Turn In*, a farce by James Kenney.
　[9]The 1842-43 Tremont Theatre opened on September 5.
　[10]Thomas Barry's first American appearance was at the Park Theatre, December 16, 1826, in *The Stranger*. Shortly, he became stage manager there, remaining until 1833. Later, he was six years at managing the Tremont Theatre, a venture that ended in financial ruin. Miss Clarendon had appeared at the Franklin Theatre, New York, April 17, 1841, as Mariana in *The Wife*. The effort was termed inauspicious by Ireland, with the public determining that "her ambition o'releaped itself." Gilbert was a native Bostonian, who had first appeared at the Federal Street Theatre, November 28, 1828. He became an outstanding player of second parts in tragedy.
　[11]The Chatham Theatre opened July 20, 1843, with *The Soldier's Daughter*—Greene as Governor Heartall, Mrs. Greene as Widow Cheerly. The sequence that followed is somewhat confusing in the text. Welch was at the Park Theatre with his Olympic Circus prior to Duverna's management of the Chatham. Welch began his season January 5, 1843. By March 13 the regular theatre fare was being offered under Simpson's proprietorship. After a stint in Philadelphia with the circus, the Greenes returned to New York and performed briefly at the Chatham for Thorne, beginning July 20, 1843. They were at the Arch Street Theatre, Philadelphia, as regular members of the company for the season opening, August 10. The Arch Street business being poor, Greene joined Duverna at the Chatham in September. The couple were probably working apart much of the fall season, Mrs. Greene in Philadelphia and John in New York. Greene was at the Chestnut Street in November; and by mid-December was a regular member of the Arch Street again, perhaps joining his

*Theatrical Rambles of Mr. & Mrs. Greene*, Charles Durang

wife in the company. Duverna held the lease for both Arch Street and Chatham Theatres at this time. In September of 1844 they were back at the Chatham. On October 12, 1847, Duverna fell from a private box at the Chatham, incurring injuries that soon led to his death.

[12]*The Cobbler's Wife* may be a revision of *The Cobbler's Daughter* or J. R. Planche's *The Cobbler's Will*.

*Theatrical Rambles of Mr. & Mrs. Greene*, Charles Durang

## XXVIII.

JOSEPHINE CLIFTON — FROM GAY TO THE GRAVE — A CORPSE — FORREST'S FAREWELL TO NEW ORLEANS — THE MC VICKERS — THE DRAMA, ITS EARLIER HISTORY IN CHICAGO — MRS. HUNT IN *MACBETH* — CHICAGO SCAVENGER LAW — BACK TO NEW ORLEANS — THE CASE OF THE ANGRY CANINE AND DEAD RICHARD III — BRIEF BIOGRAPHY OF BOOTH THE ELDER.

When the Greenes arrived at New Orleans they found among the list of performers Mrs. Coleman Pope, Miss Dudley, Mrs. Johnston, Mrs. G. Rowe, Mrs. Walters, George W. Jamieson, William Placide, Charles Grierson, and the late Josephine Clifton, afterwards Mrs. Place.

One evening this lady (Place) came behind the scenes, seeming in quite a laughing mood and pleased with all. Addressing Mrs. Greene in a merry vein, she remarked to her, "Ah! my lady, you are playing my favorite parts now. Wait until the stars come, then I shall get them all back again."

"Ah, then," replied Mrs. G., "I shall have a chance to rest," in the same cheerful vein.

Mrs. Greene says she never saw her look better or in more animated spirits. During the week she was almost every evening behind the scenes, merrily jesting with the performers. On the Saturday night it was casually said that she felt a little indisposed. Nothing more was heard until the Monday morning following, when her death was announced. While Mrs. Greene was at breakfast the news of her death was brought to her. This was on the 22$^{nd}$ of November. Astounded at the intelligence, Mrs. Greene ran to her house and

*Theatrical Rambles of Mr. & Mrs. Greene*, Charles Durang

found her a corpse, but much changed. The entire company were here assembled. Her features were distorted, her hands drawn up and fast clenched. All the body bore evident marks that cramps and violent pains had cause a most painful death.[4]

The weather was sultry, warm and damp, a fatal state of atmosphere in Orleans. It was necessary to bury her *instanter*. A great delay occurred in procuring a metallic coffin, during which the body began to swell frightfully. Poor Josephine's funeral rites were few and quickly performed, not from coldness from those around her, but from imperious circumstances. As her corpse I was brought to the cemetery, its gates were being closed. She was placed in a vault until it was convenient to remove her remains to Ronaldson's burial ground at Philadelphia, where they now rest by the side of her sister, Miss Missouri.[5] A handsome broken marble column marks the spot with suitable inscriptions.

The theatre was opened that night. The company strongly disapproved of it. No one felt like performing. They would all have sooner relinquished their night's salary than to have appeared. It would have been a silent homage due to her memory.

There was little or no inharmonious business action in this company. Each one of the leading performers, nay, even the message deliverer, had their lines defined in their articles of agreement, so that no murmuring in their business relations was ever heard, nothing of the injustice that was often exercised in other theatres. No grumbling about managerial favoritism.

At the termination of this engagement the Greenes entered into one with Messrs. Smith and Ludlow, lessees of the St. Charles Theatre, New Orleans. At this period, Mr. Edwin Forrest, the reigning American star, played his farewell engagement at New Orleans, taking a final leave of the audience on his last benefit night in a brief speech of four or five lines. The substance still lingers on the memory, after a lapse of some years:

My friends, we now part theatrically forever. The prompter, in one moment hence, will tingle his little

## *Theatrical Rambles of Mr. & Mrs. Greene*, Charles Durang

bell and the curtain of this theatre will fall forever on my mimic life. It was here my earliest professional essays were made and enthusiastically cherished by you. It is for your individual and public welfare that the latest pulses of my heart will beat.

The house was crowded to excess. He never appeared on those boards again, although often solicited to do so. The sum of $20,000 was pledged to him and amply guaranteed to him for a fulfillment of the engagement. He refused the call. He could not prove false to his word; his farewell pledge was his reply.

At the end of the season Mr. Greene and wife left for St. Louis, where Greene endeavored to obtain a building to convert into a temporary theatre, so as to offer Forrest an engagement, as its inhabitants were irrepressibly anxious to have him play there for a series of nights. Mrs. Henry Hunt, the present Mrs. John Drew, was the leading lady; but no suitable building could be obtained, except an old church, the alterations of which would have been attended with so great an outlay and waste of time as put the speculation to rest at once.

This idea being abandoned, they adopted a new plan of operations, concluding to wear through the summer with a small selected company in itinerant movements. Thus traveling, they reached Cincinnati and made offers to several performers who were too busy doing nothing not to be willing to engage in doing anything.

At this point they met with Mr. McVicker and wife.[6] This gentleman gave great promise of becoming one of our first comedians, and has since made a star reputation in Yankee parts. Greene broached his plans to him that he purposed to visit the new city of Chicago, which, since his first visit to that city *incog.* after the war of 1812, has magically sprung into a western metropolitan commercial port of beauty. Mr. McVicker and lady at once agreed to accompany the Greene *corps*. They found the once aboriginal village of wigwams, which rested on boggy swamps, now covered with squares of substantial warehouses, located on wide avenues, and quays

*Theatrical Rambles of Mr. & Mrs. Greene*, Charles Durang

protruding into Late Michigan, the harbor lined with ships, steamboats and other vessels. The growth of this place is truly miraculous, it having passed into a proverb: "Grown as fast as Chicago!"

Here they found a neat little theatre under the management of Mr. John B. Rice. He and his company were now playing at Milwaukee, where he had another similar theatre. He thus occupied the year between the two places, alternately playing in them as circumstances directed. Meeting an old New York acquaintance, he advised them to telegraph to Mr. Rice on the subject of engagements, as he wanted recruits. They did so and immediately received offers which Greene and company readily accepted.

They put up at a large hotel built of brick, said to be the best house of entertainment west of New York, belonging to a gentleman who,
from a very humble beginning, had in this Aladdin region of magical operations made a colossal fortune, while he was still in the prime of life with many years ahead to enjoy it and probably government honors.

The Chicago dramatic horizon was studded with stars of all colors, from tragedy to broad comedy. The first that shone forth was Mrs. Henry Hunt, followed by Dibden Pitt, Barney Williams and wife, Mrs. George Farren, Mr. and Mrs. E. Conner, Mr. E. Forrest, and Mr. and Miss Wemyss.

Some queer affairs occurred in their playing *Macbeth*. This play requires numerical force as well as good talent to perform. The witches are a vocal or operatic body of themselves. This *corps* was rather sparse in numbers. Mrs. H. Hunt was the Lady Macbeth, so she and some of the principal parts had to double and triple, as phrased behind the scenes. They had to assume the witches' garb in addition to their proper one, a change easily made, only throwing a gown over the other dress and mossy wig over the head; Mrs. Hunt assisted in the chorus and in solos of the principal singing witches. For the first scene of the witches that sometimes ends the second act and which agreeable to Shakespeare begins the third act, Mrs. Hunt donned a weird woman's gown and wild headdress and was ready for the principal singing witch.

## *Theatrical Rambles of Mr. & Mrs. Greene*, Charles Durang

"Speak, sister, speak, is the deed done?" etc., etc.

King Duncan, who had just been murdered, was alive again as a witch, singing with wand in hand. Macduff, Banquo, etc., were all transformed into vocal spirits and weird supernaturals.

All our readers may not know that what is called the music, the operatic part of Macbeth, is not all Shakespeare's, but the work of Davenant and Locke, who composed the music for Charles II's entree into London. The scenes of Hecate and the weird women with ether sprites, are Shakespeare's, on which were grated the songs, choruses, and dances of the witches with brooms in their hands, suitable in some measure to the witchery ideas of the great bard. The music of itself, no doubt, adds greatly to the supernatural sublimities of the tragedy. It receives from the vast improved instrumentation of our day a further lyric impressiveness. But it is a pity that Davenant and his co-authors should have adulterated Shakespeare's scenes of this tragedy with many silly ones of action of ghosts and language of rhyme.

Mrs. H. Hunt's dexterity in these doubles was clever and droll, not apparent to the spectators but visible to the performers to their infinite amusement. Proteus for shape and mocking bird for tongue, she was either the pretty but truculent Lady Macbeth or a lovely, smiling Esmenidia to scourge wickedness. She dodged about the stage from L. H. to R. H. to sing a solo. But in thus aiding the musical requirements of the choruses and solos, in flying to right, left, and center, she toppled into the cauldron and was near being burned alive by the flaming spirits of wine with which the sponge was saturated within the seething magic pot. The alarm was prodigious! The incantation scene suddenly collapsed and finished in grotesque wildness. Rice, the manager, feared that the tragedy could not be ended by reason of this mishap. But Mrs. Hunt recovered soon from her alarm and injury of person and finished Lady Macbeth with Siddonsian grace.

It would seem that a kind of conscription scavenger law existed in Chicago. It was something of a road repairing rule, such as prevailed in our rural districts in early days, that the inhabitants should keep their own neighborhoods in order

## *Theatrical Rambles of Mr. & Mrs. Greene*, Charles Durang

and clean. Agreeable to this custom or rule, Greene and McVicker received a notice the day after their arrival to appear at a named rendezvous, each with a spade and hoe, to work three days on the street to cleanse it of its muddy encumbrances. This was a reasonable requisition. Although they were strangers, they were there to elicit patrons for their show. It was certain that the public, the pedestrians, and those conveyed in vehicles could not reach the theatre after night while the thoroughfares were so clogged. But the proud representation of Irish characters, of Teague, Looney, etc., conceived that a gross insult had been offered to the drama in his person. Indeed, that the authorities thought, as the honor of making our first turnpikes, digging our canals, and building railroads belonged exclusively to Irishmen, the honor of cleansing Chicago of mud pertained to the artistes who sustained that character in the mimic world. Greene and McVicker petitioned the authorities to procure the machinery of a suction hose and pumps. And faith, they agreed to the project as a most sensible arrangement. So the actors were not conscripted to expel the rebellious mud.

The summer passed, the Greenes descended once more the mighty father of rivers to New Orleans to fulfill an engagement with Mr. Place. Their clever associate, Mr. McVicker, is now sole proprietor and effective manager of a fine, large, and handsome new theatre at Chicago where his inimitable comic abilities, blended with a good temper, integrity and liberality, with his enthusiastic political speeches, have given him a popularity with the citizens of the western commercial metropolis unprecedented by any citizen or actor of the great west. A share of that public favor was fully enjoyed by his wonderfully, talented daughter, "Little Mary," who was unrivalled as Eva in *Uncle Tom's Cabin* and in other pieces adapted for her years.[1]

On the Greene's arrival, they met for the first time the beautiful and talented Miss Julia Dean, a model woman.[2] Mrs. Greene had a very severe illness just before leaving Chicago, which came near terminating her existence. She recovered partially during the trip but continued weak and dispirited on her arrival at New Orleans, although the sight of that (to her loved) place did much to restore her.

*Theatrical Rambles of Mr. & Mrs. Greene*, Charles Durang

The company was much the same as that of the last season. Mr. Henry Grafton was engaged as stage manager, Miss Jane Davenport and father were there. The lady was engaged for a few nights. Mr. Booth was starring it. He opened in the *Iron Chest*. The next night he played *Richard III*. Mr. Greene was cast for King Henry.[3]

He had just finished his dying speech and was dead when a dog ran howling on the stage, making directly for the defunct monarch, smelling the body all over, and thus performed a stage miracle. For the dead majesty rose slowly and emphatically, and by way of a whisper, exclaimed: "Get out!" The animal, dropping his tail, made his exit at the opposite wing. The King then composed his limbs with decency, calmed his features and again departed in peace. The dog again entered, with howling noises, and with similar gyrations nosed the body. This irritated the dead King, who majestically arose to his legs and with a forcible kick put to flight the animal, who vamoosed again through Booth's legs and off. By that time the whole house was in an uproar of shouts, laughter and cheering screams. When Greene had driven his canine annoyance away, he very coolly laid himself down on the stage and died for the third time. The scene was thus more ludicrous than that of Don Whiskerandos in the *Critic*.[7]

When Greene was thus deceased for the third time, the dog again entered. This time he was chased by the scene shifters with ropes and whips to secure him if possible. He dodged through the scenes and apertures of the wings so that it was impossible to catch him. He again made for the dead King, and as he entered, Greene in a rage arose, seized him by the hind legs and, so secured, handed this hounded dog over to his pursuers.

It appeared afterwards that the dog belonged to the keeper of the back door, who had him tied up in a room. Some person for malicious mischief let him loose at that particular scene. It was said that Booth was very angry at this event, which destroyed the scene and caused jocularity to run through the audience for the balance of the tragedy, a most annoying tease to a tragedian who requires the serious atten-

*Theatrical Rambles of Mr. & Mrs. Greene*, Charles Durang

tion of his spectators, but not their smiles and vulgar, loud laughter.

Imagine poor Booth's situation. He had to stand as Richard, a silent and mortified auditor throughout this farcical scene, himself, the great object of all reverted to ludicrous sports. Booth under similar circumstances was remarkable for restraint of temper and placidity of mien. He never assumed haughty airs or displayed ostentatious anger. But Booth for once lost his temper and proved very angry. In his business intercourse with the profession, on the stage, at rehearsal, or in social relations, he was all urbanity and easy politeness. He was so different in his behavior towards his brethren from the too often conceited foreigners, that it was a pleasure, rather than labor, to rehearse and act with him. And, we may say *en passant* that all the American stars are much more affable and polite in their manners than those of England.

Poor Mrs. Greene, we remember on one occasion was playing Lady Macbeth to Booth's Thane. She ventured to ask him his meaning of several of her passages and the mode of acting some of its stereotyped or traditional points. Booth, as modest in such matters as he was a master to answer such questions, took her to the rear of the stage and imparted his ideas and experiences. Mrs. Greene came running into the green room elated with his instructions, and followed them at night, and gained infinite approbation for the conception and execution. She had an audience of the actors behind to behold them and gained their approval. Mrs. Greene was a plain, modest woman herself, with instinctive talent, of good sense, and willing to learn.

It was said that Booth was an imitator of Edmund Kean. If so (which we deny), he was no servile one. He was like him, short in figure, in his manner and mobility of facial expression, dressed in the same costume. The similitude was strong and striking. Kean had many defects, as voice and figure. The former was at times very ragged but his towering genius voided these asperities and became beauties that dazzled. Many remember the saying of Dowton, the London actor, when Kean's first appearance at Drury Lane produced so great a mania in public judgment: "'Tis only necessary now-

*Theatrical Rambles of Mr. & Mrs. Greene*, Charles Durang

a-days to be under five feet, have bandy legs, and a hoarse voice, and inflamed liver; but you'll be thought a great tragedian." Quin said something of the same kind about Garrick when he first appeared and restored Nature and Shakespeare to the stage, putting to flight monotonous tones of speech.

Thus it was towards Booth. All his private actions were a subject of ill-natured remark. His rustic views of life, when he took a farm near the village of Bel Air in Maryland to cultivate the earth and live retired during his professional relaxations, were the subject of tart and ludicrous observations; and many extravagant stories are told of his going with his hog and hominy to market and then to rehearsal at the Holliday Street Theatre.

## NOTES

[1] Josephine Clifton died on November 22, 1847.

[2] Louisa Missouri Miller (born 1821) first appeared on stage at the National Theatre, New York, in 1838. Contrary to her mother's wishes she became a pupil of Thomas Hamblin and a member of his household. Her brother, Nelson H. Miller, published a card accusing Hamblin of improprieties. Upon reading the notice, she is said to have swooned, grown sick, and died of "inflammation of the brain" on June 16, 1838.

[3] McVicker (born 1822) was working as a printer in St. Louis before he entered into the theatrical business as a call boy in 1843 for Ludlow and Smith in New Orleans. He joined J. B. Rice's Chicago Company, 1848, as first low comedian. In 1850 he purchased Dan Marble's Yankee plays from his widow and made a starring tour in both the United States and England. Since then he was primarily connected with Chicago theatricals as manager.

[4] Mary McVicker became the wife of Edwin Booth.

[5] Julia Dean (born 1830) made her first appearance on the New York stage as Julia in *The Hunchback*. Coming from two generations of actors, she was graceful, pretty, and intelligent. Her popularity was excessive.

[6] Henry Grafton may in reality be Harry P. Grattan, who

*Theatrical Rambles of Mr. & Mrs. Greene*, Charles Durang made an American debut in *Hamlet* at the Park Theatre, May 11, 1842. Although he failed in New York, he established himself in lesser roles with the small theatres of the West. He sometimes used the name of Harry Plunkett. *The Iron Chest* was a melodrama by Colman the younger.

[7]*The Critic*, a farce by R. B. Sheridan.

*Theatrical Rambles of Mr. & Mrs. Greene*, Charles Durang

## XXIX.

ILLNESS AND DEATH OF THE ELDER BOOTH — GREENE'S PERSONAL APPEARANCE — THE MAYOR OF TRENTON RECEIVES A BLESSING — A MANAGEMENT SPECULATION — THE CHOLERA — JULIA DEAN AND ELIZA LOGAN — A BREAKFAST SCENE — MISS CHARLOTTE CUSHMAN.

The management of Drury Lane at London was preparing a magnificent revival of *King Lear* for Kean as Lear. The lessees or conductors of Covent Garden, the great rival of the other house, determined to forestall this grand effort. They hit upon Booth for Lear, a quasi-rival of the great actor, a name that hung in supposed equipoise against him. Booth was thus engaged for a limited number of nights, depending on the success of the play for its continuance at £20 per night and a benefit, his part on that night to be selected by himself.

The play of *Lear* was thus cast: Lear, J. B. Booth; Edgar, Charles Kemble; Edmund, Mr. Macready; Cordelia, Mrs. Bartley. After a few nights the receipts so diminished that the play was discontinued.

After a consultation with the parties some new arrangements were made, Booth agreeing to a reduction of £10 per night. The experiment was renewed on these conditions. The play drew its slow length along for a few losing nights. Booth now took a benefit, announcing himself for *Richard III*. This also proved a failure and, agreeably to star engagements there, he was obliged to pay on the ensuing morning into the treasury the sum of £80 to make up the deficiency of the night's expenses. This consumed all his earnings on the former performances. He then visited the Provinces, making up, in a measure, his London losses and kept his laurels

*Theatrical Rambles of Mr. & Mrs. Greene*, Charles Durang

green. And so came to America, where, after he had many fitful wanderings over the continent, on the 30$^{th}$ of November, 1852, he died on board the steamer *J. W. Chenoworth*. We are indebted to a fellow passenger of his, of Salem, New Jersey, who attended him in his last moments and closed his eyes on the waters of the Ohio, for the following narrative of the event. It is plain but eloquently affective. It will speak for itself, and deserves a record in any dramatic work. It was published in the Philadelphia *Ledger*. The writer was a benevolent, religious man, and of liberal views in theatricals:

Salem, N. J., July 16$^{th}$, 1856

MESSERS. EDITORS.—

Gentlemen: Excuse me for this intrusion upon your time, as this is the only means I have of [relating the facts of] the great tragedian, J. B. Booth, the circumstances of his death. As I am the only person that was with him and nursed him during his short but fatal illness, listened to his last words, and saw him die, I feel this information would be gratifying to his family at least, be it ever so meanly expressed, or however humble the source. I had taken passage on the steamer *J. W. Chenoworth* from New Orleans to Cincinnati, at the same time that Booth did, though at that time unknown to me save by reputation. We had been one day out from New Orleans, when I noticed a man walking back and forth in the saloon, with his hands behind him, his head bowed in deep thought. I sat observing him closely, trying to recollect when and where I had seen him, for that I had certainly seen that man I was fully convinced. A gentleman came up to me and remarked, "That is the tragedian, Booth." I then remembered having seen him in his last play at the St. Charles Theatre, N.O. The second day out he was absent from the saloon, and, on inquiry, I found that he was confined to his state room very sick of a diarrhea. Well knowing

## Theatrical Rambles of Mr. & Mrs. Greene, Charles Durang

the careless regard strangers have on those boats for one that is sick, I at once visited his room, apologizing for my intrusion, and offered my services to him in any manner that might be useful. After scanning me with a look of penetration and surprise that I can never forget, he accepted the offer. On examining his room I found he had been neglected. I immediately called the porter, had the room cleaned out, clean linen put on him and on the bed; ordered some gruel to be made for him, as he was too weak for stronger nourishment; but there was no medical attendant at hand, and he wasted away very fast. The third day after he was taken he could not turn over without help. I saw that he was getting in a hopeless condition, and thinking to stimulate his energies, gave him some brandy and water, having to saturate a rag and place it between his teeth, his jaws having become rigid; but on tasting it he made an effort to remove it from his lips, and spoke with difficulty, "No more in this world." I saw that he had no hopes of living, and felt anxious in regard to his hope for the future, but being a young man and an entire stranger, I felt it to be a very delicate situation for one of my inexperience; but with a mental prayer that I might be sustained, I commenced by asking him if he had a wife; he answered, with a look of astonishment, and an emphatic "Certainly I have;" I then asked him if he had any message to send to her, but I could not understand him, but he seemed to say, in his look and features, "Oh, that I could talk!" But, poor man, his power of utterance was so impaired, that he could scarcely utter a word distinctly. He attempted to tell me of his travels in California, but I could understand nothing but that he had suffered a great deal, and had been exposed very much. On the fourth day after he was taken I asked him if I should read to him from my Testament; he seemed anxious that I should, when I selected an encouraging chapter, and read, while he gave the deepest attention. I then asked him if I might pray for him; his eyes became dim with moisture, and he signified

## Theatrical Rambles of Mr. & Mrs. Greene, Charles Durang

his consent, when I knelt by his bunk, and besought the Great Father of us all, before whom he was so shortly to appear, to receive him, though at this late hour, for the sake of Him that died that sinners might trust in his mercy. He seemed very grateful, and attempted to put his arms around my neck, as I bent over him to smooth his pillow. But the fifth day, about one o'clock, he died. I was with him all the morning until the bell rang for dinner, when he repeated the words several times, distinctly, "pray, pray, pray," accompanied by a beseeching look. We were then below Louisville, Kentucky, where, upon arriving, the captain procured a metallic coffin, and telegraphed to his wife in Baltimore to meet the corpse in Cincinnati, which she did, taking it to Baltimore for interment. But as I myself was sick by watching on arriving at Cincinnati, and immediately left the boat, I saw none of his friends, and on recovering, went south, so that I have had no opportunity of making this known to them.

—J. H. S.

His last appearance on the stage was at the St. Charles Theatre, New Orleans, on the 10th of November, 1852. On that occasion he performed Sir Edward Mortimer in the *Iron Chest* and John Lump in the *Review*.

John Greene was not only the most absent of men but equally careless of his property and interests, too often the characteristics of the player, doubtless the effect of ideal impersonation giving the habit of ideal impressions. When he married he put himself out to nurse to his wife. He never put up his own dresses or his properties for the stage, which preparations were all made by her. She packed up everything for traveling or for the use of the performances.

Greene, having an engagement at Cincinnati for a week's time, knowing his unfortunate wont of system in such matters, she carefully packed up all his acting properties in the order he might want the articles each night, as she was not to accompany him herself. In less than a week he wrote "My dear Anne, I have most unfortunately lost my carpet bag." In a few days another missive came, "I have lost my

## Theatrical Rambles of Mr. & Mrs. Greene, Charles Durang

new hat and boots." And a third of a similar tenor, "My trunk and its contents are missing, *non est*." Mrs. Greene concluded the next news would be the announcement of his lost person. At length he returned with his lost trunk, minus half of its contents. This was luck, for she generally had to go in search of him when going alone upon one of these expeditions.

John Greene's personal appearance was unique. There was a striking individuality about him that at once struck the curious eye, and, in his plain but genteel garb, imparted something of the puritan character. One day, being attired in a long, black surtout coat, pants and waistcoat, with white cravat, which gave him a very clerical aspect, he was taken for a Catholic priest by a man who addressed him with reverence as, "Father! I have delivered those books as you desired."

To which Green replied in a solemn tone and air, "Son, you have done well." Thus they separated.

John Greene was clearly not a stationary manager. Ever on the *qui vive* to give variety to his profession, if he could not pack a trunk, he could portray a low Irishman. Again on a start he hastily collected a small company and went to Clarksville, a thriving little town below Nashville. This company consisted of Mr. Hield, Mr. Claude, Mr. Hamilton, Mr. Renzi, Mr. Greene, Mrs. Greene, Miss Kate Macgloire, etc.

The Clarksvillians did not like the company's acting. Mr. Greene, not being able to succeed in Nashville, had brought his miserable, seedy company to Clarksville; but he soon found out they knew what was what. If they did not live in a city, they knew good acting from bad and were not to be taken in.

As the critics of that town were too enlightened for Greene's company, they decamped for other parts, known and unknown, where the people were less Aristotelian in their Thespian ideas. Therefore they bent their way to a land of promise called Evansville.

On their way they called at the small town of Trenton, where the Mayor forbade their bills being posted. Therefore

## Theatrical Rambles of Mr. & Mrs. Greene, Charles Durang

the company beat a hasty retreat from the place. Hield, from its center square, pronounced his parting blessing on the mayor and its corporation! Their object being Evansville, they hurried on to it.

The letters they had received from there while they were at Nashville led them to believe that a handsome theatre, with every other requisite, would greet them at this place, that a set of new scenery had been painted, stuffed seats, an orchestra of ability, etc. This led to sanguine expectations of noble patronage. The reverse of all this was the new scene to behold. On the company's arrival, they hastened with full speed and glee to see this temple of Thalia and Melpomene, when to their astonished gaze they beheld an old lager beer saloon in its most noisome and greasy state. The was stage floored with unplanned boards, the wings made of soiled Dutch figured paper, the drop curtain a faded piece of yellow muslin not reaching the stage by a foot and a-half. The scenes, (all drops, not flats like the flat-headed persons who planned it all) were mere daubs of red and yellow watercolors, and made up of fancy wall paper of figures and Chinese views. There was a rag-carpet of many particolors for a drawing-room Brussels carpeting, etc.

They opened with the *Lady of Lyons*, Hield, as Claude; Mrs. Greene as Pauline. The house was thin and the applause as meager. To cap the climax, during the most interesting scene of the play, *viz.*, the parting of Claude and Pauline in the fourth act, the entire scene fell down, leaving nothing to view but the bare brick dingy wall at the back. As Pauline was fainting and Claude and Damas were in attitudes, two darkies played the usual Marseilles hymn on a violin and a banjo.

Waiting for a boat for several weeks to take them to Nashville, the Greenes were obliged to remain in very uncomfortable lodgings, among a rude and very ill-bred set of people. At length the desired boat arrived and the Greenes made their *exeunt* in her up the Cumberland River.

Travel on, travel like the Wandering Jew, seemed the fate of Mr. John Greene and wife. While they were professionally sojourning in Baltimore in 1850, he received an invitation from the proprietors of the Nashville Theatre to go

## Theatrical Rambles of Mr. & Mrs. Greene, Charles Durang

and rent it. The project was backed by many of his friends with flattering views of successful patronage. Mrs. Greene opposed the scheme, its responsibilities, its cares, its anxieties. The risks were great and numerous, as nothing in the category of business transactions are more precarious than that of theatricals. Her advice was unheeded and thither they went.

The theatre was just finished and numerous applicants were bidding for it, some of whom offered a much larger rent than did Greene. For many reasons the preference was given to him. But the theatre was without the necessary stock of scenery, wardrobe, properties, etc., so indispensable to active operations. Greene employed extra hands at his own expense to complete the stage department for the opening. Mrs. Greene took charge and supervised the construction of the wardrobe, while Greene went to Cincinnati and engaged a company. The organization was very perfect, a talented company, a most effective orchestra and splendid scenery, etc.

The opening night came and with it came the cholera! The event was in July, 1850. A general stampede of the citizens took place. Nashville was truly a city of the dead. Thus situated, after four representations the theatre closed. Mr. Greene in this public calamity was a heavy loser; the musicians absconded without rendering services equal to the advance of money to enable them to travel upon to meet their engagements. The actors remained at their posts, awaiting with their manager the result or the abatement of the pestilence so that they could make another beginning.

The disease gradually lessened in virulence, so that business resumed its sway. And with this sign of returning health and confidence, Greene commenced an opening. This was deemed rash and imprudent, but the people in his employ must live, or die of starvation, despite the cholera. Besides, in all calamities, that people will eat, drink and be merry if they can is a maxim that seems established in truth by history. So up went the green curtain to a very fair audience, and the business rapidly increased from spare audiences to crowded houses before the second week was out.

*Theatrical Rambles of Mr. & Mrs. Greene*, Charles Durang

Mrs. Estelle Potter, as the leading lady, became an immense favorite; Mrs. Henry Ryner,[2] also, as well as Mrs. Bernard.

The first star was the lucky Julia Dean, who took the town by *coup de main*. All the young men were in love with her, the old men were lost in admiration recalling their faded passions, while woman's curiosity and jealous vanities were elicited "to see what on earth was the matter," and flocked in masses to see her beauty and attractive manner. Such was her magnetic powers over the public that Greene re-engaged her for a repetition of her characters.

The elite of Nashville fashionables filled the dress circle nightly, ladies occupying the seats of the parquet where they did not often go. Such was the sensation this delightful actress created, that the strictly pious of the church ventured to pluck the forbidden fruit and to partake of its taste. Julia Dean, with great personal requisites, and they of a soft, gentle nature, blended with infinite power and winning expression, was certainly very perfect and attractive. She always impressed the auditor with the idea that modesty and virtue were her paramount principles.

Then followed another blooming native plant, Miss Eliza Logan, a great card also. No one claimed great personal loveliness for her, of course; but her genius, her talent, amply made up for all such deficiencies. Let it be remembered that she had such requisites, but it became a question of comparison. Both of these young ladies were always accompanied by their fathers. Their lives were ever marked by the strictest good conduct. Miss Logan married and retired from the stage. Miss Dean married and is known as Mrs. Julia Dean Hayne, but labors yet in her vocation.

Mr. Greene's success at Nashville this season was a triumph and he closed late in November. The company went to Mobile in the winter, where Mr. Joseph Field opened a theatre.[1] The Greenes accompanied Miss Dean as far as Louisville, where she had an engagement.

In this journey they stopped at Tyre Springs for breakfast. At this repast quite a funny incident occurred. Miss Dean ate her breakfast very slowly, occasionally conversing with those around her. A gentleman at this *table d'hôte*, a stranger to her and her friends, sat opposite, taking

## *Theatrical Rambles of Mr. & Mrs. Greene*, Charles Durang

his meal and sipping his coffee quite leisurely, but gazing furtively at the fair actress in seeming ecstasies. She was rather the feast for his eyes than the food was for his appetite. The landlord seemed quite impatient at this prolonged meal. In his selfish, stingy disposition, fearing that his larder would be too far infringed upon, he watched the table, walking around it several times.

At last, not being able to restrain his brutal manners, he approached the table and thus rudely addressed the divine tragedienne and ladylike Julia, "Come, ain't you done eatin' yet?"

Astonishment seized upon all. It was as startling as the ghost of Don Guzman in *Don Juan*. While the young enamored gentleman who sat statue-like opposite dropped his saucer and looked as if he could have devoured this ill-mannered Boniface with a Jonah swallow. The lady, at this vulgar assault, rose with a dignity so peculiar to herself and, viewing the boor from head to feet, gave him a withering, scornful look that would have shrunk the blunted nature of a Hottentot into shame (but strange to say hardly phased his brutalities), and made her indignant exit. The gentlemen present gave him a severe castigation. One pulled his nose, another threw the sediment of their coffee cups, etc., into his saucy snub face till it was spottedly bronzed.

Mr. and Mrs. Greene, in about a fortnight after this, arrived at Mobile, where they just saw Miss Cushman in her celebrated character of Meg Merrilies, which she has made on the stage as conspicuous and as tangible to public admiration as Walter Scott's most perfect delineation of that wild character in the novel. Both are efforts of genius. If we may be allowed to parody a well-known saying, "That Shakespeare was made for Garrick and Garrick for Shakespeare," Scott was made for Cushman and Cushman for Scott. To be sure the comparison is meager, for she only impersonates one of Sir Walter's great ones, while Garrick was the general representative of Shakespeare's magnates. Of all the parts she played in London during her first season there at the Princess' Theatre in 1846 in an engagement extending altogether through eighty-four nights, in none did she acquire more true

*Theatrical Rambles of Mr. & Mrs. Greene*, Charles Durang

fame from the critics and public than in Meg Merrilies.

She opened as Bianca in *Fazio*. During her engagement she appeared as Emilia and Lady Macbeth; with Mr. Forrest, playing Julia in the *Hunchback*; Mrs. Haller, Lady Teazle, Beatrice, Rosalind and Juliana in the *Honey Moon*. This inimitable artiste, whose grand and forcible delineations have long been the boast of the American public, had retired, but from loyal motives and love of country, re-appeared in our principal cities in a series of her characters for the benefit of its defenders in the field who might be wounded and disabled. Her course was as laudable as it is justly appreciated. As a woman of talent, of energetic purposes and daring zeal, of family affections most true and delicate as such, she deserves the good fortune that has attended her exertions through life. In her professional aspirations she left no department of the stage untouched, for comedy, tragedy, melodrama, opera and farce, all received her attention and wooing. She even became a stage manageress; not in name only at the head of the bill, but in fact and personal superintendence of the office, cast the pieces, attended to the stage business at rehearsals by the side of the prompter, saw to the scene, plots, etc. In all this she exhibited the masculine gender in manner and command, but she fully developed the woman, for she would have the last say. Her judgment was good. She could talk learnedly on costumes to the costumer of the theatre, to the prompter and master carpenter on the essential points of appropriate scenery to be used in a drama as to historical or architectural correctness. She could also give a sound opinion in orthoepy and the reading of Shakespeare, the proper requisites for a stage manager but which very few of our modern officials know. But this petticoat government, with all its tact, did not answer Mr. F. A. Marshall's interests and she resigned the stage management of the Walnut Street Theatre of 1842 and 1843 to the administration of W. R. Blake, who as such was efficient and inefficient, an antithesis of capabilities that we leave our readers to judge of themselves.

Blake was a fine actor and as a manager catered well for the public. He spared no money where talent offered. When he first opened the Walnut Street Theatre after the in-

*Theatrical Rambles of Mr. & Mrs. Greene*, Charles Durang

terior was rebuilt, he had one of the largest salary lists of extravagant amounts that were ever known to the theatres in that city. His stock company embraced the leading talent of the country. But his rate of expenditure could not be sustained. At first, however, it was a success. The rent of the theatre was not then what it is now, or anything of the nature that Mr. W. Wheatley recently paid for the New Chestnut Street Theatre, Philadelphia, said to be $14,000, a rent that may be sustained in New York, but not in Philadelphia.

## NOTES

[1] Joseph M. Field (born in England, 1810) made his New York debut at the Park Theatre in 1830. He managed Field's Varieties in St. Louis, in 1852. He had a journalist's career as assistant editor for the New York *Evening Post*; later, as editor of the St. Louis *Reveille*; and, as "Straws," he wrote humorous sketches and essays for the New Orleans *Picayune*.

[2] Mrs. Henry Ryner, formerly Kate Meadows, made her debut in 1835 at the Walnut Street Theatre. She was formerly married to Proctor.

*Theatrical Rambles of Mr. & Mrs. Greene*, Charles Durang

## XXX.

CHARLOTTE CUSHMAN CRITICIZED — AN ACCIDENT TAKEN ADVANTAGE OF — THE DRAMA AT NASHVILLE — CHANFRAU'S SUCCESS — A TERPSICHORIAN SHERIFF — A GENEROUS OFFER — LAST DAYS AND DEATH OF JOHN GREENE — DFATH OF MRS. GREENE — THE END.

Miss Charlotte Cushman at this time, 1842, was full of youthful vigor and its pleasant freshness. We can't say that her face possessed what may be termed a spiritual expression of a Raphael's virgin; but it was animated with a vivid blue eye, an expanded forehead of intellectual form, the nose, unfortunately, of the short snub form, but the skin of alabaster tint, while her cheeks of desirable fullness were beautifully flushed roseate hues, and the hair of auburn color fell in waving profusion, as desired. Her figure is very tall but symmetrical. On the whole she is a very striking female of versatile powers and commanding presence. We feel that we cannot accord her that great element of the human mind. Alas! she is founded more on the imitative than originality of action; for she at once, and probably without knowing it, formed her acting on the Macready style after having acted with him, even to his Scottish sound of letters and other little Macreadyish peculiarities, some of which were beauties in the Roscius, but sad abominations in his imitators.

But we must say, when she put the breeches on and assumed the *toga virilis*, she was every inch a man of good proportions. Mary Howitt of England has written glowingly of "our Charlotte," so also has that distinguished London littérateur and lecturer, W. J. Fox, M.P., who, in speaking of stage artistes, said that "the best Romeo on the English stage or that I ever saw on the London boards is Miss Cushman,

*Theatrical Rambles of Mr. & Mrs. Greene*, Charles Durang

the American."

A lady in London being asked her opinion of Miss Cushman's Romeo, answered with great simplicity, "Oh! Miss Cushman is a very dangerous young man." Although Miss Cushman may not possess the pathetic sweetness or tranquility of Miss Ellen Tree, the lady-like impressiveness and tenderness of Miss Fanny Jarman, nor the electrical intellectuality of Miss Fanny Kemble, whose impassioned passages never partook of the vehement exaggerations in action or speech but in exquisite elocution, in subdued graceful action would quietly mirror the passions to sympathetic effect, Miss Cushman is tremendously great in declamatory passages and effective in her acting and, although she may have lacked sentiment and the feminine manner so enchanting in the above ladies, she was otherwise powerfully great in what may be termed Miltonic in tone and harmony.

During Miss Cushman's engagement at Greene's Nashville Theatre she performed *Meg Merrilies*. Greene played Dandie Dinmont. In the dying scene of *Meg* he has to hold the maniac in his arms. Her death struggles are long and painful. But, as Miss Cushman portrayed and vigorously acted these struggles, it was more than Greene's strength of muscle could stand, though he was by no means weak. The last and closing scene of poor Meg was so terrific and vigorous that she broke from his grasp and over went Dandie Dinmont, falling prostrate on the stage, making a final end before Meg Merrilies herself. Greene resolved that if she played the part again during his management he would not play his again with her vigorous acting.

Miss Cushman in one of her engagements at Nashville played Lady Macbeth, which was deemed one of her *chefs d'oeuvre*. A curious accident befell in the letter scene. After reading it she comments on its import in soliloquy, prophesying results, exclaiming, "Glamis thou art, and Cawdor; and shalt be what thou art promised."

In walking, or rather on a kind of sudden turn, the train of her robes got entangled in her feet, and in the effort to disengage it she slipped, and fell down on the stage. A dead silence reigned through the auditory, for they thought it was a new point of the actress and in breathless silence awaited the conclusion of the speech. With infinite tact Miss Cushman collected her thoughts and really turned the mishap into a telling point. She continued her soliloquy thus prostrate, gradually raising her person with one hand on the boards, while occasionally taking a furtive glance at the letter, till the attendant announced the news of the King's approach to the castle. At that moment she started up erect on her feet. She was rapturously applauded for the effect. Never was an accident so effectually covered.

Mr. Greene closed his Nashville season and went to Mobile as usual. On his return he found the theatre torn to pieces by Barnum, who had rented it for the purpose of introducing the vocalist, Jenny Lind, and finding that it was not large enough to meet the crowds that rushed to see this nightingale, he took the liberty of making such extensive alterations that it required great expenditure to restore it to its original shape.[1]

Greene now first introduced gas into the theatre at a heavy outlay of several hundred dollars, supplanting the old oil lamps. Thus, with the restoration of the building, involved Greene in debt to such an extent that he had better have built a new theatre. Nothing in the busy speculations of this world is so uncertain as that of theatrical operations.

Mr. Greene made but little here, although he averaged a good business. The stars, generally speaking, take away the manager's profits. One of the disappointments of this season was the sudden death of Mr. Graham, a tragedian. He was engaged as a star by Mr. Greene for Nashville. He was still performing at St. Louis but was announced in Nashville to appear in *Hamlet*. The office was open for the sale of tickets, seats were taken, and half the tickets were sold, when news of his sudden death was received.[2] A postponement was the result.

John Greene was very fond of Nashville. He liked its society, he liked its localities, its cheer and its plenty, and he determined to make it his home in future, with occasional sojourns in other adjacent places. The Nashville season could not be prolonged over four months and then there were eight more to be provided for. During all this time there was no

## *Theatrical Rambles of Mr. & Mrs. Greene*, Charles Durang

abatement of rent for the recess. It was still going on. The theatre was sometimes let out for concerts, minstrels, and exhibitions of various sorts, but the business affairs of the theatre often looked gloomy, the houses very poor, and the receipts did not always meet the expenses.

During one of these melancholy periods of non-paying houses it was suggested to engage Mr. and Mrs. Charles Howard. They came with Mr. Dawson.[3] They were favorites, especially Mrs. Howard. All were sanguine as to the success of these arrangements. Everybody seemed delighted. The lady would certainly prove as attractive as a gold mine. Greene was constantly accosted everywhere with, "Get Mrs. Howard. She will fill your houses." Well, she came, was engaged, she pleased those who came, but they were a few. She did not draw. The houses were poor and her engagement dragged heavily and unprofitably along. Those who were so desirous to see the lady did not come more than one night. This arrangement failed.

Then followed Miss Julia Bennett, or rather Mrs. Barrow, a most finished comedy actress who made a hit in London at the Haymarket Theatre in 1843 as the Widow Cheerly.[4] Her first appearance in America was at Marshall's theatre, Broadway, New York. This fine actress played to hardly the expenses at Nashville.

Then Charles Burke played to nearly empty benches. The popular Ravels came. This company of great excellence was engaged at a very large sum. They performed two weeks, out of which Greene cleared about one hundred and fifty dollars. Greene tried the little Batemans, who were always deemed "good for so much," but all proved of no avail. Then came George Jamieson with his fame and sonorous voice and for the first week scarcely any had the curiosity to look in at the doors, much less sit a performance out. It was strictly private theatricals, friends only being admitted, and few of them taking the trouble to come at all. Then the *Old Plantation* was brought out by Jamieson, when it had a tremendous success.[5]

Then followed James Murdoch, who was immensely attractive and who continued ever since a great favorite with

## Theatrical Rambles of Mr. & Mrs. Greene, Charles Durang

the good citizens of Nashville. There is no better card than James Murdoch, the citizen, actor, elocutionist and farmer of Ohio. His sun rose in the East with radiant splendor and, we opine, will set in the West in glorious majesty.

Mr. Chanfrau wrote for an engagement for himself and Miss Albertine.[6] Mr. Greene was not disposed to negotiate for this engagement. However, it was concluded and he was most agreeably disappointed by their drawing wonderfully, a success beyond measure. Chanfrau and Albertine were very clever. Indeed their fame was most deserved.

The lady met with a very serious accident during one of the performances. She ran from the stage to her dressing room to make a quick change of dress in the *French Spy*, where a trap door behind the scenes had been left open. She, not seeing it, fell through, hurting her leg and bruising herself otherwise. After some delay it was bound up and she in a very lame state finished the part. With her wounded limb bandaged nightly did she finish her engagement. She proved rather a lame Spy but a very popular one.

Miss Eliza Logan was one of our visiting stars of notoriety and very popular with the Nashvillians. She was acting one of her favorite characters on the night a jury was empanelled in the city court for some important case, and they had gone out to consult upon a verdict. Before they could agree upon it, an irresistible desire arose among them to see Miss Logan that night. How to procure a temporary deliverance from the jury room for that purpose was a question? They resolved to appeal to the sheriff, Mr. Clemens, a jolly, good matured, good hearted man. He was very fond of the theatre and dancing especially. He agreed to their request and accompanied them himself. The result was that the court fined the merry official fifty dollars. Sympathy in the sheriff's favor rose fifty per cent through the city.

John Greene perceiving that capital might be made out of this excitement, and that the fat, goodly sheriff had the reputation of being a good dancer, called on him with the novel proposition that if he would allow his name to be used in the play bills and appear in a *pas de deux* with Miss Kate Walters he would himself pay the court fine. Clemens at once agreed to it. Being very popular with all classes, for he

## Theatrical Rambles of Mr. & Mrs. Greene, Charles Durang

really was a benevolent man, this eccentric effort caused a tremendous excitement. The house overflowed with people.

The appearance of Clemens and Miss Walters gave rise to tumultuous applause. They bowed and curtsied for full four minutes and then they commenced the dance. The sheriff's dancing was loudly applauded and every step encored. It was a rich treat. After a repeat, the sheriff being tired out, he made a final double shuffle. In bowing to the audience, his cap fell into the orchestra upon the leader's violin, which caused fresh bursts of applause and laughter. His friends besieged the back door of the theatre when he had done, carried him off with yells of triumph to the hotel, making a night of hilarious sport, and Mr. Greene netted a hundred dollars over his expenses and the fine.

The citizens the next day offered a complimentary benefit to Greene as a token of respect to his worthy and energetic management, which he accepted, and it all proved a bumper as well as an honor. On this occasion a bible was presented to him from a well-known minister of the gospel. This present at first offended Greene's feelings as if offered to a benighted heathen of religious darkness who was ignorant of its divine revelations. But he learned afterwards that it was not the purpose of the reverend donor to cast any reflection on his religious natures or to reflect any aspersions on his profession, but simply to present a heavenly treasure to a man whom he thought deserved, from general report, a gift so valuable from a brother of sacerdotal order to a lay brother, as a mere expression of good will and courtesy. On this information Greene acknowledged the kindness in a note to the clergyman.

The new lessee offered the Greenes an engagement which they, accepted, but the salaries were not forthcoming so they left for the north. Soon reaching New York, the grand mart for American theatricals, they learned that the Troy theatre was to let and made application for it *ad interim*, consulting his old friend, Edwin Forrest in relation thereto. Mr. Forrest, with his wonted friendly feeling for John Greene, answered in his usual laconic but friendly style, so characteristic of his nature:

*Theatrical Rambles of Mr. & Mrs. Greene*, Charles Durang

New York, April 3rd, 1857

MY DEAR GREENE:—

I hear you are about to embark in the management of the Troy Theatre. I think you will do well there. When a regular actor in the city of Albany, some years ago, under Gilbert, I remember our theatre derived considerable support from the Trojans, who have a real love for the drama, and have an appreciative taste for good acting. Your long experience as a manager will afford the playgoers many advantages. I hope you will succeed in obtaining the theatre, and if I can assist you in any way to that end, you may command my services. It is not impossible I might even ask for an engagement.

Yours truly, Edwin Forrest

P.S.—If I can assist you in obtaining the theatre at Troy in a pecuniary way, or in any other way, I shall do it with pleasure.

After a brief sojourn at New York and a tour of the eastern theatrical circuits during the summer, they visited Troy to consult further with the proprietors of the theatre, where he found the edifice very handsome but the rent entirely too heavy, while the prices of admission were extremely low. Greene reflected calmly on the chances of success under the adverse circumstances that seemed to loom upon the perspective. It is the duty of a manager while sailing in a smooth sea to look out for breakers ahead in the event of sudden white squalls. Adverse winds too often attend prosperous gales and wreck the ship.

Greene answered the Trojan stockholders that he was about returning to Nashville and that on his arrival there he would give them a definite answer as to taking their theatre. He did so and, after due consideration and consultation with friends, declined the theatre.

The Greenes now received a liberal offer of engage-

## *Theatrical Rambles of Mr. & Mrs. Greene*, Charles Durang

ment from the manager of the Memphis Theatre, offering good salaries and benefits on fair terms, which they accepted. The manager did everything for their comfort that he could. He caused a room in the theatre to be fitted up as a dressing and a lodging room, their meals being furnished from the adjoining hotel.

They opened with *The Soldier's Daughter*. We have many hosts of soldiers' daughters now, many cheerful ones and many with drooping hearts. May the latter find paternal homes under their country's roof.

A new theatre was being built at Memphis for Mr. Crisp and was soon completed. Opening with *éclat* and popular favor, it made the other house very shaky; but "still they kept their colors flying on the outer walls" in noble competition, Miss Crampton playing Richard III, Shylock, Hamlet, etc. Mr. Collins, the Irish comedian and vocalist, drew capital houses in despite of the now powerful opposition.[7]

John Greene and his wife had long been wanderers around this world of care; from early youth to advanced age they had plied their professional art from North to South, East to West, till at length their years admonished them to seek a resting place, a blessed retreat to end their days in. And in the words of Sir Walter Scott on the retirement of a celebrated actor from the Edinburgh stage, *viz.*, Charles Kemble:

> That time creeps on, and higher duties crave
> Some space between the theatre and grave,
> That like the Roman in the capital
> I may adjust my mantle ore I fall;
> My life's brief act in public service flowing
> The last, the closing scene, must be my own.

With this heartfelt desire he sought that coveted asylum ere he was struck with the disease that occasioned his death. The many private and delicate attentions of friendship and public professional appreciation extended to himself and wife in Nashville impressed his heart that that was the de-

*Theatrical Rambles of Mr. & Mrs. Greene*, Charles Durang

sired resting place of Home, sweet home. But in making this decision he was swayed by conscientious feeling of being able, in the event of his becoming a permanent lessee of the Nashville theatre, whether he would be able to sustain his managerial career through a series of years. The same motives rendered him undetermined as to the Troy theatre. He was a man of great integrity of character. His word was his bond, never forfeited. His promises were as sacred as his registered oath.

He positively sacrificed his life to conscientious scruples. The fear of not being enabled to fulfill his managerial obligations so preyed upon his mind as to superinduce his mental disease, *viz.*, a softening of the brain long ere his physical frame gave way. While debating and weighing all these business matters, he was playing an engagement at Memphis, which was the last he ever played on this great stage of life, when that grand and mysterious cord that connects the mind to the body suddenly snapped without a moment's warning.

On the day of this sore affliction that soon eventuated in his death, he appeared in his usual health and spirits and attended rehearsal. As was his wonted custom of an afternoon, he took a short walk. On his return he seemed fatigued. He threw off his upper garments, laid down to rest, and fell into a slumber. Mrs. Greene, not seeing anything unusual in his personal habits, left him so resting till tea time, when she attempted to awake him. But to her horror she found that he was speechless and insensible. In her distracted state of mind she became almost frantic. A physician was immediately summoned, who administered such remedies as the case required. The doctor declared the attack to be paralysis of the brain. And in order to assuage the wife's distress, he added that in a short time he would be restored to his faculties and reason.

This assurance served to sooth her sorrows for a time, as the angel Hope ever does. Her situation seemed insupportable. As she sat night and day, watching for a glimmering return of reason, a faint response, or a silent look in answer to the devoted wife's ardent entreaties from the bereft senses of a paralyzed husband. Who could have wished, who could

## *Theatrical Rambles of Mr. & Mrs. Greene*, Charles Durang

have had the heart and in that heart the courage to say to her that her hopes are vain? To her, and to the world, he was henceforth an imbecile, a dead man. He cried like a child at seeing objects, but gave no sign of recognition of anyone being known to him.

Mr. John Roberts,[8] the tragedian, and Mrs. Farren and daughter were those on whom she looked with hope that he would know them, as they had been dear, respected, loved friends. But alas! he knew them not.

Mrs. Greene removed him to the country, hoping the air might be beneficial. She would have him propped in an armchair and carried into the garden, where he would seemingly watch her; and if she disappeared he would show signs of uneasiness by sobs, moans, and sometimes painful shrieks.

Several months were passed in this secluded rural place, but it brought no change to poor Greene. At length his physician recommended a removal to Nashville, where the sight of old faces and familiar scenes that once entranced his heart seemed for a season to revive his health. She flattered herself that he would again be blessed with speech, but the scene was nearer the closing than she imagined. One day he was more restless than usual. Anxious friends attended her and offered to sit up all night, but she thankfully declined, knowing that strange faces annoyed him. During the night, death dropped his curtain over poor John Greene. He died on the 28$^{th}$ of May, 1860, and was interred in Mount Olivet Cemetery agreeably to his expressed wish that his last resting place should be among people and a spot he loved and honored during his life.

After Mr. Greene's death, Mrs. Greene remained in Nashville for some months. In the summer of 1861 she paid a visit to her friends and relatives at and near Philadelphia. During her visit to the East she sojourned with her sister-in-law, Mrs. E. T. Hall, whose husband, Mr. E. T. Hall keeps the Old Red Lion Inn, Bucks County, on the Bristol turnpike, a well-known, quaint, old-fashioned edifice of revolutionary history in the early days of our republic.

It was a breakfast and dining depot for stage passengers between New York and Philadelphia in their transit in

*Theatrical Rambles of Mr. & Mrs. Greene*, Charles Durang

the jolting old stage-wagon drawn by four smart looking nags, changing such teams every ten miles. This ancient colonial tavern stands there an object of interest. The volcanic rumblings of our appalling rebellion were now audible, and especially lowering over Tennessee.

When at last all regular commination was about being broken up, Mrs. Greene received a notice from her friends in Nashville recommending her to return or else all the funds she had invested there would be confiscated. This was a destructive blow to her. In three weeks time she seemed to have aged twenty years. Her nervous system received a shock it never recovered from. She had lost her protector and she had to struggle through the world by herself. She left Philadelphia in trembling anxiety in September and died in Nashville on the 19$^{th}$ of January, 1862.

Thus did these Thespian wanderers close their lives in Nashville, Tennessee at advanced ages, after "double toil and trouble," but accompanied by the attributes that ever pay homage to an honored old age—honor, respect and a host of friends. So they rest in the same grave at Mount Olivet, where the Christian symbol of our holy religion, the simple cross, marks their last resting place.

> There they alike in trembling Hope repose,
> Within the bosom of their father and their God.

## NOTES

[1] Jenny Lind gave two concerts in Nashville, with tickets sold at auction to satisfy immense public demand.

[2] Richard L. Graham died on May 27, 1851.

[3] Charles D. S. Howard was a light comedian of little note in the New York theatres but was held in high esteem by audiences in the South and West. Mrs. Howard, the former Rosina Shaw, was, according to Ireland, "for many years the pet comedienne of New Orleans and St. Louis. Dawson may be J. M. Dawson who made his American debut, September 27, 1847, at the Broadway Theatre and was performing at the Bowery as late as 1859.

[4] Julia Bennett first appeared in America as Lady Teazle,

*Theatrical Rambles of Mr. & Mrs. Greene*, Charles Durang

February 24, 1851, at the Broadway Theatre, New York, where she was recognized as a first-class comedienne.

[5]*The Old Plantation* was written by George Jamieson for himself.

[6]Miss Albertine traveled professionally with F. S. Chanfrau for several years. Small in stature but with amazing physical endurance, she was popular in breeches parts.

[7]W. H. Crisp (born 1820), a light and eccentric comedian from the Dublin theatre, first appeared in America at the Park as Jermey Diddle. He was a leading man for Cora Mowatt at Mobile and New Orleans, 1845-46, and was well-known in the South and West. Miss Crampton (born 1816) made her debut in Cincinnati at age 15. Although petite and lovely, she chose to play robust roles. It was said that the "Little Siddons," as she was called in the West, could have been better than Cushman but for her undisciplined and intemperate nature. Mr. Collins first appeared in New York on October 23, 1809. Best suited for low comedy and old men, he was popular in the Western theatres.

[8]Roberts is most probably the J. B. Roberts (born 1818) who first appeared as Richmond to Booth's Richard III at the Walnut Street Theatre, January 20, 1836. He worked with the Greenes at the Chatham, 1846-47. Later, he traveled as a star throughout the country.

*Theatrical Rambles of Mr. & Mrs. Greene*, Charles Durang

# BIBLIOGRAPHY

### BOOKS

Barnum, P. T. *Struggles and Triumphs.* Hartford (Conn.): J. B. Burr & Company., 1870.
Beirne, Francis F. *The War of 1812.* New York: F. P. Dutton & Company, 1949.
Bernard, John. *Retrospections of America, 1797-1811.* New York; Benjamin Blom (reissue), 1969.
Brown, Col. T. Allston. *History of the American Stage.* New York: Benjamin Blom (reissue) 1969.
Brown. *History of the New York Stage.* 3 vols. New York: Benjamin Blom (reissue), 1964.
Carson, William G. B. The Theatre on the Frontier, the Early Years of the St. Louis Stage. New York: Benjamin Blom (reissue), 1965.
Chindahl, George L. *A History of the Circus in America.* Caldwell (Idaho): The Caxton Printers, Ltd., 1959.
Clapp, William W., Jr.. *A Record of the Boston Stage.* New York: Greenwood Press (reissue), 1969.
Cowell, Joseph Leathly. *Thirty Years Passed Among the Players in England and America.* 2 v. New York: Harper and Brothers, 1844.
Delafield, Major Joseph. *The Unfortified Boundary*, II. Privately printed in New York, 1943.
Dunlap, William. *History of the American Theatre and Anecdotes of the Principal Actors.* New York: Burt Franklin (reissue), 1963.
Graham, Philip. *Showboats.* Austin: University of Texas Press, 1951.
Grimsted, David. *Melodrama Unveiled.* Chicago: University of Chicago Press, 1968.
Ireland, Joseph N. *Records of the New York Stage from 1750 to 1860.* 2 vols. New York: T. H. Morrell, 1867.
James, Reese, D. *Old Drury of Philadelphia, a History of the Philadelphia Stage, 1800-1835.* Philadelphia: University of Pennsylvania Press, 1932.
Jefferson, Joseph.. *The Autobiography of Joseph Jefferson.* New York: The Century Company, 1889.
Kendall, John S. *The Golden Age of the New Orleans Theatre.* Baton Rouge (La.): Louisiana State University Press, 1952.
Ludlow, Noah Miller. *Dramatic Life as I Found It: A Record of Personal Experiences.* St. Louis: G. I. Jones & Company, 1880.
Mates, Julian. *The American Musical Stage Before 1800.* New Brunswick

*Theatrical Rambles of Mr. & Mrs. Greene*, Charles Durang (N.J.): Rutgers University Press, 1962.

Minnigerode, Meade. *The Fabulous Forties.* New York: G. Putnam's Sons, 1924.

Odell, George C. D. *Annals of the New York Stage*, Vols. I-VII. New York: Columbia University Press, 1927-31.

Overmyer, Grace. *America's First Hamlet.* New York: New York University Press, 1957.

Phelps, H. P. *Players of a Century, a Record of the Albany Stage.* New York: Benjamin Blom (reissue), 1972.

Rees, James. *The Dramatic Authors of America.* Philadelphia: G. B. Zieber & Company, 1845.

Rees. *The Life of Edwin Forrest, with Reminiscences and Personal Recollections.* Philadelphia: T. B. Peterson & Brothers, 1874.

Russell, W. Clark. *Representative Actors.* London: Frederick Warne & Company.

Seilhamer, George O. *History of the American Theatre.* 3 vols. New York: Benjamin Blom (reissue), 1968.

Sherman, Robert L. *Drama Cyclopedia, a Biography of Plays and Players.* Chicago: Published by the author, 1944.

Smith, Solomon Franklin. *The Theatrical Journey-Work and Anecdotal Recollections of Sol. Smith, Comedian, Attorney at Law, Etc., Etc.* Philadelphia: B. Peterson, 1854.

Smith. *Theatrical Management in the West and South for Thirty Years.* New York: Harper & Brothers, 1868.

Smither, Nelle Kroger. *A History of the English Theatre in New Orleans.* New York: Benjamin Blom (reissue), 1967.

Stone, Henry Dickinson. *Personal Recollections of the Drama, or Theatrical Reminiscences, Embracing Sketches of Prominent Actors and Actresses, Their Chief Characteristics, Original Anecdotes of Them, and Incidents Connected Therewith.* Albany: Charles Van Benthuysen & Sons, 1873.

Taylor, Douglas (ed.). *Autobiography of Clara Fisher Maeder.* New York: The Dunlap Society, 1897.

Vandenhoff, George. *Leaves from an Actor's Note-Book, with Reminiscences and Chit-Chat of the Green-Room and the Stage, in England and America.* New York: D. Appleton & Company, 1860.

Wallack, Lester. *Memories of Fifty Years.* New York: Charles Scribner's Sons, 1889.

Wemyss, Francis Courtney. *Chronology of the American Stage from 1752 to 1852.* New York: Benjamin Blom (reissue), 1968.

Wemyss. *Twenty-Six Years of the Life of an Actor and Manager.* New York: Burgess, Stringer & Company, 1847.

Willard, George O. *History of the Providence Stage, 1762-1891.* Providence: The Rhode Island News Company, 1891.

Willis, Eola. *The Charleston Stage in the XVIII Century.* New York: Benjamin Blom (reissue), 1968.

Wilson, Arthur Herman. *A History of the Philadelphia Theatre, 1835 to 1855.* Philadelphia: University of Pennsylvania Press, 1935.

*Theatrical Rambles of Mr. & Mrs. Greene*, Charles Durang

Wilson, Garff B. *A History of American Acting.* Bloomington (Ind.): Indiana University Press, 1966.
Wood, William Burk. *Personal Recollections of the Stage, Embracing Notices of Actors, Authors, and Auditors, During a Period of Forty Years.* Philadelphia: Henry Carey Baird, 1855.

### ARTICLES

"The Bowery Theatre Nearly a Half Century Ago," New York *Clipper*, February 24, 1877, p. 381.
"Brief Reminiscence of the Circus in Days of Yore: The Old Richmond Hill," New York *Clipper*, October 8, 1864, p. 201.
"Broadway a Quarter of a Century Since," New York, *Clipper*, January 16, 1869, p. 322.
"The Broadway Circus," New York *Clipper*, November 30, 1878, p. 284.
Brown, Col. T. Allston, "History of the American Stage," New York *Clipper*, July 28, 1860-November 17, 1860.
Brown, "Theatrical Reminiscences of George Stone," New York *Clipper*, February 16, 1861, p. 348; February 23, 1861, p. 357; March 2, 1861, p. 365.
"The Charleston Stage Sixty Years Ago," New York *Clipper*, February 17, 1877, p. 373.
"Charlotte Cushman: the Versatilities of a Great Career," New York *Clipper*, May 13, 1876, p. 52.
"Dan Marble's Last Appearance," New York *Clipper*, April 18, 1874, p. 20.
"The Declining Days of the Old Chatham," New York *Clipper*, January 19, 1878, p. 341.
"The Drama in Gotham Forty-Eight Years Ago," New York *Clipper*, November 29, 1884, p. 589.
Durang, Charles, "The Philadelphia Stage from the Year 1794 to the Year 1855," Philadelphia *Weekly Dispatch*, 1854-60. Microfilm in three parts, beginning with issue of May 7, 1854.
"The Early Days of the Chicago Stage," New York *Clipper*, November 25, 1876, p. 277.
"Echoes of a Famous Ring: The Gala Days of the Old Bowery Amphitheatre," New York *Clipper*, April 8, 1876, p. 12.
"An East Side Theatre," New York *Clipper*, January 3, 1863, p. 297.
"English Actors in America," New York *Clipper*, September 19, 1868, p. 188.
"The Fannyellslermaniaphobia," New York *Clipper*, January 12, 1878, p. 333.
"Fanny Ellsler's Debut in New Orleans," New York *Clipper*, October 23, 1897, p. 555.
Hamilton, William B., "The Theatre in the Old Southwest: The First Decade at Natchez," *American Literature*, XII (January, 1941), pp.

*Theatrical Rambles of Mr. & Mrs. Greene*, Charles Durang 471-85.

"Heenan-Sayers Fight," New York *Clipper*, May 28, 1870, p. 60.

"The Hields: Father, Mother and Son, the End of a Long Life," New York *Clipper*, June 16, 1877, p. 92.

"History of the American Turf," *Spirit of the Times*, May 29, 1858, p. 184.

"Holliday Street Theatre," New York *Clipper*, July 25, 1874, p. 132.

"Interesting Dramatic Reminiscences, a Glimpse at the Stage in 1840," New York *Clipper*, August 8, 1868, p. 140.

"The Jeffersons Sixty Years Ago," New York *Clipper*, November 17, 1877, p. 269.

"The Last Appearance of the Late John M. Scott," New York *Clipper*, December 12, 1874, p. 292.

Picton, Col. Tom, "'London Assurance' and Who Played It," New York *Clipper*, July 11, 1868, p. 108.

Picton, "Memories of the Park Theatre," New York *Clipper*, July 4, 1868, p. 100.

Picton, "More Than Thirty Years Ago: Our Drama's Semi-Centennial," New York *Clipper*, April 8, 1876, p. 12.

Picton, "Noted Daughters of Terpsichore, the Fascinating Fanny Ellsler in America," New York *Clipper*, April 23, 1881, p. 73.

Picton, "Old Drury," New York *Clipper*, June 27, 1868, p. 92.

Picton, "Richmond Hill and the Tivoli," New York *Clipper*, August 1, 1868, p. 132.

Reichmann, Felix, "Amusements in Lancaster, 1750-1940," Papers of the Lancaster County Historical Society. XLV (1941), pp. 25-55.

"A Reminiscence in the Early History of the Cincinnati Stage," New York *Clipper*, April 16, 1870, pp. 9-10.

"A Reminiscence of the First Theatre in Chicago, Ill.," New York *Clipper*, May 9, 1874, p. 44.

"Reminiscences of Actors and Actresses: Theatres and Theatricals Thirty-five and Forty-five Years Ago in Montréal, Canada," New York *Clipper*, November 25, 1865, p. 260.

Renauld, J. B., "The Richmond Theatre," New York *Clipper*, June 8, 1872, p. 73; June 15, 1872, p. 84.

Smither, Nelle Kroger, "Charlotte Cushman's Apprenticeship in New Orleans," *Louisiana Historical Quarterly*, XXXI (October, 1948), pp. 973-80.

"A Theatrical Celebrity of the Olden Time," New York *Clipper*, February 13, 1869, p. 356.

"Theatricals in Alabama: Some Amusing Dramatic Reminiscences of Mobile," New York *Clipper*, December 20, 1873, p. 300.

Wilmeth, Don B., "The Mackenzie-Jefferson Theatrical Company in Galena, 1838-39," *Journal of the Illinois State Historical Society*, LX (Spring, 1967), pp. 23-36.

*Theatrical Rambles of Mr. & Mrs. Greene*, Charles Durang

## PERIODICALS

*Dramatic Mirror and Literary Companion*, Vols. 1-2, October 14, 1841-May 7, 1842.
New York *Clipper*, Vols. 1-62, May 7, 1853-July 12, 1924.
New York *Mirror*, Vols. 1-6, 1844-47.
New York *Mirror and Ladies Literary Gazette*, Vols. 3-7, 1825-30.
*Spirit of the Times*, Vols. 1-30, December 10, 1831-February 2, 1861.
*Thespian Mirror*, 14 issues, December, 1805-May, 1806.

*Theatrical Rambles of Mr. & Mrs. Greene*, Charles Durang

# INDEX

Abbott, William, 197, 199
Abercrombie, Dr., 18, 24
Academy of Music, Philadelphia, 246
Adams, John Jay, 131, 137, 248
Adams, Mr., 225
Addams, Augustus A., 183, 190
Adelphi Theatre, 172
Adincourt, Mr., 197, 199
*Agreeable Surprise, The*, 114, 115, 234
*Aladdin*, 155
Albany Amphitheatre, 248
Albertine, Miss, 279, 286
*Alexander the Great*, 23, 25
Alexandria Theatre, 43
*All the World's a Stage*, 217
Allen, Andrew Jackson, 153, 155
Allport, Joseph, 80, 81
Almar, George, 217
American Theatre, 235, 236, 239, 250
Anderson, James, 229, 246, 250
Anderson, Mrs. James, 184
Anthony Street Theatre, 34, 87
*Apostate, The*, 131, 137
Arch Street Theatre, 148, 153, 154, 178, 183, 202, 208, 238, 240, 249, 252
Arnold, S. J., 124, 135
*As You Like It*, 250
Astor Place Opera House, 251
Astor Place Opera House, 58
Austin, Mrs., 144, 145, 242
*Babes in the Woods*, 110, 114
Bailey, Judge, 93
Bainbridge, 52
Banim, John, 97
Barbiere, Mons., 151

Barnes, Charlotte, 209
Barnes, John, 179, 181, 182
Barnes, Mr. and Mrs. John, 183
Barnes, Mrs. John, 180
Barnum, P. T., 277
Barrett, George, 25, 129, 135, 212, 241, 246, 247
Barrett, Georgiana, 129
Barrett, Mrs. George, 206, 212, 213
Barrett, Mrs. George, 135
Barrett, Mrs. Giles, 135
Barrow, Mrs., 278
Barry, Thomas, 248, 252
Barrymore, William, 202, 208
Bartley, Mrs., 264
Barton, Mr., 212
Bate's Theatre, Cincinnati, 251
Bateman sisters, 278
Bateman, Miss, 207
Bateman, Mrs., 210
Battersby, Mrs., 99, 100, 103, 106, 109
*Battle of Waterloo, The*, 140
Beaumont, de Jersey, 29, 34
Beaumont, Mrs., 29, 34
Beekman, Mr., 96
Bellamy, 250
Bendall, G. Wilkins, 212
Bennett, Julia, 278, 285
Bently, Mr., 172
Bernard, John, 80, 81, 87
Bernard, Mrs., 271
Bernard, W. B., 175
*Bertram*, 164, 215
Bickerstaff, Isaac, 114, 137
Bignall family, 31, 35
Bignall, John, 31, 35
Bignall, Mr. and Mrs. John, 92
Bignall, Mrs., 35, 147

*Theatrical Rambles of Mr. & Mrs. Greene*, Charles Durang

Bird, Robert Montgomery, 74, 164
*Birth Day, The*, 103
Bishop, Henry R., 124, 138
Black and Inslee, 154
*Black-Eyed Susan*, 160, 161, 162, 173
Blake, Mr. and Mrs. William Rufus, 183
Blake, Mrs. William Rufus, 101
Blake, William Rufus, 148, 202, 273
Blanchard, Master G., 80
Blanchard, Miss, 78, 80
Blanchard, William, 75, 76, 79, 80, 82, 83, 84, 165, 191
Bloxton, Mrs., 111, 113, 115
*Blue Beard*, 200, 208
*Bohemian Mother, The*, 182, 204
Booth, Edwin, 262
Booth, Junius Brutus, 130, 260, 261, 264, 265
Booth, Junius Brutus, 265
Boston Museum, 249
Boucicault, Dion, 251
Bowers, Mrs., 165
Bowery Theatre, 35, 75, 103, 104, 107, 114, 115, 136, 145, 150, 151, 154, 162, 164, 177, 190, 191, 203, 204, 209, 217, 240, 251, 285, 289
Braydon, Mr., 62
Brichta, Madame, 241, 251
Bridges, Mr., 229
Broadway Amphitheatre, 130
Broadway Circus, 124, 136
Broadway Theatre, 278, 285, 286
*Bronze Horse, The*, 202, 208
Brooke, Mrs., 135
Brougham, Mr. and Mrs. John, 248
Brougham, Mrs. John, 57, 207
Browne, James S., 165, 241, 246
Brunton, 24

Buckstone, J. B., 175, 182, 199, 236, 239, 240
*Budget of Blunders, The*, 35
Buffalo Theatre, 191
Burke, Charles, 93, 97, 225, 278
Burke, Master, 183
Burke, Mrs. Thomas, 92, 132
Burke, Thomas, 92, 93, 97, 101, 102
Burroughs, Watkins, 133, 134, 137
Burton, William, 35, 249
Butler, R., 175
Byron, Lord, 136
*Cabin Boy and His Monkey, The*, 191
*Cabinet, The*, 134, 138
Caldwell, James, 43, 52, 53, 54, 55, 56, 57, 102, 103, 105, 107, 109, 132, 212, 217, 226, 236, 237, 238, 246, 287
Camp Street Theatre, 105, 207, 210, 211
*Carmelite*, 136
*Cataract of the Ganges, The*, 109, 114
Celeste, Madame, 55, 172, 175, 176, 213
*Cenerentola*, 57
Chanfrau, F. S., 279, 286
Chapman family, 64, 149
Chapman, Mrs. Samuel, 226
Chapman, Samuel, 141, 145, 149
Chapman, William, 61, 64
Charles Street Theatre, 217
Charleston Theatre, 34, 41, 97, 101, 132
Chatham Theatre, 44, 135, 162, 177, 182, 209, 248, 250, 252, 286
Cherry, Andrew, 58
Chestnut Street Theatre, 18, 24, 25, 29, 34, 35, 36, 41, 43, 68, 80, 92, 93, 96, 97, 98, 100, 102, 113, 121, 123, 124, 125, 129, 135, 145, 157, 158, 181,

293

191, 198, 203, 208, 249, 252, 274
Cibber, Colly, 107
Cibber, Theophilus, 176
Cincinnati Theatre, 223
*Cinderella*, 54, 57
City Theatre, 137
Clarendon, Miss, 248, 252
Clarke, John Henry, 179, 180, 181, 182
Clarke, N. B., 202, 209
Claude, 268
Clawson, Isaac, 133, 137
Clemens, 279
Clifton, Josephine, 150, 151, 152, 155, 159, 161, 162, 164, 248, 254, 255, 262
Cline, Herr, 149, 154, 171, 176
*Cobbler's Daughter, The*, 253
*Cobbler's Wife, The*, 249, 253
*Cobbler's Will, The*, 253
Coburg Theatre, 171
Collingbourne, W., 200, 208
Collins, 282, 286
Colman, George, 44, 56, 124, 155, 168, 175, 208
Columbian Gardens, 97
*Committee, The*, 175
Cone, Spencer H., 17, 18, 19, 20, 21, 22, 23, 24, 25
Connell, Capt., 121
Conner, Edmund, 202, 203, 208, 225, 227, 232, 236, 257
Conway, Mr., 104
Cooke, George Frederick, 33, 35
Cooke, George Frederick, 23
Cooke, T. P., 173
Cooper, James F., 164
Cooper, Pricilla, 183, 190
Cooper, Thomas A., 17, 23, 24, 52, 56, 98, 126, 127, 131, 141, 142, 145, 154, 164, 186, 190
Copeland, Fanny, 239
*Coriolanus*, 135

Covent Garden Theatre, 29, 57, 58, 172, 173, 190, 197, 198, 207, 264
Cowell, Joe, 125, 130, 136, 137, 139, 140, 141, 142, 143, 144, 145, 164, 210, 227, 228, 229, 232, 238, 241, 242, 243, 244, 245, 246, 252, 287
Cowell, Mr. and Mrs. Joe, 207
Cowell, Sidney, 207
Cowper, William, 87
Crampton, Miss, 282, 286
Cripps, Mr., 247
Crisp, W. H., 282, 286
*Critic, The*, 23, 25, 129, 260, 263
Crooke, Mr., 34
Cumberland, Richard, 57, 136, 175
*Cure for the Heart Ache, A*, 146, 153
Cushman, Charlotte, 213, 217, 272, 273, 275, 276, 277, 286, 289, 290
*Cymbeline*, 244
Daley, Mrs., 172
Dallas, Alexander James, 74
Dallas, George M., 68, 74
*Damon and Pythias*, 92, 189
Dance, Charles, 217
Darley, Mrs., 97, 100
Davenport, E. L., 165
Davenport, Miss, 213
Dawson, J. M., 278, 285
Dean, Julia, 259, 262, 271, 272, 273
*Deep Deep Sea, The*, 217
*Deep, Deep Sea, The*, 217
*Deluge*, 245
DeVandal, Mr., 226
*Devil's Bridge, The*, 120, 121, 124, 134, 138
*Devil's Daughter, The*, 213, 217
Dibdin, Thomas, 107, 138, 145, 199
Dibdin, W. J., 25

*Theatrical Rambles of Mr. & Mrs. Greene*, Charles Durang

Dimond, William (or Diamond), 25
Dinneford, William, 138, 199
*Don Giovanni*, 141, 145
*Don Juan*, 272
*Douglas*, 136, 144, 145, 251
Dowton, 261
Drake, Mrs., 84, 87, 92, 213, 214
*Dramatist, The*, 55, 58
Drew, John, 144
Drew, Mrs. John, 144, 256
Drummond, Sir Gordon, 81
Drury Lane Theatre, 25, 57, 63, 100, 129, 137, 141, 145, 147, 164, 190, 191, 264
Dudley, Miss, 254
*Duenna, The*, 134, 138
Duff, John, 22, 23, 25, 56, 135
Duff, Mary, 100, 179, 190
Duffy, William, 149, 150, 153, 154, 178, 180, 183, 186, 189, 191, 192, 193, 194, 195, 196, 199, 201
Dumas, Jules, 227
*Dumb Savayard and His Monkey, The*, 191
Dunham, Elmira, 183, 190
Dunham, Emeline, 190
Dunham, Miss, 193
Dunlap, William, 107
Durang, Charles, 43
Durang, Charles, 34
Durang, Ferdinand, 17, 34
Duverna, William, 248, 250, 252
Dwyer, 23
Eagle Theatre, 186, 192, 199
Eberle, Miss E., 208
Edes, Col. Benjamin, 122
Edmonds, 149
Edwards, Jonathan, 163
Egerton, Mrs., 198
*El Hyder*, 200
*Ellen Wareham*, 193, 199
Elliston, 22
Ellsler, Fanny, 237
Emery, Miss, 141, 145

English Opera Co., 243, 251
Entwistle, 27, 34, 36, 37, 43
*Fair Penitent, The*, 36, 43
*Fairy Queen, The*, 57
*Family Jars*, 217
Farquhar, George, 199
Farren, Fanny Fitz, 110, 114
Farren, George, 103, 107, 110, 114
Farren, Mrs. George, 110, 257
Farren, Mrs. George, 236
Farren, William, 107, 173
*Fatal Dowry, The*, 130, 136
Fawcett, Mr., 197, 207
*Fazio*, 216, 217, 273
Federal Street Theatre, 41, 252
Fenwick, Mrs., 190
Ferron, Mrs. George, 149, 154, 183
Field, J. M., 54, 57, 179, 180, 271, 274
Field's Varieties, St. Louis, 274
Fields, Irish, 200
Finn, Henry, 176, 183, 190
Fisher, Charles, 226, 227, 232, 235
Fisher, Clara, 144, 145, 226, 232, 240
Fitzwilliam, Fanny, 172, 236, 237, 238, 239, 247, 252
Fletcher, John, 35
Flynn, Mrs., 250
Foote, John Forrester, 123, 124
Forrest, Edwin, 43, 64, 85, 102, 103, 104, 106, 107, 108, 109, 110, 130, 144, 150, 154, 164, 183, 213, 220, 248, 255, 257, 280, 281
Forrest, William, 35, 92, 97, 109, 111, 117, 178, 181, 202
*Forty Thieves, The*, 97
Fox, W. J., 275
Francis, Mr. and Mrs., 24
Franklin Theatre, 155, 252
*Fraternal Discord*, 107
*French Spy, The*, 213, 217, 251, 279
*Gamesters, The*, 34, 136, 199

295

*Theatrical Rambles of Mr. & Mrs. Greene*, Charles Durang

Garner, 103
Garrick, David, 24, 30, 44, 101, 173, 262, 272
Gates, William, 179
Germon, Mr. and Mrs., 225, 227, 229, 232, 246
Gilbert, John, 252
Gilbert, Mr. and Mrs. John, 248
Gilfert, Charles, 104, 107
*Gladiator, The*, 74
*Golden Farmer, The*, 141, 145
Goldsmith, Oliver, 217
Gouffe, Mons., 191
Goward, Miss, 172
Grafton, Henry, 260, 262
Graham, Richard L., 277, 285
Grattan, Harry P., 262
Green, Mr. and Mrs. Charles, 186, 191
Greffulhe, 35
Grey, Jackson, 103
Grierson, 139
Grierson, Charles, 254
Grierson, Thomas, 139, 140, 142, 144
Grundy, Felix, 221
*Gulliver in Lilliput*, 44
*Guy Mannering*, 65, 224
Hackett, James, 144, 154, 164
Haines, J. T., 217
Hall, Mr. and Mrs. E. T., 284
Hallam, John, 101, 139, 140, 144
Hallam, Mr. and Mrs. John, 139
Hallam's company, 101
Hamblin, Mr. and Mrs. Thomas, 141
Hamblin, Mrs. Thomas, 75, 173, 179
Hamblin, Thomas, 136, 145, 150, 154, 162, 178, 179, 204, 262
Hamilton, John, 192, 193, 194, 199, 201, 268
Hamilton, John, 192
*Hamlet*, 63, 86, 99, 190, 242, 277
Hardy, Col., 162

Harris, Joseph, 17, 24
Harrison, James J., 98
Haymarket Theatre, 81, 137, 278
*Heart of Midlothian, The*, 198, 199
*Heir at Law*, The, 64
Henderson, John, 87
*Henry VIII*, 123
Hield, 268, 269
Higgins, 103
Higgins, Mrs., 103
Hill, Yankee, 164
Hilson, Mr. and Mrs., 179, 180
Hoare, Prince, 25
Hodges, Mr. and Mrs., 207, 216, 227
Hodgkinson, 44
Holland, George, 212, 217, 238, 239
Holliday Street Theatre, 27, 34, 102, 122, 262
Holman, George, 30, 132
Holman, Joseph, 52, 53, 56, 57, 131
Holman, Joseph, 52
Holman, Mrs., 133
Holman, Mrs. (Miss Latimer), 131
Home, 144
*Honest Thieves*, 175
*Honey Moon, The*, 51, 56, 273
*How Sweet is Rest on Sunday*, 211
Howard, Mr. and Mrs. Charles, 278, 285
Howard, Robert, 175
Howitt, Mary, 275
Hughes, 197
Hughes, Elizabeth, 190
Hughes, Miss, 183
*Hunchback, The*, 180, 191, 262, 273
Hunt, Henry Blaine, 144
Hunt, Leigh, 63, 67
Hunt, Mrs. Henry, 256, 257, 258

*Theatrical Rambles of Mr. & Mrs. Greene*, Charles Durang

Hunter, James, 138, 170, 171, 175
Hurtan, Madame, 151
*Husband at Sight, A*, 193, 199
Hutchings, Mr. and Mrs., 161, 162
Hutin, Madame, 155
*Hypocrite, The*, 218, 224
*Ice Witch*, 182
*Imposter, The"*, 24
Inchbald, Mrs., 35
Incledon, Charles, 132, 137
*Inconstant, The*, 199
*Inconstant,The*, 198
Ingersoll, David, 200, 208
*Irish Tutor, The*, 172, 175
Irish, Charles, 139, 140
*Irishman in London, The*, 172, 175, 189
*Iron Chest, The*, 260, 263, 267
Isherwood, William, 148, 153
Jackson, A. W., 150, 151, 202
Jackson, Capt., 111
Jackson, Gen. Andrew, 221, 222
Jackson, Mr., 248
Jameson, A., 162
Jameson, Sandy, 157, 162
Jamieson, George W., 254, 278, 286
Jarman, Fanny, 186, 191, 197, 276
Jarman, Miss, 198
Jefferson family, 225, 226, 235, 236
Jefferson, Cornelia, 225, 227
Jefferson, Elizabeth, 145, 226, 229, 235
Jefferson, Hetty, 232
Jefferson, John, 101
Jefferson, Joseph, 149, 225, 226, 227, 232, 234
Jefferson, Joseph, 130
Jefferson, Joseph Jr., 204
Jefferson, Mary Ann, 232
Jefferson, Mrs. Joseph, 97, 100, 225
Jefferson, Thomas, 101
Jerrold, Douglas, 162
*John Bull*, 56, 125, 145
*John of Paris*, 105, 107
John Street Theatre, 101, 115
*Johnny Gilpin's Journey to London*, 86, 87
Johnson, David, 183, 190
Johnson, R. M., 84
Johnson, Richard Kantor, 87
Johnston, Mrs., 254
Johnston, S., 250
Johnstone, 172
Jones, 178, 202
Jones, George, 179, 181
Jones, Samuel, 120, 124
Jonson, Ben, 33
Juda, Mrs., 250
*Julius Caesar*, 154
Kean, Edmund, 92, 121, 122, 123, 124, 173, 261
Keeley, Mrs., 172
Kelly, Fanny, 179
Kelly, Lydia, 125, 135
Kelly, Miss, 144
Kelsey, 103
Kemble, Charles, 74, 198, 264, 282
Kemble, Fanny, 172, 191, 198, 276
Kenna family, 34
Kenney, James, 25, 252
Kent, Mr. and Mrs., 200, 208
*King John*, 126, 127
*King Lear*, 110, 264
Kinlock, Mrs., 139
Kisacush, 231
Knight, Henry, 184, 191
Knight, Mr. and Mrs. Henry, 197
Knight, Mrs. E., 130, 144
Knight, Mrs. E. (Mary Ann Povey), 136
Knight, Thomas, 175
Knowles, Sheridan, 180, 181, 191, 208, 213, 217, 232
Kotzebue, 107
*La Peyrouse*, 191
Lacy, M. R., 199, 252

297

*Theatrical Rambles of Mr. & Mrs. Greene*, Charles Durang

*Lady of Lyons, The*, 85, 206, 219, 269
*Lady of the Lake, The*, 23, 25
*LaFavorita*, 252
Lafayette Circus, 133, 137
Lafayette Theatre, 153, 154
Lafayette, Gen., 104
Lafolle, Mrs., 99, 100, 101
LaForrest, Mrs., 250
Lane, Louisa, 139, 144
Lardner, Dr., 212, 217
*Last Days of Pompeii, The*, 203, 209
Latimer, Miss, 57, 131, 132, 137
Lee, Charles, 140, 144
Lee, Nathaniel, 25
Leech, Harvey, 191
Lehr, Charles, 150, 152, 155, 160, 161
Lennox, Thomas, 161, 162
Leon, Mons., 149, 154
Lewis, Henry, 29, 30, 31, 34
Lewis, M. G., 35, 81
Lewis, William Thomas "Gentleman", 35
Lewyllen, Mr. and Mrs., 197, 199
Lind, Jenny, 277, 285
Lion Theatre, 200, 208
Lockwood, Mr., 92
Logan, 251
Logan, Celia, 189
Logan, Cornelius A., 189
Logan, Eliza, 189, 251, 271, 279
Logan, Mr. and Mrs., 183
Logan, Olive, 189
*London Assurance*, 241, 242, 245, 251
*Long Rifle, The*, 173
Lopez, Mr., 126
*Love*, 181, 225
*Love Chase, The*, 217
*Love in a Village*, 133, 134, 137, 173
Lucas, 52
Ludlow, Mrs. Noah, 52, 117

Ludlow, Noah, 51, 56, 115, 117, 119, 124, 190, 225, 229, 232, 235, 237, 238, 255
*Macbeth*, 44, 56, 86, 110, 128, 147, 217, 257
Macgloire, Kate, 268
Mackay, 165
MacKenzie, Alexander, 232
MacKenzie, Mr. and Mrs. Alexander, 227
MacKenzie, Mrs. Alexander, 229
Macready, William C., 128, 129, 130, 135, 136, 144, 147, 164, 175, 264, 275
*Mad Anthony Wayne*, 248
Madery, Col., 69
Maeder, Gaspard, 115
*Mahomet, the Imposter*, 18, 97
*Mahomet, the Impostert*, 92
Malfort, Mrs., 106
*Man and Wife*, 125, 135
*Man of Fortune, The*, 44
Manders, Mr., 251
*Manfred*, 164
Mann, Col. Alvah, 129, 136
Mann, Mrs. W., 101
Manvers, Mr., 241, 244, 245
Marble, Dan, 177, 179, 182, 262
Marshall, F. A., 273
Martine, 106
Mason, Mrs., 27, 34, 43
Massinger, Philip, 136
Maywood, Mrs., 148, 153
Maywood, Robert, 153
McCafferty, 103
McKenzie, 20, 24
McKinney, 107
McVicker, 259
McVicker, John H., 35, 259
McVicker, Mary, 259, 262
McVicker, Mr. and Mrs. John, 256
Meadows, Kate, 274
Meadows, Mr., 172
Medina, Louisa, 208, 209
*Meg Merrilles*, 276

298

*Theatrical Rambles of Mr. & Mrs. Greene*, Charles Durang

Memphis Theatre, 282
*Merchant of Venice*, 178
Merry, Robert, 24
Mestayer, Mr., 136
*Metamora*, 150, 154, 219
*Midnight Hour, The*, 31
Miller, Louisa Missouri, 262
Miller, Nelson H., 262
Milman, H. M., 217
Miss Nelson's Theatre, 57
Missouri, Miss, 255
Mitchell, Mr. and Mrs., 139, 140, 142
Mitford, Miss, 208
Mobile Theatre, 162
Moncrieff, W. T., 114
*Monk, The*, 31, 35
Montgomery, Gen., 131, 137
Montgomery, Mayor, 122
Montreal Theatre, 80
Moore, Edward, 34, 136
Moore, John, 103
Moreton, John Pollard, 36, 43
Moretonian Dramatic Society, 36, 43
Morgan, 52
Morgan, Mrs., 52
Morrel, Miss, 22
Morton, Mr., 227, 229
Morton, Thomas, 25, 114, 153, 217
Mossop, George, 144
*Mountain Sylph, The*, 217
*Mountaineers, The*, 40, 44
Mowatt, Mrs. Cora, 164, 286
Mueller, Mrs., 246
Murdoch, James, 165, 279
Muse, Dr., 93
Myers, John H., 107
Nano, Signor Hervio, 191
National Theatre, 44, 115, 249, 262
*Nature and Philosophy*, 161, 162
Nelson, 182
Nelson, Miss, 54, 57, 207
*New Hay at the Old Market*, 124

New Orleans Theatre, 105
Niblo's Garden, 251
Nichols, Mr., 92, 132
Nichols, Mrs., 250
Norwich Theatre, 24
Nowel, John, 22
Nuskey, Anne, 16, 28, 29, 30, 32
O'Keeffe, John, 115
O'Neil, P., 62, 64
*Old Plantation, The*, 278, 286
Oldmixon, Mrs., 132, 137
Olympic Circus, 252
*Constitution*, 33
*Midnight Hour*, 35
*John Bull*, 56
*Othello*, 107, 174
Owen, Robert Dale, 44
Oxley, John, 183, 190
Page, Joseph, 103
Park, 190, 191
Park Theatre, 25, 34, 35, 41, 44, 57, 81, 96, 98, 107, 109, 115, 124, 131, 134, 136, 137, 142, 144, 153, 154, 158, 179, 199, 240, 248, 250, 251, 252, 263, 274, 286, 290
Parodi, Signorina Teresa, 58
Parsloe, Charles, 184, 191
Parsons, Charles, 214, 218, 219, 223
*Paul Jones, the Pilot of the German Ocean*, 44
Paul Street Theatre, 202
Paulding, 164
Payne, John Howard, 23, 162
Pearl Street Theatre, 107, 153, 183, 189
Pearlman, Mrs., 154
Pearman, Mrs., 149
Pearson, Mr., 241
*Peasant Boy, The*, 23, 25
Pelby, William, 92, 131, 136, 164
Pepin's circus, 43
Philips, Miss, 250
Phillips, Aaron, 52, 56, 134, 154

299

Phillips, Aaron', 52
Phillips, J. B., 208
Phillips, Lydia, 183, 190
Phillips, Moses, 177, 179, 181, 182
Phillips, T., 134, 135, 138
Pickering, Alexander, 183, 190
Pierson, Mr., 246
Pitt, Dibden, 257
*Pizarro*, 58, 62, 64, 109, 115, 143, 153, 195
Place, Robert, 155, 250, 259
Placide family, 101
Placide, Alexander, 41, 101, 106, 132
Placide, Alice, 101
Placide, Henry, 101
Placide, Jane, 54, 55, 58, 101, 103, 109
Placide, Mrs., 101
Placide, Thomas, 101, 110, 120
Placide, William, 254
Placido, 106
Planche, J. R., 253
*Planter and His Dogs, The*, 191
Plunkett, Harry, 263
*Pocahontas*, 38, 40, 44
Pocock, 107
*Point of Honor, The*, 73, 74
*Poor Soldier, The*, 162
Pope, Mrs. Colemen, 254
Porter, Charles S., 35, 36, 37, 38, 39, 44, 136, 167, 183
Potter, Mrs. Estelle, 271
Power, Tyrone, 172, 176
Pownall, Miss, 101
Pownall, Mrs., 100, 101
*Presumptive Evidence*, 178, 182
Price and Simpson, 133, 134
Price, Chandler, 22
Price, Stephen, 96, 98, 133, 134, 141
Pritchard, Mr., 131, 137
Proctor, Joseph, 202
*Provoked Husband, The*, 104, 107
Prune Street Theatre, 91, 97, 102

Putnam, 163, 248
*Raising the Wind"*, 25
Randall, George W., 211
Rannie, 56
Ravel, Gabriel, 184
Ravels, 278
Raymond, Mr., 136, 218
Reader, Mr., 241
Redige, Paulo, 106
Reeves, Jack, 172
*Rendezvous, The*, 97, 184, 191
*Rent Day*, 179
Renzi, 268
*Review, The*, 155, 175, 267
Reynolds, Frederick, 58
Reynolds, Miss, 250
Rice, J. B., 203, 209, 257
Rice, T. D., 248
*Richard III*, 20, 23, 86, 122, 124, 145, 146, 260, 264
Richardson, Elizabeth, 235
Richardson, Mr., 226
Richardson, Mrs., 227
Richmond Hill Theatre, 35, 57, 179, 180, 182
Riddle, Eliza, 57, 124
Riddle, Mrs., 102
Riddle, Sally, 120, 124
*Rienzi*, 200, 208
*Rival Queens, The*, 25
Roberts, J. B., 284, 286
Roberts, Mr. and Mrs., 148
Rock, Mary, 235, 238, 240
Rockwell, 251
*Romeo and Juliet*, 39, 64, 78
*Rosina*, 125, 135
Rossi, Signora, 245
Rossini, 54, 57
Rowe, J. S., 115
Rowe, James, 55, 57, 213, 214
Rowe, Miss, 55, 251
Rowe, Mr., 54
Rowe, Mrs., 54
Rowe, Mrs. (Rosina Seymour), 57
Rowe, Mrs. G., 254
Rowe, Mrs. J., 103
Rowe, Nicholas, 43

*Theatrical Rambles of Mr. & Mrs. Greene*, Charles Durang

*Rule a Wife*, 29, 35
Russel, Mrs. Richard, 103
Russell, Marian, 103, 110
Russell, Marian, 110
Russell, Mr., 54
Russell, Mrs., 54
Russell, Richard, 57, 103, 107, 110, 180, 246
Ryner, Mrs. Henry, 271, 274
Sadlers Wells, 106
Salvi, Sig., 245, 251
*Sam Patch*, 182
Sandford, Charles, 132, 133, 134, 138, 148
Sandford, Mrs. (Miss Latimer), 132, 134
Schaeffer's Washington Garden Theatre, 84, 87
*School for Scandal, The*, 93, 98
*School of Reform, The*, 23, 25, 212, 217
Scott, John M., 37, 38, 44, 57, 117, 124, 148, 213, 218, 272, 290
Scott, Moses, 111
Scott, Sir Walter, 25, 65, 198, 282
Sedley, William Henry, 124, 139
Sefton, John, 139, 140, 142, 144, 211
Seilhamer, 106
Sergeant, Mr. and Mrs., 241, 246
Seymour, Count, 114, 115
Seymour, Rosina, 57, 111, 113, 115
*She Stoops to Conquer*, 217
Shea, Martin Arthur, 31
Sheridan, R. B., 25, 138, 263
Shiel, R. S., 137
Siddons, Mrs., 173, 214
Simpson, Edmund, 133, 136, 139, 140, 142, 252
Sinclair, Daniel, 204
*Single Life*, 240
*Sleeping Beauty, The*, 141, 145
*Sleeping Draught, The*, 190
Sloman, Mr. and Mrs. John, 238, 240, 241
Smith, Henry, 124
Smith, Lemuel, 103
Smith, Mrs. Harry, 120
Smith, O., 172
Smith, Sol, 57, 103, 255
Smith, William Henry, 139, 140, 141
*Soldier's Daughter, The*, 33, 55, 58, 106, 107, 120, 252, 282
Sollee, Mons., 101
Somerville, 150, 153, 154, 156, 157, 158, 161
Somerville, Mrs., 157
South Street Theatre, 36, 44
Southey, 208
Southwark Theatre, 24
Southwell, Henry, 141, 145, 157, 160
Southwell, Miss, 148
Southwell, Mr. and Mrs. Henry, 150, 158
*Speed the Plough*, 190
*Spoiled Child, The*, 114
*Spoiled Child, The*, 110
Sprague, Charles, 98
St. Charles Street Theatre, 206
St. Charles Theatre, 53, 55, 57, 162, 210, 236, 243, 245, 251, 252, 255, 265, 267
St. Philips Street Theatre, 52, 56
Stadts, Dr., 194
Stafford, 250
Stannard, Rachel, 139, 142, 144
Stevens, Major, 183, 190
Stewart, John, 27, 34
Stewart, Mrs. John, 227
Stone, John Augustus, 154
*Stranger, The*, 33, 135, 172, 216, 241, 243, 252
Stuart, Gilbert, 36
Stuart, Mary, 118
Sully, Matthew, Sr., 34
Sully, Thomas, 34
Surin, Stanislaus, 89, 97

301

*Theatrical Rambles of Mr. & Mrs. Greene*, Charles Durang

Surrey Theatre, 145
*Sylla*, 136
*Tales of Calas, The*, 154
Tatnall, 133
Terry, Daniel, 65
*Thalaba*, 202, 208
Theatre d'Orleans, 52
*Theresa*, 161, 162
Thomas, Capt., 165
Thomas, Miss, 97
Thompson, E. H., 182
Thorne, Charles, 252
Thorne, James, 54, 57
Thorne, Mr. and Mrs. Charles, 177
Thornton, Jack, 80, 118, 119
Thornton, Jack, 119
Thornton, Mrs. Jack, 80, 84
*Three and the Deuce*, 23, 53
Tiernan, Mr. and Mrs., 197, 198
*Titus Andronicus*, 68, 74
Tobin, John, 56
*Tom Thumb*, 110, 114, 190
Tree, Ellen, 165, 197, 206, 276
Tremont Theatre, 137, 248, 252
*Tribute to Departed Genius; or, The Tears of Thalia Helponene*, 33
*Turn Out or Turn In*, 248, 252
Turnbull, Captain, 80, 81, 82
Turnbull, Julia, 81
Turnbull, Miss C., 81
*Twelfth Night*, 206
*Two Friends, The*, 192, 199, 247, 252
Twomley (Mrs. Caldwell), 55
Tyler, John, 190
Tyler, Robert, 190
*Uncle Tom's Cabin*, 259
Undine, 92, 97
Vache, Mr., 203, 204, 205, 206
Vallee, Lieutenant, 80
Van Buren, Martin, 247
Vandenhoff, George, 165, 248
Vaughan, Henry, 52, 56
Vaughan, John, 52
Vaughan, John, 56
Vaughan, Mrs., 52

*Venice Preserved*, 141, 145, 155, 162, 164, 196, 204
*Victorine*, 172, 175
*Virginius*, 190, 213
*Voice of Nature, The*, 97
Vos, Mrs., 118, 124
Walker, 141
Wallack, Henry, 92, 97, 134
Wallack, James, 92, 97, 149, 172
Wallack, Mrs. Henry, 92
Wallack, Mrs. James, 101
Wallack, W. H., 44
Walnut Street Circus, 90
Walnut Street Theatre, 23, 29, 44, 90, 91, 92, 96, 97, 115, 124, 130, 136, 139, 141, 142, 143, 149, 154, 202, 203, 204, 207, 208, 209, 273, 274, 286
Walters, Kate, 279
Walters, Mrs., 254
Ward, Thomas, 197
Ward, William, 199
Warde, Mr., 172
Waring, Miss, 178
Waring, Mrs., 103, 109, 111, 179
Warren Theatre, 137
Warren, Mary Anne, 203, 209
Warren, Mrs. William, 19, 24
Warren, Philip, 129
Warren, William, 20, 21, 24, 27, 31, 34, 90, 92, 93, 96, 97, 125, 130, 135, 136, 139, 140, 142, 149, 203
Washington Theatre, 93
Watson, Mr., 214
Webb, Charles, 43, 73, 195, 196, 213
Webster, Benjamin, 145
Welch, Rufus, 200, 208, 248, 252
Wells, Miss Sarah, 139, 142, 144
Wells, Mr., 142, 145
Wemyss, Francis C., 122, 123, 139, 140, 141, 186, 202, 208, 219

*Theatrical Rambles of Mr. & Mrs. Greene*, Charles Durang

Wemyss', Francis C., 206
*Wept of the Wish-ton-Wish, The*, 172, 175
*Werner*, 130, 136
*West Indian, The*, 53, 57, 175
West, Mrs. William, 35, 165
Westray, Juliana, 24
Wheatley, Emma, 150, 155, 158, 186, 191
Wheatley, William, 129, 136, 186, 187, 274
Whitney, Mr., 197, 199
*Widow Wiggins*, 236, 240
Wieland, Master, 191
*Wife, The*, 186, 191, 252
Wignell, Thomas, 24, 43, 81
Wiley, 163
*William Tell*, 54, 103, 129
*William Tell*, 136
Williams, Mr. and Mrs. Barney, 257
Williams, Mrs. H. A., 153
Willis Mr., 36
Willis, Mr., 33, 41
Willis, Mr. and Mrs., 35
Willis, Mrs., 35, 36, 37, 38, 39, 50, 51, 59, 288
Wilson, Alexander, 109, 111, 115, 116, 117
Wilson, Mrs., 111

Winans, John, 250
Winter Trivoli, 97
Wisdom, Mr., 143
*Wood Demon, The*, 80, 81
Wood, Mr. and Mrs., 173
Wood, Mr. and Mrs. A., 243
Wood, mr. and Mrs. William, 149
Wood, Mr. and Mrs. William, 148
Wood, Mrs., 128, 145
Wood, Mrs. John, 38
Wood, William, 20, 21, 24, 27, 31, 34, 43, 90, 92, 93, 96, 97, 98, 99, 115, 126, 130, 134, 148, 180, 215, 243
Woodhall, Clara, 189
Woodhall, Jacob, 189
Woodhull, Clara, 183
Woodhull, Jacob, 107, 109, 179, 180, 183
Woodruff, Mr., 75, 83
*Wrecker's Daughter, The*, 202, 208
Wright, Mr. and Mrs., 227, 229, 232
Wrighten, Mrs., 100
Yates, 172
Young, Charles, 30, 31, 35, 172, 179

www.ingramcontent.com/pod-product-compliance
Lightning Source LLC
Chambersburg PA
CBHW031559110426
42742CB00036B/246